AF531545

POLITICAL THEORY

Supreme Court ruled in favour of the federal government, permitting the Drug Enforcement Administration (DEA) to arrest medical marijuana patients and caregivers. In Gonzales v. Oregon, the Supreme court ruled the practice of physician-assisted suicide in Oregon is legal.

States' Rights as "Code Word"

The term "states' rights," some have argued, was used as a code word by defenders of segregation. It was the official name of the "Dixiecrat" party led by white supremacist presidential candidate Strom Thurmond. George Wallace, the Alabama governor—who famously declared in his inaugural address, "Segregation now! Segregation tomorrow! Segregation forever!"—later remarked that he should have said, "States' rights now! States' rights tomorrow! States' rights forever!" Wallace, however, claimed that segregation was but one issue symbolic of a larger struggle for states' rights; in that view, which some historians dispute, his replacement of *segregation* with *states' rights* would be more of a clarification than a euphemism.

States' Rights and the Rehnquist Court

The Supreme Court's University of Alabama v. Garrett (2001) and Kimel v. Florida Board of Regents (2000) decisions allowed states to use a rational basis review for discrimination against the aged and disabled, arguing that these types of discrimination were rationally related to a legitimate state interest, and that no "razorlike precision" was needed." The Supreme Court's United States v. Morrison (2000) decision limited the ability of rape victims to sue their attackers in federal court. Chief Justice William H. Rehnquist explained that "States historically have been sovereign" in the area of law enforcement, which in the Court's opinion required narrow interpretations of the Commerce Clause and Fourteenth Amendment.

Kimel, *Garrett* and *Morrison* indicated that the Court's previous decisions in favour of enumerated powers and limits on Congressional power over the states, such as United States v. Lopez (1995), Seminole Tribe v. Florida (1996) and City of Boerne v. Flores (1997) were more than one-time flukes. In the past, Congress relied on the Commerce Clause and the Equal Protection

POLITICAL THEORY

Mukesh Kumar Singh

ANMOL PUBLICATIONS PVT. LTD.
NEW DELHI-110 002 (INDIA)

ANMOL PUBLICATIONS PVT. LTD.
Regd. Office: 4360/4, Ansari Road, Daryaganj,
New Delhi-110002 (India)
Tel.: 23278000, 23261597, 23286875, 23255577
Fax: 91-11-23280289
Email: anmolpub@gmail.com
Visit us at: www.anmolpublications.com

Branch Office: No. 1015, Ist Main Road, BSK IIIrd Stage
IIIrd Phase, IIIrd Block, Bangalore-560 085 (India)
Tel.: 080-41723429 • Fax: 080-26723604
Email: anmolpublicationsbangalore@gmail.com

Political Theory

First Edition, 2010

ISBN 978-81-261-4548-5

PRINTED IN INDIA

Printed at Mehra Offset Press, Delhi.

Contents

occupation. Other states may have sovereignty over a territory but they lack international recognition; are *de facto* states only. Somaliland is commonly considered to be such a state, as well as Taiwan.

State (Polity)

A state is a set of institutions that possess the authority to make the rules that govern the people in one or more societies, having internal and external sovereignty over a definite territory. In Max Weber's influential definition, it is that organization that has a "monopoly on the legitimate use of physical force within a given territory," which may include the armed forces, civil service or state bureaucracy, courts, and police.

Although the term often refers broadly to all institutions of government or rule—ancient and modern—the modern state system bears a number of characteristics that were first consolidated in Western Europe, beginning in earnest in the 15th century, when the term "state" also acquired its current meaning. Thus the word is often used in a strict sense to refer only to modern political systems.

Within a federal system, the term state also refers to political units not sovereign themselves, but subject to the authority of the larger state, or federal union, such as the "states and territories of Australia" and the "states" in the United States. Within a monarchy, two or more states may share personal union under the same monarch, but retain an individual identity, even unto a separate legislature and/or government.

In casual usage, the terms "country," "nation," and "state" are often used as if they were synonymous; but in a more strict usage they can be distinguished:

- *Country* denotes a geographical area.
- *Nation* denotes a people who share common customs, origins, and history. However, the adjectives *national* and *international* also refer to matters pertaining to what are strictly *states*, as in *national capital*, *international law*.
- *State* refers to set of governing institutions that has sovereignty over a definite territory.

Preface

Politics is a process by which groups of people make decisions. The term is generally applied to behaviour within civil governments, but politics has been observed in all human group interactions, including corporate, academic and religious institutions. It consists of "social relations involving authority or power" and refers to the regulation of a political unit, and to the methods and tactics used to formulate and apply policy. From a historical perspective, societies in need of government have moved from the primitive to the patriarchal state and finally to the military, the real politics of modern times. The origin and development of government institutions is the most visible subject for the study of politics and its history.

Political theory unlike political thought is the speculation of a single individual who is attempting to offer us a theoretical explanation of political reality, namely, the phenomena of the state. Every theory by its very nature is an explanation built upon certain hypotheses which may or may not be valid and which are always open to criticism. Political theories are of two types—normative or prescriptive and empirical or descriptive. As the words indicate, the prescriptive theory relates, in a general way, to suggest the model by which an imperfect political or social order could be made perfect. The empirical or descriptive political theory is primarily concerned with the things such as state structure, political process, etc.

The aims of this book is to provide our readers the latest research inputs on the complexities of the theories of national and international politics.

—Author

1

Nature and Significance of Political Theory

Politics

Politics is a process by which groups of people make decisions. The term is generally applied to behaviour within civil governments, but politics has been observed in all human group interactions, including corporate, academic and religious institutions. It consists of "social relations involving authority or power" and refers to the regulation of a political unit, and to the methods and tactics used to formulate and apply policy.

History

From a historical perspective, societies in need of government have moved from the primitive to the patriarchal state and finally to the military, the real politics of modern times. The origin and development of government institutions is the most visible subject for the study of Politics and its history.

Primitive Societies

Regardless of how civilized the world is, there are still large numbers of people living in the most primitive conditions. The most important of these because most scientifically studied are the "aborigines" of Australia. The scientific study of the aboriginal Australian forms the basis of what is best known of primitive societies in general.

The aboriginal Australian understands neither the cultivation of the land nor the rearing of sheep and cattle. The dog is their only "domestic" animal. They take shelter in caves and in primitive huts. They have no food but the natural products of the earth. They know a very primitive form of fire-making and their cooking is very crude. They have no knowledge of metal work. Their weapons are the flint-headed spear, the axe and the wooden boomerang. They wear no clothing at all. Living like this on the point of starvation may have gone on for thousands of years. It could be said that isolation is the only single factor in the aboriginal Australian state of stagnation.

The Totem group is the real social unit of the aboriginal Australian. The Totem is not an Australian word but it is generally accepted to designate the name of an institution which is found everywhere among primitive people. The Totem group is primarily a group of people distinguished by the sign of a natural object, such as an animal or tree, who may not intermarry with one another — this is the first rule of primitive social organization; its origin is lost in antiquity ("Alcheringa") but its object iș certainly to prevent the intermarriage of close relatives. Marriage takes place between men and women of differen Totems; the husband belongs to all the women of his wife's totem and the wife belongs to all the men of the husband's totem at the same time that a communal marriage is established between the men and women of the two different Totems—the men and women being of the same generation. This presents a most valuable objective lesson in social history. There are no unmarried couples; marriage for them is part of the natural order into which they are born.

The ceremonies are kept secret and are directed by a "Birraark" or sorcerer, usually an old man. The candidates are instructed in the history of their Totem and on the power of the Birraark. They are initiated into the mystery of the Totem, usually accompanied by an ordeal such as circumcision and then they are tattooed with a seal of identity that marks them for a given Totem and a given generation in that Totem. In this way is constructed the simple system of relationship of the aboriginal Australian. The mother takes a predominant role, for descent is almost always reckoned through females. Parent, child, brother and sister are the only recognized relationships. Rudimentary as this system may appear to be, it is widely spread among the Malay Archipelago and prevails widely among primitive peoples everywhere. The Totem serves the purpose of forbidding intermarriage between close relatives and will deal destruction if this rule is not strictly enforced. These are the rudiments of two of the most important factors in human progress: Religion and Law. The rudimentary notion of Law is very specific about what is prohibited or Taboo. Primitive people do not recognize any duties towards strangers unless there is an abundant food supply in a given area. It is a sure sign of progress if the same area is able to maintain an ever larger number of people. In his own milieu, close to nature, the savage outwits the civilized man but both are subject to natural law.

Lewis H. Morgan author of *Ancient Society* considers the American Indians to be the link between the primitive and patriarchal state of society.

Patriarchal Societies

All patriarchal societies are known by certain characteristic features:

1. Male kinship is prevalent. Men are counted as kin because they are descended from the same male ancestor.
2. Marriage is permanent. It is not until one woman is married to one man that certainty of fatherhood appears in society but it is not a general rule of patriarchal society for polygamy does exist in the earlier stages of social development.
3. Paternal authority is the ruling principle of the social order. In ancient Rome, the patria potestas extended to all descendants of one living male ancestor; it comprised control and punishment not to mention questions of life and death.

These features of the development of the patriarchal state of society are as common among the Jews as among the Arabs, among the Aryans as among the Dravidians and even among the Germanic and Celtic races.

The patriarchal state of society consists of two stages, tribe and clan. The tribe is a large group of hundreds of members who descend from one common male ancestor, sometimes from a fictitious character satisfying the etiquette that descent from the male is the only basis of society. The clan, on the other hand, is a smaller group reaching back into the past for only four generations or so to a common well-known male ancestor. The clan always breaks down into smaller units when its limit is reached. According to the Scottish historian W. F. Skene in volume 3 of *Celtic Scotland*, the tribe or larger unit is the oldest. When the tribe breaks down, clans are formed. When the clan system breaks down, it leaves the households or families as independent units. Finally, with the withering away of patriarchal society, the family is dissolved and the individual comes into existence.

The State

The origin of the State is to be found in the development of the art of warfare. Historically speaking, there is not the slightest difficulty in proving that all political communities of the modern type owe their existence to successful warfare. As a result, the new states are forced to organize on military principles. The life of the new community is military allegiance. The military by nature is competitive. The establishment of the western State is coincident to the spread of Christianity as a universal religion. Though Christianity in its early beginnings was a message to the meek and lowly, its great conquests in northern and western Europe were due to the conversion of kings and princes not to mention the conquest of American Indian civilizations. Under the cry of "one church one nation", England became a nation with church and state in intimate alliance.

Of the institutions by which the state is ruled, that of kingship stands foremost until the French Revolution put an end to the "divine right of kings". Nevertheless, kingship is perhaps the most succesful institution of Politics. However, the first kings were not institutions but individuals. The earliest kings were successful militarily. They were men not only of great military genius but also great administrators. Kingship becomes an institution through heredity. However, constitutional monarchies are not successful at all. Elective monarchy is one of the chimeras of political utopia. Chosen by an electorate, the best they become is obedient puppets like the newly elected president of a Republic, obedient to whoever would pull the strings behind the scenes.

The king rules his kingdom with the aid of his Council, without it he could not hold his territories. The Council is the king's master mind. The Council is the germ of constitutional government. Long before the council became a bulwark of democracy, it rendered invaluable aid to the institution of kingship by:

1. Preserving the institution of kingship through heredity.
2. Preserving the traditions of the social order.
3. Being able to withstand criticism as an impersonal authority.
4. Being able to manage a greater deal of knowledge and action than a single individual such as the king.

The greatest of the king's subordinates, the earls in England and Scotland, the dukes and counts in the Continent, always sat as a right on the Council. A conqueror wages war upon the vanquished for vengeance or for plunder but an established kingdom exacts tribute. One of the functions of the Council is to keep the confers of the king full. Another is the satisfaction of military service and the establishment of lordships by the king to satisfy the task of collecting taxes and soldiers.

The State and Property

No political institution is of greater importance than the institution of property. Property is the right vested on the individual or a group of people to enjoy the benefits of an object be it material or intellectual. A right is a power enforced by public trust. Sometimes it happens that the exercise of a right is opposed to public trust. Nevertheless, a right is really the creation of public trust, past, present or future. The growth of knowledge is the key to the history of property as an institution. The more man becomes knowledgeable of an object be it physical or intellectual, the more it is appropriated. The appearance of the State brought about the final stage in the evolution of property from wildlife to husbandry. In the presence of the State, man can hold landed property. The State began granting lordships and ended up conferring property and with it came inheritance. With landed property came rent and in the exchange of goods, profit, so that in modern times, the "lord of the land" of long ago becomes the landlord. If it is wrongly assumed that the value of land is always the same, then there is of course no evolution of property whatever. However, the price of land goes up with every increase in population benefitting the landlord. The landlordism of large land owners has been the most rewarded of all political services. In industry, the position of the landlord is less important but in towns which have grown out of an industry, the fortunate landlord has reaped an enormous profit. Towards the latter part of the Middle Ages in Europe, both the State—the State would use the instrument of confiscation for the first time to satisfy a debt-and the Church—the Church succeeded in acquiring immense quantities of land—were allied against the village community to displace the small landlord and they were successful to the extent that today, the village has become the ideal of the individualist, a place in which every man "does what he wills with his own." The State has been the most important factor in the evolution of the institution of property be it public or private.

The State and the Justice System

As a military institution, the State is concerned with the allegiance of its subjects. Betrayal or defiance of allegiance is a risk to its national security. Thus arises the law of treason. Criminal acts in general, breaking the peace and treason make up the whole of criminal law enforced by the State as distinguished from the law enforced by private individuals. State justice has taken the place of clan, feudal, merchant and ecclesiastical justice due to its strength, skill and simplicity. One very striking evidence of the superiority of the royal courts over the feudal and popular courts in the matter of official skill is the fact that, until comparatively late in history, the royal courts alone kept written records of their proceedings. The most innovative proceeding introduced by the royal courts was trial by jury becoming not only popular but also the bulwark of liberty. By the time of the reformation, with the separation of Church and State, in the most progressive countries, the State succeeded in dealing with the business of administering justice.

The State and the Legislative System

The making of laws was unknown to primitive societies. That most persistent of all patriarchal societies, the Jewish, retains to a certain extent its tribal law in the Gentile cities of the West. This tribal law is the rudimentary idea of law as it presented itsel to people in the patriarchal stage of society, it was custom or observance sanctioned by the approval and practice of ancestors.

The intolerable state of affairs in the 10th century in France, Germany, Spain and England where every little town had its own laws and nations like France, Germany, Spain and other countries had no national law till the end of the 18th century, came to an end, thanks to three great agencies that helped to create the modern system of law and legislation:

1. Records. From the early Middle Ages in Europe there come what are called folk-laws and they appear exactly at the time when the patriarchal is becoming the State. They are due almost universally to one cause: the desire of the king to know the custom of his subjects. These are not legislation in the sense of law-making but statements or declarations of custom. They are drawn from a knowledge of the custom of the people. Unwritten custom changes imperceptibly but not the written. It is always possible to point to the exact text and show what it says. Nevertheless, the written text can change by addition with every new edition.
2. Law Courts. By taking some general rule which seemed to be common to all the communities and ignoring the differences, English common law was modelled after such a practice so that the law became common in all the districts of the kingdom. The reason why in the rest of Europe, there was no common law till centuries later is because the State in those countries did not get hold of the administration of justice when England did. One of the shrewdest moves by which the English judges pushed their plan of making a common law was by limiting the verdict of the jury in every case to questions of fact. At first, the jury used to give answers both on law and fact; and being a purely local body, they followed local custom. A famous division came to pass: the province of the judge and the province of the jury.
3. Fictions. Records and Law Courts were valuable in helping the people adapt to law-making but like Fictions, they

were slow and imperfect. Though slowly, fictions work because it is a well known fact that people will accept a change in the form of a fiction while they would resist it to the end if the fact is out in the open.

Finally, there is the enactment of laws or legislation. When progress and development is rapid, the faster method of political representation is adopted. This method does not originate in primitive society but in the State need for money and its use of an assembly to raise the same. From the town assembly, a national assembly and the progress of commerce sprang Parliament all over Europe around the end of the 12th century but not entirely representative or homogenous for the nobility and the clergy. The clergy had amassed a fortune in land, about one-fifth of all Christendom but at the time, in the 12th and 13th centuries, the Church was following a policy of isolation; they adopted the rule of celibacy and cut themselves from domestic life; they refused to plead in a secular court; they refused to pay taxes to the State on the grounds that they had already paid it to the Pope. Since the main object of the king in holding a national assembly was to collect money, the Church could not be left out and so they came to Parliament. The Church did not like it but in most cases they had to come.

The medieval Parliament was complete when it represented all the states in the realm: nobles, clergy, peasants and craftsmen but it was not a popular institution mainly because it meant taxation. Only by the strongest pressure of the Crown were Parliaments maintained during the first century of their existence and the best proof of this assertion lies in the fact that in those countries where the Crown was weak, Parliament ceased to exist. The notion that Parliaments were the result of a democratic movement cannot be supported by historial facts. Originally, the representative side of Parliament was solely concerned with money; representation in Parliament was a liability rather than a privilige. It is not uncommon that an institution created for one purpose begins to serve another. People who were asked to contribute with large sums of money began to petition. Pretty soon, sessions in Parliament would turn into bargaining tables, the king granting petitions in exchange for money. However, there were two kinds of petitions, one private and the other public and it was from this last that laws were adopted or legislation originated. The king as head of State could give orders to preserve territorial integrity but not until these royal enactments were combined with public petition that successful legislation ever took place. Even to the present day, this has always been the basis of all successful legislation: public custom is adopted and enforced by the State.

In the early days of political representation, the majority did not necessarily carry the day and there was very little need for contested elections but by the beginning of the 15th century, a seat in Parliament was something to be cherished. Historically speaking, the dogma of the equality of man is the result of the adoption of the purely practical machinery of the majority but the adoption of the majority principle is also responsible for another institution of modern times: the party system. The party system is an elaborate piece of machinery that pits at least two political candidates against each other for the vote of an electorate; its advantage being equal representation interesting a large number of people in politics; it provides effective criticism of the government in power and it affords an outlet for the ambition of a large number of wealthy and educated people guaranteeing a consistent policy in government.

These three institutions: political representation, majority rule and the party system are the basic components of modern political machinery; they are applicable to both central and local governments and are becoming by their adaptability ends in themselves rather than a machinery to achieve some purpose.

The State and the Executive System

The administration is one of the most difficult aspects of government. In the enactment and enforcement of laws, the victory of the State is complete but not so in regards to administration the reason being that it is easy to see the advantage of the enactment and enforcement of laws but not the administration of domestic, religious and business affairs which should be kept to a minimum by government.

Originally, the State was a military organization. For many years, it was just a territory ruled by a king who was surrounded by a small elite group of warriors and court officials and it was basically rule by force over a larger mass of people. Slowly, however, the people gained political representation for none can really be said to be a member of the State without the right of having a voice in the direction of policy making.

One of the basic functions of the State in regards to administration is maintaining peace and internal order; it has no other excuse for interfering in the lives of its citizens. To maintain law and order, the State develops means of communication. Historically, the "king's highway" was laid down and maintained for the convenience of the royal armies not as an incentive to commerce.

In almost all countries, the State jealously maintains the control of the means of communication and special freedoms such as those delineated in the First Amendment to the United States Constitution are rather limited. The State's original function of maintaining law and order within its borders gave rise to police administration which is a branch of the dispensation of justice but on its preventive side, police jurisdiction has a special character of its own, which distinguishes it from ordinary judicial work. In the curfew, the State shows early in history the importance of preventing disorder.

In early days, next to maintaining law and order, the State was concerned with the raising of revenue. This led eventually to modern State socialism. It was then useful to the State to establish a standard of weights and measures so that value could be generally accepted and finally the State acquired a monopoly of coinage. The regulation of labor by the State as one of its functions dates from the 15th century, when the plague or black death decimated most of Europe.

The invariable policy of the State has always being to break down all intermediate authorities and to deal directly with the individual. This was the policy until Adam Smith's *The Wealth of Nations* was published promoting a strong public reaction against State interference. By its own action, the State raised the issue of the poor or the State relief of the indigent. The State, of course, did not create poverty but by destroying the chief agencies which dealt with it such as the village, the church and the guilds, it practically assumed full responsibility for the poor without exercising any power over it. The Great Poor Law Report of 1834 showed that communism ran rampant in the rural areas of England. In newly developed countries such as the colonies of the British Empire, the State has refused to take responsibility for the poor and the relief of poverty in spite of the fact, that the poor classes lean heavily towards State socialism.

Recognizing the great power of the State, it is only natural that in times of great crisis such as an overwhelming calamity, the people should invoke general State aid.

Political representation has helped to shape State administration. When the voice of the individual can be heard, the danger of arbitrary interference by the State is greatly reduced. To that extent is the increase of State activity popular. There are no hard and fast rules to limit State administration but it is a fallacy to believe that the State is the nation and what the State does is necessarily for the good of the nation.

In the first place, even in modern times, the State and the nation are never identical. Even where "universal suffrage" prevails, the fact remains that an extension of State administration means an increased interference of some by others, limiting freedom of action. Even if it is admitted that State and nation are one and the same, it is sometimes difficult to admit that State administration is necessarily good. Finally, the modern indiscriminate advocacy of State administration conceals the fallacy that State officials must necessarily prove more effective in their action than private enterprise. Herein lies the basic difference between Public and Business Administration; the first deals with the public deal while the second deals basically in profit but both require a great deal of education and ethical conduct to avoid the mishaps inherent in the relationship not only of business and labor but also the State and the Administration.

The Varieties of Political Experience

According to Aristotle, States are classified into monarchies, aristocracies and democracies. Due to an increase in knowledge of the history of politics, this classification has been abandoned. Generally speaking, no form of government could be considered the best if the best is considered to be the one that is most appropriate under the circumstances. All States are varieties of a single type, the sovereign State. All the Great Powers of the modern world rule on the principle of sovereignty. Sovereign power may be vested on an individual as in an autocratic government or it may be vested on a group as in a constitutional government. Constitutions are written documents that specify and limit the powers of the different branches of government. Although a Constitution is a written document, there is also an unwritten Constitution.

The unwritten constitution is continually being written by the Legislative branch of government; this is just one of those cases in which the nature of the circumstances determines the form of government that is most appropriate. Nevertheless, the written constitution is essential. England did set the fashion of written constitutions during the Civil War but after the Restoration abandoned them to be taken up later by the American Colonies after their emancipation and then France after the Revolution and the rest of Europe including the European colonies.

There are two forms of government, one a strong central government as in France and the other a local government such as the ancient divisions in England that is comparatively weaker but less bureaucratic. These two forms helped to shape the Federal government, first in Switzerland, then in the United States in 1776, in Canada in 1867 and in Germany in 1870 and in the 20th century, Australia. The Federal States introduced the new principle of agreement or contract. Compared to a federation, a confederation singular weakness is that it lacks judicial power. In the American Civil War, the contention of the Confederate States that a State could secede from the Union was untenable because of the power enjoyed by the Federal government in the executive, legislative and judiciary branches.

According to professor A. V. Dicey in *An Introduction to the Study of the Law of the Constitution*, the essential features of a federal constitution are: a) A written supreme constitution in order to prevent disputes between the jurisdictions of the Federal and State authorities; b) A distibution of power between the Federal and State governments and c) A Supreme Court vested with the power to interpret the Constitution and enforce the law of the land remaining independent of both the executive and legislative branches.

As an Academic Discipline

Political science, the study of politics, examines the acquisition and application of power and "power corrupts". Related areas of study include political philosophy, which seeks a rationale for politics and an ethic of public behaviour, political economy, which attempts to develop understandings of the relationships between politics and the economy and the governance of the two, and public administration, which examines the practices of governance.

The first academic chair devoted to politics in the United States was the chair of history and political science at Columbia University, first occupied by Prussian émigré Francis Lieber in 1857.

Spectra

"Politics: A strife of interests masquerading as a contest of principles. The conduct of public affairs for private advantage." — Ambrose Bierce

"Unlimited power is apt to corrupt the minds of those who possess it." — William Pitt the Elder

Left-right Politics

Recently in history, political analysts and politicians divide politics into left wing and right wing politics, often also using the idea of centre politics as a middle path of policy between the right and left. This classification is comparatively recent (it was not used by Aristotle or Hobbes, for instance), and dates from the French Revolution era, when those members of the National Assembly who supported the republic, the common people and a secular society sat on the left and supporters of the monarchy, aristocratic privilege and the Church sat on the right.

The meanings behind the labels have become more complicated over the years. A particularly influential event was the publication of the Communist Manifesto by Karl Marx and Frederick Engels in 1848. The *Manifesto* suggested a course of action for a proletarian revolution to overthrow the bourgeois society and abolish private property, in the belief that this would lead to a classless and stateless society.

The meaning of left-wing and right-wing varies considerably between different countries and at different times, but generally speaking, it can be said that the right wing often values tradition and capitalism while the left wing often values reform and socialism, with the centre seeking a balance between the two such as with social democracy or regulated capitalism.

According to Norberto Bobbio, one of the major exponents of this distinction, the Left believes in attempting to eradicate social inequality, while the Right regards most social inequality as the result of ineradicable natural inequalities, and sees attempts to enforce social equality as utopian or authoritarian.

Some ideologies, notably Christian Democracy, claim to combine left and right wing politics; according to Geoffrey K. Roberts and Patricia Hogwood, "In terms of ideology, Christian Democracy has incorporated many of the views held by liberals, conservatives and socialists within a wider framework of moral and Christian principles." Movements which claim or formerly claimed to be above the left-right divide include Fascist Third-position economic politics in Italy, Gaullism in France, Peronism in Argentina, and National Action Politics in Mexico.

Authoritarian-libertarian Politics

Authoritarianism and libertarianism refer to the amount of individual freedom each person possesses in that society relative to the state. One author describes authoritarian political systems as those where "individual rights and goals are subjugated to group goals, expectations and conformities", while a libertarian political system is one in which individual rights and civil liberties are paramount. More extreme than libertarians are anarchists, who argue for the total abolition of government, while the most extreme authoritarians are totalitarians who support state control over all aspects of society.

For instance, classical liberalism (also known as laissez-faire *liberalism*, or, in much of the world, simply *liberalism*) is a doctrine stressing individual freedom and limited government. This includes the importance of human rationality, individual property rights, free markets, natural rights, the protection of civil liberties, constitutional limitation of government, and individual freedom from restraint as exemplified in the writings of John Locke, Adam Smith, David Hume, David Ricardo, Voltaire, Montesquieu and others. According to the libertarian Institute for Humane Studies, "the libertarian, or 'classical liberal,' perspective is that individual well-being, prosperity, and social harmony are fostered by 'as much liberty as possible' and 'as little government as necessary.'"

World Politics

The 20th century witnessed the outcome of two world wars and not only the rise and fall of the Third Reich but also the rise and fall of communism. The development of the Atomic bomb gave the United States the victory in World War II. Later, the development of the Hydrogen bomb became the ultimate weapon of mass destruction. The United Nations has served as a forum for peace in a world threatened by nuclear war. "The invention of nuclear and space weapons has made war unacceptable as an instrument for achieving political ends." Although an all-out final nuclear holocaust is out of the question for man, "nuclear blackmail" comes into question not only on the issue of world peace but also on the issue of national sovereignity. On a Sunday in 1962, the world stood still at the brink of nuclear war during the October Cuban missile crisis from the implementation of U.S. vs U.S.S.R. nuclear blackmail policy.

Former President Ronald Reagan was horrified by nuclear weapons and believed in the probable existence of life on other planets. For the President, the fantasy of an invasion from outer space that would force the nations of the world to unite against a common enemy was strong enough to convince anyone that mankind could unite in a common interest such as world peace. At their first meeting in Geneva in 1985, president Reagan brought up the subject of an invasion from outer space to Gorbachev. General Powell was convinced Reagan peace proposal to Gorbachev was inspired by the 1951 science-fiction film, *The Day the Earth Stood Still*. On September 21, 1987, Reagan told the General Assembly of the United Nations: "...I occasionally think how quickly our differences worldwide would vanish if we were facing an alien threat from outside this world."

9/11

President George W. Bush declared America's war on terrorism as the aftermath of the attack on the World Trade Centre on September 11, 2001. What came to be known as the Bush Doctrine, which was originally the policy voiced by President Bush after 9/11 that essentially there is no difference between the terrorists and the countries that harbour them, would rally the international community behind the United States in its war against the Taliban in Afghanistan harboring Osama bin Laden and other Al-Qaeda terrorists but would distance the same community in the U.S. invasion of Iraq.

2

Power, Politics and Society

Communication Power: A Theory of Power in the Network Society

In this chapter, Manuel Castells will present a set of grounded hypotheses on the relationship between communication and power relationships in the technological context that characterizes the network society.

He will argue that the media has become the social space where power is decided and discuss the direct link between politics, media politics, the politics of scandal, and the crisis of political legitimacy in a global perspective.

He will assert that the development of interactive, horizontal networks of communication has induced the rise of a new form of communication – mass self-communication over the Internet and wireless communication networks.

Insurgent politics and social movements are able to intervene more decisively in this new communication space. However, corporate media and mainstream politics have also invested in this new space; as a result, mass media and horizontal communication networks are converging. The net outcome of this evolution is a historical shift of the public sphere from the institutional realm to the new communication space.

Manuel Castells

Manuel Castells is Research Professor at the Open University of Catalonia in Barcelona as well as Professor Emeritus of Sociology and Professor Emeritus of City and Regional Planning at the

University of California in Berkeley. He has held the position of Visiting Professor at 29 universities worldwide and has been a guest lecturer at academic and professional institutions in 43 countries.

Professor Castells has authored 22 books, including the trilogy "The Information Age: Economy, Society, and Culture" (1996-2003, Blackwell), which has been translated in 23 languages. He has co-authored and edited an additional 23 books.

He holds the Wallis Annenberg Chair of Communication Technology and Society at the University of Southern California, Distinguished Professor of Technology and Society at the Massachusetts Institute of Technology and Distinguished Visiting Professor of Internet Studies at Oxford University.

In addition, he has received many distinctions including: the Guggenheim Fellowship; the American Society for the Study of Social Problems' C. Wright Mills Award; the American Sociological Association's Robert and Helen Lynd Award; the American Political Science Association's Ithiel Sola Pool Award; Spain's national prize for Sociology and Political Science; the National Medal of Science of Catalonia; the Order of the Lion of Finland; the French Government's Order of Arts and Letters; the Order Gabriela Mistral from Chile; the President of Portugal's Order of Santiago; the Government of Catalonia's Cross of St Jordi.

He has also received Honorary Doctorates from 13 universities and several honorary professorships and university medals. He was a member of the United Nations Secretary General's Advisory Board on Information Technology and Global Development and a member of the United Nations Secretary General's Advisory Panel on the Global Civil Society. In 2005, he was appointed by the European Commission to be a founding member of the Scientific Council of the European Research Council.

He is a member of the Spanish Royal Academy of Economics and Finance, a member of Academia Europea and Corresponding Fellow of the British Academy. He was a founding member of the Scientific Council of the European Research Council and a member of the Governing Board of the European Institute of Innovation and Technology.

Feminist Perspectives on Power

Although any general definition of feminism would no doubt be controversial, it seems undeniable that much work in feminist theory is devoted to the tasks of critiquing women's subordination, analyzing the intersections between sexism and other forms of subordination such as racism, heterosexism, and class oppression, and envisioning the possibilities for both individual and collective resistance to such subordination. Insofar as the concept of power is central to each of these theoretical tasks, power is clearly a central concept for feminist theory as well. And yet, curiously, it is one that is not often explicitly discussed in feminist work (exceptions include Allen 1998, 1999, Hartsock 1983 and 1996, Yeatmann 1997, and Young 1992). This poses a challenge for assessing feminist perspectives on power, as those perspectives often have to be reconstructed from feminist discussions of other topics. Nevertheless, it is possible to identify three main ways in which feminists have conceptualized power: as a resource to be (re)distributed, as domination, and as empowerment, both individual and collective. After a brief discussion of theoretical debates amongst social and political theorists over how to define power, this entry will survey each of these feminist conceptions; it will concentrate, as does the literature, on feminist conceptions of domination.

Defining Power

In social and political theory, power is often regarded as an essentially contested concept. Although, we use the term "power" frequently in our everyday lives and seem to have little trouble understanding what is meant by it, the concept has sparked widespread and seemingly intractable disagreements amongst those philosophers and social and political theorists who have devoted their careers to analyzing and conceptualizing it.

For example, the literature on power is marked by a deep disagreement over the basic definition of power. Some theorists define power as getting someone else to do what you want them to do (power-over) whereas others define it more broadly as an ability or a capacity to act (power-to). Many very important analyses of power in political science, sociology, and philosophy presuppose the former definition of power (power-over). For example, Max Weber defines power as "the probability that one actor within a social relationship will be in a position to carry out his own will despite resistance..." (1978, 53). Robert Dahl offers what he calls an "intuitive idea of power" according to which "A has power over B to the extent that he can get B to do something that B would not otherwise do" (1957, 202-03). Dahl's definition sparked a vigorous debate that continued until the mid-1970s, but even Dahl's best-known critics seemed to agree with his basic equation of power with power-over. As Steven Lukes notes, Dahl's one-dimensional view of power, Bachrach and Baratz's two-dimensional view, and his own three-dimensional view are all variations of "the same underlying conception of power, according to which A exercises power over B when A affects B in a manner contrary to B's interests" (1974, 30). Similarly, but from a very different theoretical background, Michel Foucault's highly influential analysis presupposes that power is a kind of power-over; and he puts it, "if we speak of the structures or the mechanisms of power, it is only insofar as we suppose that certain persons exercise power over others" (1983, 217).

Others define power as an ability or capacity to do something (power-to). Thomas Hobbes's definition of power as a person's "present means...to obtain some future apparent Good"(Hobbes 1985 (1641), 150) is a classic example of this understanding of power, as is Hannah Arendt's definition of power as "the human ability not just to act but to act in concert" (1970, 44). Hanna Pitkin notes that power is related etymologically to the French word pouvoir and the Latin potere, both of which mean to be able. "That suggests, in turn, that power is a something — anything — which makes or renders somebody able to do, capable of doing something. Power is capacity, potential, ability, or wherewithal" (1972, 276). Similarly, Peter Morriss (2002) and Lukes (2005) define power as a dispositional concept, meaning, as Lukes puts it, that power "is a potentiality, not an actuality — indeed a potentiality that may never be actualized" (2005, 69). (This statement amounts to a significant revision of Lukes's earlier analysis of power, in which he argued against defining power as power-to on the grounds that such a definition obscures "the conflictual aspect of power — the fact that it is exercised over people" and thus fails to address what we care about most when we decide to study power (2005, 34)). Some of the theorists who analyse power as power-to leave power-over entirely out of their analysis. For example, Arendt distinguishes power sharply from authority, strength, force, and violence, and offers a normative account in which power is understood as an end in itself (1970). As Jürgen Habermas has argued, this has the effect of screening any and all strategic understandings of power (where power is understood in the Weberian sense as imposing one's will on another) out of her analysis (Habermas 1994). Others suggest that both aspects of power are important, but then focus their attention on either power-over (e.g., Connolly 1993) or power-to (e.g., Morriss 2002). Still others define power-over as a particular type of capacity, namely, the capacity to impose one's will on others; thus, power-over is a derivative form of power-to (Allen 1999, Lukes 2005). However, others have argued power-over and power-to refer to fundamentally different meanings of the word "power" and that it is a mistake to try to develop an account of power that integrates these two concepts (Pitkin 1972, Wartenberg 1990).

What accounts for the highly contested nature of the concept of power? One explanation is that how we conceptualize power is shaped by the political and theoretical interests that we bring to the study of power (Lukes 1986, Said 1986). For example, political scientists who study international relations bring different interests to the study of power than do democratic theorists or social movement theorists, and so forth. For the most part, feminists who are interested in power are interested in understanding and critiquing social relations of domination and subordination and thinking about how such relations can be transformed through individual and collective resistance. This means that, for the most part, feminist discussions of power focus on social rather than political power understood in terms of the power of the state (but see Yeatmann, 1997).

Lukes suggests another, more radical, explanation for the essentially contested nature of the concept of power: our conceptions of power are, according to him, themselves shaped by power relations. As he puts it, "how we think about power may serve to reproduce and reinforce power structures and relations, or alternatively it may challenge and subvert them. It may contribute to their continued functioning, or it may unmask their principles of operation, whose effectiveness is increased by their being hidden from view. To the extent that this is so, conceptual and methodological questions are inescapably political and so what 'power' means is 'essentially contested'…" (Lukes 2005, 63). The idea that conceptions of power are themselves shaped by power relations is behind the claim, made by many feminists, that the influential conception of power as power-over is itself a product of male domination.

Although there are relatively few explicit discussions of how to conceptualize power in the feminist literature, we will see that the basic distinction between power-over and power-to runs through and structures much of the feminist discussion of power.

Power as Resource: Liberal Feminist Approaches

Those who conceptualize power as a resource understand it as a positive social good that is currently unequally distributed amongst women and men. For feminists who understand power in this way, the goal is to redistribute this resource so that women will have power equal to men. Implicit in this view is the assumption that power is "a kind of stuff that can be possessed by individuals in greater or lesser amounts" (Young 1990, 31).

The conception of power as a resource can be found in the work of some liberal feminists. For example, in Justice, Gender, and the Family, Susan Moller Okin argues that the contemporary gender-structured family unjustly distributes the benefits and burdens of familial life amongst husbands and wives. Okin includes power on her list of benefits, which she calls "critical social goods." As she puts it, "when we look seriously at the distribution between husbands and wives of such critical social goods as work (paid and unpaid), power, prestige, self-esteem, opportunities for self-development, and both physical and economic security, we find socially constructed inequalities between them, right down the list" (Okin, 1989, 136). Here, Okin seems to presuppose that power is a resource that is unequally and unjustly distributed between men and women; hence, one of the goals of feminism would be to redistribute this resource in more equitable ways.

Although she doesn't discuss Okin's work explicitly, Iris Marion Young argues against this way of understanding power, which she refers to as a distributive model of power. First, Young maintains that it is wrong to think of power as a kind of stuff that can be possessed; on her view, power is a relation, not a thing that can be distributed or redistributed. Second, she claims that the distributive model tends to presuppose a dyadic, atomistic understanding of power; as a result, it fails to illuminate the broader social, institutional and structural contexts that shape individual relations of power. According to Young, this makes the distributive model unhelpful for understanding the structural features of domination. Third, the distributive model conceives of power statically, as a pattern of distribution, whereas Young, following Foucault (1980), claims that power exists only in action, and thus must be understood dynamically, as existing in ongoing processes or interactions. Finally, Young argues that the distributive model of power tends to view domination as the concentration of power in the hands of a few. According to Young, although this model might be appropriate for some forms of domination, it is not appropriate for the forms that domination takes in contemporary industrial societies such as the United States (Young 1990a, 31-33). On her view, in contemporary industrial societies, power is "widely dispersed and diffused" and yet it is nonetheless true that "social relations are tightly defined by domination and oppression" (Young 1990a, 32-33).

Power as Domination

Young's critique of the distributive model points toward an alternative way of conceptualizing power, one that understands power not as a resource or critical social good, but instead views it as a relation of domination. Although feminists have often used a variety of terms to refer to this kind of relation — including 'oppression', 'patriarchy', 'subjection', and so forth —the common thread in these analyses is an understanding of power not only as power-over, but as a specific kind of power-over relation, namely, one that is unjust and oppressive to those over whom power is exercised. In what follows, I use the term 'domination' to refer to such unjust or oppressive power-over relations. In the following section, I discuss the specific ways in which feminists with different political and philosophical commitments — influenced by phenomenology, radical feminism, socialist feminism, and post-structuralism — have conceptualized domination.

Phenomenological Feminist Approaches

The locus classicus of feminist phenomenological approaches to theorizing male domination is Simone de Beauvoir's *The Second Sex*. Beauvoir's text provides a brilliant analysis of the situation of women, the social, cultural, historical and economic conditions that define their existence. Beauvoir's basic diagnosis of women's situation relies on the distinction between being for-itself — self-conscious subjectivity that is capable of freedom and transcendence — and being in-itself — the un-self-conscious things that are incapable of freedom and mired in immanence. Beauvoir argues that whereas men have assumed the status of the transcendent subject, women have been relegated to the status of the immanent Other. As she puts it in a famous passage from the *Introduction to The Second Sex*: "She is defined and differentiated with reference to man and not he with reference to her; she is the incidental, the inessential as opposed to the essential. He is the Subject, he is the Absolute — she is the Other" (Beauvoir, xxii). This distinction — between man as Subject and woman as Other — is the key to Beauvoir's understanding of domination or oppression. She writes, "every time transcendence falls back into immanence, stagnation, there is a degradation of existence into the 'en-soi' — the brutish life of subjection to given conditions — and liberty into constraint and contingence. This downfall represents a moral fault if the subject consents to it; if it is inflicted upon him, it spells frustration and oppression. In both cases it is an absolute evil" (Beauvoir, xxxv). Although Beauvoir suggests that women are partly responsible for submitting to the status of the Other in order to avoid the anguish of authentic existence (hence, they are in bad faith), she maintains that women are oppressed because they are compelled to assume the status of the Other, doomed to immanence (xxxv). Women's situation is thus marked by a basic tension between transcendence and immanence; as self-conscious human beings, they are capable of transcendence, but they are compelled into immanence by cultural and social conditions that deny them that transcendence.

More recently, feminist phenomenologists have engaged critically with Beauvoir's ground-breaking work, and, in so doing, have extended her insights into power. For example, Iris Young argues that Beauvoir pays relatively little attention to the role that female embodiment plays in women's oppression. Although Beauvoir does discuss women's bodies in relation to their status as immanent Other, she tends to focus on women's physiology, and how physiological features such as menstruation and pregnancy tie women more closely to nature, thus, to immanence. In her essay, "Throwing Like a Girl," Young concentrates instead on "the situatedness of the woman's actual bodily movement and orientation to its surroundings and its world". She notes that girls and women often fail to use fully the spatial potential of their bodies (for example, they throw like girls), they try not to take up too much space, and they tend to approach physical activity tentatively and uncertainly. Young argues that feminine bodily comportment, movement and spatial orientation exhibit the same tension between transcendence and immanence that Beauvoir diagnoses in The Second Sex. "At the root of those modalities," Young writes, "is the fact that the woman lives her body as object as well as subject. The source of this is that patriarchal society defines woman as object, as a mere body, and that in sexist society women are in fact frequently regarded by others as objects and mere bodies" (Young 1990b, 155). And yet women are also subjects, and, thus, cannot think of themselves as mere bodily objects. As a result, woman "cannot be in unity with herself" (Young 1990b, 155). Young explores the tension between transcendence and immanence and the lack of unity characteristic of feminine subjectivity in more detail in several other essays that explore pregnant embodiment, women's experience with their clothes, and breasted experience.

Many feminists have engaged in similar phenomenological analyses of the tension between transcendence and immanence that is, on this view, characteristic of women's subordination.

Radical Feminist Approaches

Unlike liberal feminists, who view power as a positive social resource that ought to be fairly distributed, and feminist phenomenologists, who understand domination in terms of a tension between transcendence and immanence, radical feminists tend to understand power in terms of dyadic relations of dominance/subordination, often understood on analogy with the relationship between master and slave.

For example, in the work of Catharine MacKinnon, domination is closely bound up with her understanding of gender difference. According to MacKinnon, gender difference is simply the reified effect of domination. As she puts it, "difference is the velvet glove on the iron fist of domination. The problem is not that differences are not valued; the problem is that they are defined by power" (MacKinnon 1989, 219). If gender difference is itself a function of domination, then the implication is that men are powerful and women are powerless by definition. As MacKinnon puts it, "women/men is a distinction not just of difference, but of power and powerlessness....Power/powerlessness is the sex difference" (MacKinnon 1987, 123). (In this passage, MacKinnon glosses over the distinction, articulated by many second-wave feminists, between sex — the biologically rooted traits that make one male or female, traits that are often presumed to be natural and immutable — and gender — the socially and culturally rooted, hence contingent and mutable, traits, characteristics, dispositions, and practices that make one a woman or a man. This passage suggests that MacKinnon, like Judith Butler (1990) and other critics of the sex/gender distinction, thinks that sex difference, no less than gender difference, is socially constructed and shaped by relations of power.) If men are powerful and women powerless as such, then male domination is, on this view, pervasive. Indeed, MacKinnon claims that it is a basic "fact of male supremacy" that "no woman escapes the meaning of being a woman within a gendered social system, and sex inequality is not only pervasive but may be universal (in the sense of never having not been in some form" (MacKinnon 1989, 104-05). For MacKinnon, heterosexual intercourse is the paradigm of male domination; as she puts it, "the social relation between the sexes is organized so that men may dominate and women must submit and this relation is sexual — in fact, is sex". As a result, she tends to presuppose a dyadic conception of domination, according to which individual women are subject to the will of individual men. If male domination is pervasive and women are powerless by definition, then it follows that female power is "a contradiction in terms, socially speaking" (MacKinnon 1987, 53). The claim that female power is a contradiction in terms has led many feminists to criticize MacKinnon on the grounds that she denies women's agency and presents them as helpless victims.

A similar dyadic conception of male domination can be found in Carole Pateman's The Sexual Contract (1988). Like MacKinnon, Pateman claims that gender difference is constituted by domination; as she puts it, "the patriarchal construction of the difference between masculinity and femininity is the political difference between freedom and subjection" (Pateman 1988, 207). She also claims that male domination is pervasive, and she explicitly appeals to a master/subject model to understand it; as she puts it, "in modern civil society all men are deemed good enough to be women's masters" (Pateman 1988, 219). In Pateman's view, the social contract that initiates civil society and provides for the legitimate exercise of political rights is also a sexual contract that establishes what she calls "the law of male sex-right," securing male sexual access to and dominance over women (1988, 182). As Nancy Fraser has argued, on Pateman's view, the sexual contract "institutes a series of male/female master/subject dyads" (Fraser 1993, 173). Fraser is highly critical of Pateman's analysis, which she terms the "master/subject model," a model that presents women's subordination "first and foremost as the condition of being subject to the direct command of an individual man" (1993, 173). The problem with this dyadic account of women's subordination, according to Fraser, is that "gender inequality is today being transformed by a shift from dyadic relations of mastery and subjection to more impersonal structural mechanisms that are lived through more fluid cultural forms" (1993, 180). Fraser suggests that, in order to understand women's subordination in contemporary Western societies, feminists will have to move beyond the master/subject model to analyse how women's subordination is secured through cultural norms, social practices, and other impersonal structural mechanisms.

Marilyn Frye likewise offers a radical feminist analysis of power that seems to presuppose a dyadic model of domination. Frye identifies several faces of power, one of the most important of which is access. As Frye puts it, "total power is unconditional access; total powerlessness is being unconditionally accessible. The creation and manipulation of power is constituted of the manipulation and control of access" (Frye 1983, 103). If access is one of the most important faces of power, then feminist separatism, insofar as it is a way of denying access to women's bodies, emotional support, domestic labor, and so forth, represents a profound challenge to male power. For this reason, Frye maintains that all feminism that is worth the name entails some form of separatism. She also suggests that this is the real reason that men get so upset by acts of separatism: "if you are doing something that is so strictly forbidden by the patriarchs, you must be doing something right" (Frye 1983, 98). Frye frequently compares male domination to a master/slave relationship, and she defines oppression as "a system of interrelated barriers and forces which reduce, immobilize, and mold people who belong to a certain group, and effect their subordination to another group (individually to individuals of the other group, and as a group, to that group)" (Frye 1983, 33). In addition to access, Frye discusses definition as another, related, face of power. Frye claims that "the powerful normally determine what is said and sayable". For example, "when the Secretary of Defence calls something a peace negotiation...then whatever it is that he called a peace negotiation is an instance of negotiating peace". Under conditions of subordination, women typically do not have the power to define the terms of their situation, but by controlling access, Frye argues, they can begin to assert control over their own self-definition. Both of these — controlling access and definition — are ways of taking power. Although she does not go so far as MacKinnon does in claiming that female power is a contradiction in terms, Frye does claim that "if there is one thing women are queasy about it is actually taking power".

Socialist Feminist Approaches

According to the traditional Marxist account of power, domination is understood on the model of class exploitation; domination results from the capitalist appropriation of the surplus value that is produced by the workers. As many second wave feminist critics of Marx have pointed out, however, Marx's categories are gender-blind. Marx ignores the ways in which class exploitation and gender subordination are intertwined; because he focuses solely on economic production, Marx overlooks women's reproductive labor in the home and the exploitation of this labor in capitalist modes of production. As a result of this gender-blindness, socialist feminists have argued that Marx's analysis of class domination must be supplemented with a radical feminist critique of patriarchy in order to yield a satisfactory account of women's oppression; the resulting theory is referred to as dual systems theory. As Iris Young puts it, "dual systems theory says that women's oppression arises from two distinct and relatively autonomous systems. The system of male domination, most often called 'patriarchy', produces the specific gender oppression of women; the system of the mode of production and class relations produces the class oppression and work alienation of most women" (Young 1990b, 21). Although Young agrees with the aim of theorizing class and gender domination in a single theory, she is critical of dual systems theory on the grounds that "it allows Marxism to retain in basically unchanged form its theory of economic and social relations, on to which it merely grafts a theory of gender relations" (Young 1990b, 24). Young calls instead for a more unified theory, a truly feminist historical materialism that would offer a critique of society and social relations of power as a whole.

In a later essay, Young offers a more systematic analysis of oppression, an analysis that is grounded in her earlier call for a comprehensive socialist feminism. Young identifies five faces of oppression: economic exploitation, socio-economic marginalization, lack of power or autonomy over one's work, cultural imperialism, and systematic violence. The first three faces of oppression in this list expand on the Marxist account of economic exploitation, and the last two go beyond that account, bringing out other aspects of oppression that are not well explained in economic terms. According to Young, being subject to any one of these forms of power is sufficient to call a group oppressed, but most oppressed groups in the United States experience more than one of these forms of power, and some experience all five (Young 1992, 194). She also claims that this list is comprehensive, both in the sense that "covers all the groups said by new left social movements to be oppressed" and that it "covers all the ways they are oppressed"

(Young 1992, 181). Nancy Hartsock offers a different vision of feminist historical materialism in her book Money, Sex, and Power: Toward a Feminist Historical Materialism (1983). In this book, Hartsock is concerned with "(1) how relations of domination along lines of gender are constructed and maintained and (2) whether social understandings of domination itself have been distorted by men's domination of women" (Hartsock 1983, 1). Following Marx's conception of ideology, Hartsock maintains that the prevailing ideas and theories of a time period are rooted in the material, economic relations of that society. This applies, in her view, to theories of power as well. Thus, she criticizes theories of power in mainstream political science for presupposing a market model of economic relations — a model that understands the economy primarily in terms of exchange, which is how it appears from the perspective of the ruling class rather than in terms of production, which is how it appears from the perspective of the worker. She also argues that power and domination have consistently been associated with masculinity. Because power has been understood from the position of the socially dominant — the ruling class and men — the feminist task, according to Hartsock, is to reconceptualize power from a specifically feminist standpoint, one that is rooted in women's life experience, specifically, their role in reproduction. Conceptualizing power from this standpoint can, according to Hartsock, "point beyond understandings of power as power over others" (Hartsock 1983, 12).

Post-structuralist Feminist Approaches

Most of the work on power done by post-structuralist feminists has been inspired by Foucault. In his middle period works, Foucault analyzes modern power as a mobile and constantly shifting set of force relations that emerge from every social interaction and thus pervade the social body. As he puts it, "power is everywhere, not because it embraces everything, but because it comes from everywhere" (1978, 93). Foucault endeavors to offer a "micro-physics" of modern power (1977, 26), an analysis that focuses not on the concentration of power in the hands of the sovereign or the state, but instead on how power flows through the capillaries of the social body. Foucault criticizes previous analyses of power (primarily Marxist and Freudian) for assuming that power is fundamentally repressive, a belief that he terms the "repressive hypothesis" (1978, 17-49).

Although Foucault does not deny that power sometimes functions repressively, he maintains that it is primarily productive; as he puts it, "power produces; it produces reality; it produces domains of objects and rituals of truth" (1977, 194). It also, according to Foucault, produces subjects. As he puts it, "the individual is not the vis-à-vis of power; it is, I believe, one of its prime effects" (1980, 98). According to Foucault, modern power subjects individuals, in both senses of the term; it simultaneously creates them as subjects by subjecting them to power. As we will see in a moment, Foucault's account of subjection and his account of power more generally have been extremely fruitful, but also quite controversial, for feminists interested in analyzing domination.

It should come as no surprise that so many feminists have drawn on Foucault's analysis of power. Foucault's analysis of power has arguably been the most influential discussion of the topic over the last thirty years; even those theorists of power who are highly critical of Foucault's work acknowledge this influence. Moreover, Foucault's focus on the local and capillary nature of modern power clearly resonates with feminist efforts to redefine the scope and bounds of the political, efforts that are summed up by the slogan "the personal is political." At this point, the feminist work that has been inspired by Foucault's analysis of power is so extensive and varied that it defies summarization.

Several of the most prominent Foucaultian-feminist analyses of power draw on his account of disciplinary power in order to critically analyse normative femininity. In Discipline and Punish, Foucault analyzes the disciplinary practices that were developed in prisons, schools, and factories in the 18th century — including minute regulations of bodily movements, obsessively detailed time schedules, and surveillance techniques — and how these practices shape the bodies of prisoners, students and workers into docile bodies (1977, 135-169). In her highly influential essay, Sandra Bartky criticizes Foucault for failing to notice that disciplinary practices are gendered and that, through such gendered discipline, women's bodies are rendered more docile than the bodies of men

(1990, 65). Drawing on and extending Foucault's account of disciplinary power, Bartky analyzes the disciplinary practices that engender specifically feminine docile bodies — including dieting practices, limitations on gestures and mobility, and bodily ornamentation. She also expands Foucault's analysis of the Panopticon, Jeremy Bentham's design for the ideal prison, a building whose spatial arrangement was designed to compel the inmate to surveil himself, thus becoming, as Foucault famously put it, "the principle of his own subjection" (1977, 203). With respect to gendered disciplinary practices such as dieting, restricting one's movement so as to avoid taking up too much space, and keeping one's body properly hairless, attired, ornamented and made up, Bartky observes "it is women themselves who practice this discipline on and against their own bodies....The woman who checks her make-up half a dozen times a day to see if her foundation has caked or her mascara run, who worries that the wind or rain may spoil her hairdo, who looks frequently to see if her stocking have bagged at the ankle, or who, feeling fat, monitors everything she eats, has become, just as surely as the inmate in the Panopticon, a self-policing subject, a self committed to relentless self-surveillance. This self-surveillance is a form of obedience to patriarchy" (1990, 80).

As Susan Bordo points out, this model of self-surveillance does not adequately illuminate all forms of female subordination—all too often women are actually compelled into submission by means of physical force, economic coercion, or emotional manipulation. Nevertheless, Bordo agrees with Bartky that "when it comes to the politics of appearance, such ideas are apt and illuminating" (1993, 27). Bordo explains that, in her own work, Foucault's analysis of disciplinary power has been "extremely helpful both to my analysis of the contemporary disciplines of diet and exercise and to my understanding of eating disorders as arising out of and reproducing normative feminine practices of our culture, practices which train the female body in docility and obedience to cultural demands while at the same time being experienced in terms of power and control" (ibid). Bordo also highlights and makes use of Foucault's understanding of power relations as inherently unstable, as always accompanied by, even generating, resistance. "So, for example, the woman who goes into a rigorous weight-training program in order to achieve the currently stylish look may discover that her new muscles give her the self-confidence that enables her to assert herself more forcefully at work" (1993, 28).

Whereas Bartky and Bordo focus on Foucault's account of disciplinary power, Judith Butler draws primarily on his analysis of subjection. For example, in her early and massively influential book, *Gender Trouble* (1990), Butler notes that "Foucault points out that juridical systems of power produce the subjects they subsequently come to represent. Juridical notions of power appear to regulate political life in purely negative terms.....But the subjects regulated by such structures are, by virtue of being subjected to them, formed, defined, and reproduced in accordance with the requirements of those structures" (1990, 2). The implication of this for feminists is, according to Butler, that "feminist critique ought also to understand how the category of 'women', the subject of feminism, is produced and restrained by the very structures of power through which emancipation is sought" (1990, 2). This Foucaultian insight into the nature of subjection — into the ways in which becoming a subject means at the same time being subjected to power relations — thus forms the basis for Butler's trenchant critique of the category of women, and for her call for a subversive performance of the gender norms that govern the production of gender identity. In *Bodies that Matter* (1993), Butler extends this analysis to consider the impact of subjection on the bodily materiality of the subject. As she puts is, "power operates for Foucault in the constitution of the very materiality of the subject, in the principle which simultaneously forms and regulates the 'subject' of subjectivation" (1993, 34). Thus, for Butler, power understood as subjection is implicated in the process of determining which bodies come to matter, whose lives are livable and whose deaths grievable. In *The Psychic Life of Power* (1997), Butler expands further on the Foucaultian notion of subjection, bringing it into dialogue with a Freudian account of the psyche. In the introduction to that text, Butler notes that subjection is a paradoxical form of power. It has an element of domination and subordination, to be sure, but, she writes, "if, following Foucault, we understand power as forming the subject as well, as providing the very condition of its existence and the trajectory of its desire, then power is not simply what we oppose but also, in a strong sense, what we depend on for our existence and what we harbour and preserve in the beings that we are" (1997, 2). Although Butler credits Foucault with recognizing the fundamentally ambivalent character of subjection, she also argues that he does not offer an account of the specific mechanisms by which the subjected subject is formed. For this, Butler maintains, we need an analysis of the psychic form that power takes, for only such an analysis can illuminate the passionate attachment to power that is characteristic of subjection.

Although many feminists have found Foucault's analysis of power extremely fruitful and productive, Foucault has also had his share of feminist critics. In a very influential early assessment, Nancy Fraser argues that, although Foucault's work offers some interesting empirical insights into the functioning of modern power, it is "normatively confused" (Fraser 1989, 31). In his writings on power, Foucault eschews normative categories, preferring instead to describe the way that power functions in local practices and to argue for the appropriate methodology for studying power. He even suggests that such normative notions as autonomy, legitimacy, sovereignty, and so forth, are themselves effects of modern power. Fraser claims that this attempt to remain normatively neutral or even critical of normativity is incompatible with the politically engaged character of Foucault's writings. Thus, for example, although Foucault claims that power is always accompanied by resistance, Fraser argues that he cannot explain why domination ought to be resisted. As she puts it, "only with the introduction of normative notions of some kind could Foucault begin to answer such questions. Only with the introduction of normative notions could he begin to tell us what is wrong with the modern power/knowledge regime and why we ought to oppose it" (1989, 29). Other feminists have criticized the Foucaultian claim that the subject is an effect of power; according to feminists such as Linda Martín Alcoff and Seyla Benhabib, such a claim implies a denial of agency that is incompatible with the demands of feminism as an emancipatory social movement. Finally, Nancy Hartsock (1990 and 1996) calls into question the usefulness of Foucault's work as an analytical tool. Hartsock makes two related arguments against

Foucault. First, she argues that his analysis of power is not a theory for women because it does not examine power from the epistemological point of view of the subordinated; in her view, Foucault analyzes power from the perspective of the colonizer, rather than the colonized (1990). Second, Foucault's analysis of power fails to adequately theorize structural relations of inequality and domination that undergird women's subordination; this is related to the first argument because "domination, viewed from above, is more likely to look like equality".

Despite these and other trenchant feminist critiques of Foucault, his analysis of power continues to be an extremely useful resource for feminist conceptions of domination.

Power as Empowerment

Up to this point, much of this entry has focused, as does much of the feminist literature on this topic, on power as domination, which is a form or an instance of power-over. However, a significant strand of feminist theorizing of power starts with the contention that the conception of power as power-over, domination, or control is implicitly masculinist. Many feminists from a variety of theoretical backgrounds have argued for a reconceptualization of power as a capacity or ability, specifically, the capacity to empower or transform oneself and others. Thus, these feminists have tended to understood power not as power-over but as power-to. (Wartenberg (1990) argues that this feminist understanding of power, which he calls transformative power, is actually a type of power-over, albeit one that is distinct from domination because it aims at empowering those over whom it is exercised. However, most of the feminists who embrace this transformative or empowerment-based conception of power explicitly define it as an ability or capacity and present it as an alternative to putatively masculine notions of power-over. Thus, in what follows, I will follow their usage rather than Wartenberg's.)

For example, Jean Baker Miller claims that "women's examination of power...can bring new understanding to the whole concept of power" (Miller 1992, 241). Miller rejects the definition of power as domination; instead, she defines it as "the capacity to produce a change — that is, to move anything from point A or state A to point B or state B" (Miller 1992, 241). Miller suggests that power understood as domination is particularly masculine; from women's perspective, power is understood differently: "there is enormous validity in women's not wanting to use power as it is presently conceived and used. Rather, women may want to be powerful in ways that simultaneously enhance, rather than diminish, the power of others" (Miller 1992, 247-248).

Similarly, Virginia Held argues against the masculinist conception of power as "the power to cause others to submit to one's will, the power that led men to seek hierarchical control and...contractual constraints" (Held 1993, 136). Held views women's unique experiences as mothers and caregivers as the basis for new insights into power; as she puts it, "the capacity to give birth and to nurture and empower could be the basis for new and more humanly promising conceptions than the ones that now prevail of power, empowerment, and growth" (Held 1993, 137). According to Held, "the power of a mothering person to empower others, to foster transformative growth, is a different sort of power from that of a stronger sword or a dominant will" (Held 1993, 209). On Held's view, a feminist analysis of society and politics leads to an understanding of power as the capacity to transform and empower oneself and others.

This conception of power as transformative and empowering is also a prominent theme in lesbian feminism and ecofeminism. For example, Sarah Lucia Hoagland is critical of the masculine conception of power with its focus on "state authority, police and armed forces, control of economic resources, control of technology, and hierarchy and chain of command" (Hoagland 1988, 114). Instead, Hoagland defines power as "power-from-within" which she understands as "the power of ability, of choice and engagement. It is creative; and hence it is an affecting and transforming power but not a controlling power" (Hoagland 1988, 118). Similarly, Starhawk claims that she is "on the side of the power that emerges from within, that is inherent in us as the power to grow is inherent in the seed". For both Hoagland and Starhawk, power-from-within is a positive, life-affirming, and empowering force that stands in stark contrast to power understood as domination, control or imposing one's will on another.

A similar understanding of power can also be found in the work of the prominent French feminists Luce Irigaray and Hélène Cixous. Irigaray, for example, urges feminists to question the definition of power in phallocratic cultures, for if feminists "aim simply for a change in the distribution of power, leaving intact the power structure itself, then they are resubjecting themselves, deliberately or not, to a phallocratic order" (Irigaray 1985, 81), that is, to a discursive and cultural order that privileges the masculine, represented by the phallus. If we wish to subvert the phallocratic order, according to Irigaray, we will have to reject "a definition of power of the masculine type" (Irigaray 1985, 81). Some feminists interpret Irigaray's work on sexual difference as suggesting an alternative conception of power as transformative, a conception that is not grounded in the feminine. Similarly, Cixous claims that "les pouvoirs de la femme" do not consist in mastering or exercising power over others, but instead are a form of "power over oneself".

Nancy Hartsock refers to the understanding of power "as energy and competence rather than dominance" as "the feminist theory of power" (Hartsock 1983, 224). Hartsock argues that precursors of this theory can be found in the work of some women who did not consider themselves to be feminists — most notably, Hannah Arendt, whose rejection of the command-obedience model of power and definition of 'power' as "the human ability not just to act but to act in concert" overlaps significantly with the feminist conception of power as empowerment (1970, 44). Arendt's definition of 'power' brings out another aspect of the definition of 'power' as empowerment because of her focus on community or collective empowerment. This aspect of empowerment is evident in Mary Parker Follett's distinction between power-over and power-with; for Follett, power-with is a collective ability that is a function of relationships of reciprocity between members of a group (Follett 1942). Hartsock finds it significant that the theme of power as capacity or empowerment has been so prominent in the work of women who have written about power. In her view, this points in the direction of a feminist standpoint that "should allow us to understand why the masculine community constructed...power, as domination, repression, and death, and why women's accounts of power differ in specific and systematic ways from those put forward by men....such a standpoint might allow us to put forward an understanding of power that points in more liberatory directions".

Concluding Thoughts

As this entry shows, there is a wide variety of feminist perspectives on power. If it is true, as I claimed at the outset, that power is a central concept for feminist theory, then the rich variety of feminist work on this topic should not be surprising. And yet much work remains to be done. For example, feminist conceptions of domination must be continually refined in light of the ever-changing social, cultural, and historical circumstances that the concept aims to illuminate.

At present, there is a need to refine our understanding of domination to make it more applicable to the concerns raised by recent discussions of globalization. With respect to empowerment, the challenge is for feminists to rethink this concept in ways that are not reliant on arguably essentialist conceptions of femininity, that is, conceptions that presuppose a universal essence of the feminine. More work also remains to be done to clarify the relationship between the individual and the structural, with respect to both domination and empowerment. Finally, the basic opposition in the feminist literature on power between those who define power as domination and those who define it as empowerment arguably needs to be overcome. There has not been enough work done that attempts to integrate these two conceptions of power. If we are to make these and other theoretical advances, however, feminists will have to spend more time explicitly discussing and defending the conceptions of power that up to now have been largely implicit in their work.

Political Power

Political power (*imperium* in Latin) is a type of power held by a person or group in a society. There are many ways to hold such power. Officially, political power is held by the holders of the sovereignty. Political powers are not limited to heads of states, however, and the extent to which a person or group holds such power is related to the amount of societal influence they can wield, formally or informally. In many cases this influence is not contained within a single state and it refers to international power.

Political scientists have frequently defined power as "the ability to influence the behaviour of others" with or without resistance.

For analytical reasons, MacMillan separates the concepts power:

Power is the capacity to restructure actual situations.

—I.C. Macmillan

Influence is the capacity to control and modify the perceptions of others.

—I.C. Macmillan

Abuse of Power

Throughout history there have been many examples of the destructive or senseless use of political power. This has happened most frequently when too much power has been concentrated in too few hands, without enough room for political debate, public criticism, and other types of correctives.

Examples of such regimes are despotism, tyranny, and dictatorship. To counter these potential problems, people have devised and practised different solutions, most of them related to the sharing of power (as in democracy), the placing of limitations on the extent of power one individual or group can have, and the creation of protective rights for individuals through legislation or charters (such as human rights).

Separation of Powers

Charles de Montesquieu claimed that without following a principle of containing and balancing legislative, executive and judiciary powers, there is no freedom and no protection against abuse of power. This is the separation of powers principle.

Division of Power

A similar concept, termed Division of Power, also consists of differentiated legislative, executive and judiciary powers. However, while Separation of Power prohibits one branch from interfering with another, Division of Power permits such interference. For example, in Indonesia, the President (who wields executive power) can introduce a new bill, but the People's Consultative Assembly (holding legislative power) chooses to either legalize or reject the bill.

Political Science Perspectives

Within normative political analysis, there are also various levels of power as described by academics that add depth into the understanding of the notion of power and its political implications. Robert Dahl, a prominent American political scientist, first ascribed to political power the trait of decision-making as the source and main indicator of power. Later, two other political scientists, Peter Bachrach and Morton Baratz, decided that simply ascribing decision-making as the basis of power was too simplistic and they added what they termed a 2nd dimension of power, agenda-setting by elites who worked in the backrooms and away from public scrutiny in order to exert their power upon society. Lastly, British academic Steven Lukes added a 3rd dimension of power, preference-shaping, which he claimed was another important aspect of normative power in politics which entails theoretical views similar to notions of cultural hegemony. These 3 dimensions of power are today often considered defining aspects of political power by political researchers.

A radical alternative view of the source of political power follows the formula: information plus authority permits the exercise of power. Political power is intimately related to information. Sir Francis Bacon's statement: "Nam et ipsa scientia potestas est" for knowledge itself is power, assumed authority as given. Many will know that unless someone with authority listens and acts, there is no political power.

It is said democracy is the best method of informing those entrusted with authority. They are best able to use authority without ignorance to maximize political power. Those who exercise authority in ignorance are not powerful, because they do not realize their intentions and have little control over the effects of using their authority.

Post-modernism has debated over how to define political power. Perhaps, the best known definition comes from the late Michel Foucault, whose work in Discipline and Punish (and other writings) conveys a view of power that is organic within society. This view holds that political power is more subtle and is part of a series of societal controls and 'normalizing' influences through historical institutions and definitions of normal vs. abnormal.

Foucault once characterized power as "an action over actions" (une action sur des actions), arguing that power was essentially a relation between several dots, in continuous transformation as in Nietzsche's philosophy. His view of power lent credence to the view that power in human society was part of a training process in which everyone, from a Prime Minister to a homeless person, played their role within the power structure of society. Jürgen Habermas opposed himself to Foucault's conception of discourse as a battlefield for power relations, arguing that it should be possible to achieve consensus on the fundamentals rules of discourse, in order to establish a transparent and democratic dialogue. Thenceforth, he argued against Foucault and Althusser that power was not immanent to discourse, and that philosophy could be completely distinguished from ideology. More recently, there has been a move among academics to differentiate power from a new concept of luck. Under some conditions (particularly the when examining the third dimension of power) it becomes necessary to determine who obtains a favourable result through the wielding of genuine power and who is simply "lucky". An example might be an ethnic minority who receive favourable treatment while not intentionally seeking it. A person promoted through positive discrimination would be considered "lucky" rather than "powerful". The eventual aim of such discrimination would be to eventually convert some (or all) of that luck into power. Some groups remain serially lucky without ever obtaining power.

Society

Society or human society is the manner or condition in which the members of a community live together for their mutual benefit. By extension, society denotes the people of a region or country, sometimes even the world, taken as a whole.

Used in the sense of an associaton, a society is a body of individuals outlined by the bounds of functional interdependence, possibly comprising characteristics such as national or cultural identity, social solidarity, language or hierarchical organization. Human societies are characterized by patterns of relationships between individuals sharing a distinctive culture and institutions. Like other communities or groups, a society allows its members to achieve needs or wishes they could not fulfil alone. A society, however, may be ontologically independent of, and utterly irreducible to, the qualities of constituent individuals; it may act to oppress. The urbanization and rationalization inherent in some, particularly Western capitalist, societies, has been associated with feelings of isolation and social "anomie". More broadly, a society is an economic, social or industrial infrastructure, made up of a varied collection of individuals. Members of a society may be from different ethnic groups. A society may be a particular ethnic group, such as the Saxons; a nation state, such as Bhutan; a broader cultural group, such as a Western society. The word *society* may also refer to an organized voluntary association of people for religious, benevolent, cultural, scientific, political, patriotic, or other purposes. A "society" may even, though more by means of metaphor, refer to a social organism such as an ant colony.

Evolution of Societies

According to anthropologist Maurice Godelier, one critical novelty in human society, in contrast to humanity's closest biological relatives (chimpanzees and bonobo), is the parental role assumed by the males, which were unaware of their "father" connection.

Sociologist Gerhard Lenski differentiates societies based on their level of technology, communication and economy: 1) hunters and gatherers, 2) simple agricultural, 3) advanced agricultural, 4) industrial, and 5) special (e.g. fishing societies or maritime societies). This is somewhat similar to the system earlier developed by anthropologists Morton H. Fried, a conflict theorist, and Elman Service, an integration theorist, who have produced a system of classification for societies in all human cultures based on the evolution of social inequality and the role of the state. This system of classification contains four categories:

- Hunter-gatherer bands (categorization on duties and responsibilities.)
- Tribal societies in which there are some limited instances of social rank and prestige.
- Stratified structures led by chieftains.
- Civilizations, with complex social hierarchies and organized, institutional governments.

In addition to this there are:

- Humanity, mankind, that upon which rest all the elements of society, including society's beliefs.
- Virtual society is a society based on online identity, which is evolving in the information age.

Over time, some cultures have progressed toward more-complex forms of organization and control. This cultural evolution has a profound effect on patterns of community. Hunter-gatherer tribes settled around seasonal foodstocks to become agrarian villages. Villages grew to become towns and cities. Cities turned into city-states and nation-states.

Today, anthropologists and many social scientists vigorously oppose the notion of cultural evolution and rigid "stages" such as these. In fact, much anthropological data has suggested that complexity (civilization, population growth and density, specialization, etc.) does not always take the form of hierarchical social organization or stratification.

Also, cultural relativism as a widespread approach/ethic has largely replaced notions of "primitive," better/worse, or "progress" in relation to cultures (including their material culture/technology and social organization).

Organization of Society

Human societies are often organized according to their primary means of subsistence. As noted in the section on "Evolution of societies", above, social scientists identify hunter-gatherer societies, nomadic pastoral societies, horticulturalist or simple farming societies, and intensive agricultural societies, also called civilizations. Some consider industrial and post-industrial societies to be qualitatively different from traditional agricultural societies.

One common theme for societies in general is that a lone person has rather limited means at their disposal, and societies serve to aid individuals in times of crisis. Traditionally, when an individual requires aid, for example at birth, death, sickness, or disaster, members of that society will rally others to render aid, in some form—symbolic, linguistic, physical, mental, emotional, financial, medical, or religious. Many societies will distribute largess, at the behest of some individual or some larger group of people. This type of *generosity* can be seen in all known cultures; typically, prestige accrues to the generous individual or group. Conversely, members of a society may also shun or scapegoat members of the society who violate its norms. Mechanisms such as gift-giving and scapegoating, which may be seen in various types of human groupings, tend to be institutionalized within a society. Social evolution as a phenomenon carries with itself certain elements that could be detrimental to the population it serves.

Some societies will bestow status on an individual or group of people, when that individual or group performs an admired or desired action. This type of recognition is bestowed by members of that society on the individual or group in the form of a name, title, manner of dress, or monetary reward. Males, in many societies, are particularly susceptible to this type of action and subsequent reward, even at the risk of their lives. Action by an individual or larger group in behalf of some cultural ideal is seen in all societies. The phenomena of community action, shunning, scapegoating, generosity, and shared risk and reward occur in subsistence-based societies and in more technology-based civilizations.

Societies may also be organized according to their political structure. In order of increasing size and complexity, there are bands, tribes, chiefdoms, and state societies. These structures may have varying degrees of political power, depending on the cultural geographical, and historical environments that these societies must contend with. Thus, a more isolated society with the same level of technology and culture as other societies is more likely to survive than one in closer proximity to others that may encroach on their resources. A society that is unable to offer an effective response to other societies it competes with will usually be subsumed into the culture of the competing society.

Shared Belief or Common Goal

People of many nations united by common political and cultural traditions, beliefs, or values are sometimes also said to be a society (such as Judeo-Christian, Eastern, and Western). When used in this context, the term is employed as a means of contrasting two or more "societies" whose members represent alternative conflicting and competing worldviews.

Some academic, learned and scholarly associations describe themselves as *societies* (for example, the American Mathematical Society). More commonly, professional organizations often refer to themselves as societies (e.g., the American Society of Civil Engineers, American Chemical Society). In the United Kingdom and the United States, learned societies are normally nonprofit and have charitable status. In science, they range in size to include national scientific societies (i.e., the Royal Society) to regional natural history societies. Academic societies may have interest in a wide range of subjects, including the arts, humanities and science.

In some countries (for example the United States and France), the term "society" is used in commerce to denote a partnership between investors or the start of a business. In the United Kingdom, partnerships are not called societies, but cooperatives or mutuals are often known as societies (such as friendly societies and building societies). In Latin America, the term society may be used in commerce denoting a partnership between investors, or anonymous investors; for example: "Proveedor Industrial Anahuac S.A." where S.A. stands for Anonymous Society (Sociedad Anónima); however in Mexico in other type of partnership it would be declared as S.A. de C.V. or S.A. de R.L., indicating the level of commitment of capital and the responsibilities from each member towards their own association and towards the society in general and supervised by the corresponding jurisdictional civil and judicial authorities.

Society Today

The term *society* is currently used to cover both a number of political and scientific connotations as well as a variety of associations.

Western Society

The development of the Western world has brought with it the emerging concepts of Western culture, politics and ideas, often referred to simply as *Western society*. Geographically, it covers at the very least the countries of Western Europe, North America, Australia and New Zealand and sometimes also includes South America and Israel. The cultures and lifestyles of all of these stem from Western Europe. They all enjoy relatively strong economies and stable governments, allow freedom of religion, have chosen democracy as a form of governance, favour capitalism and international trade, are heavily influenced by Judeo-Christian values, and have some form of political and military alliance or cooperation.

Information Society

Although the concept of information society has been under discussion since the 1930s, in the modern world it is almost always applied to the manner in which information technologies have impacted society and culture.

It therefore covers the effects of computers and telecommunications on the home, the workplace, schools, government and various communities and organizations, as well as the emergence of new social forms in cyberspace.

One of the European Union's areas of interest is the Information Society. Here policies are directed towards promoting an open and competitive digital economy, research into information and communication technologies, as well as their application to improve social inclusion, public services and quality of life.

The International Telecommunications Union's World Summit on the Information Society in Geneva and Tunis (2003/2005) has led to a number of policy and application areas where action is required. These include:

- promotion of ICTs for development;
- information and communication infrastructure;
- access to information and knowledge;
- capacity building;
- building confidence and security in the use of ICTs;
- enabling environment;
- ICT applications in the areas of government, business, learning, health, employment, environment, agriculture and science;
- cultural and linguistic diversity and local content;
- media;
- ethical dimensions of the Information Society;
- international and regional cooperation.

Knowledge Society

As access to electronic information resources increased at the beginning of the 21st century, special attention was extended from the Information Society to the knowledge society.

In the words of an Irish governmental analysis, "The capacity to manipulate, store and transmit large quantities of information cheaply has increased at a staggering rate over recent years. The digitisation of information and the associated pervasiveness of the Internet are facilitating a new intensity in the application of knowledge to economic activity, to the extent that it has become the predominant factor in the creation of wealth.

As much as 70 to 80 percent of economic growth is now said to be due to new and better knowledge."

The Second World Summit on the Knowledge Society, held in Chania, Crete, in September 2009, gave special attention to the following topics:

- business and enterprise computing;
- technology-enhanced learning;
- social and humanistic computing;
- culture, tourism and technology;
- e-government and e-democracy;
- innovation, sustainable development and strategic management;
- service science, management and engineering;
- intellectual and human capital development;
- ICTs for ecology and the Green Economy;
- future prospects for the Knowledge Society;
- technologies and business models for the creative industries.

Well-known Societies

While there are literally thousands of societies representing virtually every interest, a number of them are widely recognized. A few examples demonstrating the variety of a society's scope and interests are given below.

The Royal Society

The Royal Society, officially the Royal Society of London for the Improvement of Natural Knowledge, is a learned society for science that was founded in 1660 and is considered by most to be the oldest such society still in existence.

Fellowship, granted for life, is awarded to scientists after their election by existing fellows, and is considered a great honour. Fellows must be citizens or residents of a member of the Commonwealth of Nations or the Republic of Ireland, while the smaller number of Foreign Members are drawn from other countries. Up to 44 new Fellows are elected each year. The Society's statutes state that candidates for election must have made "a substantial contribution to the improvement of natural knowledge, including mathematics, engineering science and medical science."

The Fabian Society

Britain's best-known socialist society is the Fabian Society, a membership organization affiliated with the Labour Party. It was founded in 1884, some years before the creation of the Labour Party itself. Although membership is relatively small (around 7,000), the society is very influential.

It is best known for its ground-breaking work from the late 19th century until World War I. The society laid many of the foundations of the Labour Party. Today, it is a vanguard "think tank" of the New Labour movement.

Famous members have included George Bernard Shaw, H. G. Wells, Virginia Woolf, Ramsay MacDonald, Tony Benn, Harold Wilson, and more recently Tony Blair and Gordon Brown.

Society of Friends

The Society of Friends is a Christian organization whose members are commonly known as Quakers. It was founded in 17th century England by George Fox who called for a radical, egalitarian, spirit-filled Christianity that would not be oppressive of people on account of race, sex, or class. Women and men were given equal status as all were children of God. A person should not set himself up with honors and distinctions as these were meaningless in the sight of God. From this came the Quaker practices of simple living, plain dress and plain speech. Quakers maintain that the teaching of Jesus is a practical method for the guidance of the world today and that religion is concerned with the whole of life.

Friends World Committee for Consultation (FWCC) is the international Quaker organization which loosely unifies the diverse groups of Friends from around the world.

A number of leading charities today were founded with participation from Quakers, such as Oxfam and Amnesty International.

Societies for the Prevention of Cruelty to Animals

Throughout the English-speaking world, there are a considerable number of societies for the prevention of cruelty to animals, often known as SPCAs. Their operations may include protecting and providing shelter to animals in danger, striving to relieve the suffering of animals and ensuring law enforcement for the protection of animals. They are non-profit organizations that campaign for animal welfare and take in abused or abandoned animals, and help them to get adopted.

Among the large national organizations are the American ASPCA with over one million supporters across the United States and the British RSPCA with voluntary funding of over £80 million a year.

Social Class

Social classes are the hierarchical arrangements of people in society as economic or cultural groups. Class is an essential object of analysis for sociologists, anthropologists, political economists and social historians. In sociology and anthropology social class is discussed in terms of 'social stratification'.

In sociology and political philosophy, the most basic class distinction is between the powerful and the powerless. In Marxist theory and historical materialism, social class is caused by the fundamental economic structure of work and property. Various social and political theories propose that social classes with greater power attempt to cement their own ranking above the lower social classes in the social hierarchy to the detriment of the society overall. By contrast, conservatives and structural functionalists have presented class difference as intrinsic to the structure of any society and to that extent ineradicable. Social classes with a great deal of power are usually viewed as "the elites" within their own societies.

Causes and Outcomes of Social Class

In class society class is a key feature of life, and the cause and consequence of an individual's class often deeply scores their life.

Determinants of Class Position

In so-called non-stratified societies or acephalous societies, there is no concept of social class, power, or hierarchy beyond temporary or limited social statuses. In such societies, every individual has a roughly equal social standing in most situations.

In class societies a person's class status is determined by membership in a group. Theorists disagree about the determining elements, but common shared features appear in many accounts. Key shared group relationships include:

- relationships of production, ownership and consumption
- a common legal status, including ceremonial, occupational and reproductive rights
- family, kinship or tribal group structures or membership
- acculturation, including education.

The most powerful class in a society often have a distinct lifestyle that emphasize their prestige. This culture often includes markers such as intensive costume and grooming; manners and language codes that mark insiders and outsiders; unique political rights such as honorary titles; and, concepts of social honour or face that are claimed to only be applicable to the in group. These expectations can be inverted, and low-class shared group behaviour can also be observed, and often becoming defining elements of personal identity and uniting factors in group behaviour. Bourdieu suggests a notion of high and low classes with a distinction between bourgeois tastes and sensitivities and the working class tastes and sensitivities.

Fluid notions such as race can influence class standing. The association of particular ethnic groups with class statuses are common in many societies. As a result of conquest or internal ethnic differentiation, a ruling class is seen to be ethnically homogenous. Similarly, particular races or ethnic groups may be legally or customarily restricted to occupying low class positions. Which ethnicities are considered as belonging to high or low classes varies from society to society. In modern societies strict legal links between ethnicity and class have been drawn, such as in apartheid, the Caste system in Africa, and in the position of the Burakumin in Japanese society.

Defining Ascribed status versus Achieved status deals with the actual individual person's role in class identification, and on whether or not one's social standing is determined at birth or earned over a lifetime. Achieved statuses are acquired based on merit, skills, abilities, and actions. Examples of achieved status include being a doctor or even being a criminal—the status then determines a set of behaviors and expectations for the individual.

Consequences of Class Position

Different consumption of social goods is the most visible consequence of class. In modern societies, it manifests as income inequality, though in subsistence societies it manifested as malnutrition and periodic starvation. Although class status is not a causal factor for income, there is consistent data that show those in higher classes have higher incomes than those in lower classes. This inequality still persists when controlling for occupation. The conditions at work vary greatly depending on class. Those in the upper-middle class and middle-class enjoy greater freedoms in their occupations. They generally are more respected, enjoy more diversity, and are able to exhibit some authority. Those in lower classes tend to feel more alienated and have lower work satisfaction overall. The physical conditions of the workplace differ greatly between classes. While middle-class workers may "suffer alienating conditions" or "lack of job satisfaction", blue-collar workers suffer alienating, often routine, work with obvious physical health hazards, injury, and even death.

In the more social sphere, class has direct consequences on lifestyle. Lifestyle includes tastes, preferences, and a general style of living. These lifestyles could quite possibly affect educational attainment, and therefore status attainment. Class lifestyle also affects how children are raised. For example, a working-class person is more likely to raise their child to be working class and middle-class children are more likely to be raised to be middle-class. This perpetuates the idea of class for future generations.

Theoretical Models

Theoretical models of class seek to explain how class relationships come into being, and why particular class relationships exist across broadly similar societies.

Marxist

For Marx, class involves two factors:

Objective Factors

A class shares a common relationship to the means of production. That is, all people in one class make their living in a common way in terms of ownership of the things that produce social goods. A class may own things, own land, own people, be owned, own nothing but their labour. A class will extract tax, produce agriculture, enslave and work others, be enslaved and work, or work for a wage.

Subjective Factors

The members will necessarily have some perception of their similarity and common interest. Marx termed this Class consciousness. Class consciousness is not simply an awareness of one's own class interest (for instance, the maximisation of shareholder value; or, the maximisation of the wage with the minimisation of the working day), class consciousness also embodies deeply shared views of how society should be organised legally, culturally, socially and politically.

The first criteria divides a society into the owners and non-owners of means of production. In capitalism, these are capitalist (bourgeoisie) and proletariat. Finer divisions can be made, however: the most important subgroup in capitalism being petite bourgeoisie (small bourgeoisie), people who possess their own means of production but utilise it primarily by working on it themselves rather than hiring others to work on it. They include self-employed artisans, small shopkeepers, and many professionals. Jon Elster has found mention in Marx of 15 classes from various historical periods.

A prerequisite for classes is existence of sufficient surplus product. Marxists explain the history of "civilized" societies in terms of a war of classes between those who control production and those who produce the goods or services in society. In the Marxist view of capitalism, this is a conflict between capitalists (bourgeoisie) and wage-workers (the proletariat). For Marxists, class antagonism is rooted in the situation that control over social production necessarily entails control over the class which produces goods—in capitalism this is the exploitation of workers by the bourgeoisie.

Marx himself argued that it was the goal of the proletariat itself to displace the capitalist system with socialism, changing the social relationships underpinning the class system and then developing into a future communist society in which: "..the free development of each is the condition for the free development of all." (Communist Manifesto) This would mark the beginning of a classless society in which human needs rather than profit would be motive for production. In a society with democratic control and production for use, there would be no class, no state and no need for money.

Vladimir Lenin has defined classes as "large groups of people differing from each other by the place they occupy in a historically determined system of social production, by their relation (in most cases fixed and formulated in law) to the means of production, by their role in the social organisation of labour, and, consequently, by the dimensions of the share of social wealth of which they dispose and the mode of acquiring it."

Proletarianisation

The most important transformation of society for Marxists has been the massive and rapid growth of the proletariat in the world population during the last two hundred and fifty years. Starting with agricultural and domestic textile labourers in England and Flanders, more and more occupations only provide a living through wages or salaries. Private enterprise or self-employment in a variety of occupations is no longer as viable as it once was, and so many people who once controlled their own labour-time are converted into proletarians. Today groups which in the past subsisted on stipends or private wealth—like doctors, academics or lawyers—are now increasingly working as wage labourers. Marxists call this process proletarianisation, and point to it as the major factor in the proletariat being the largest class in current societies in the rich countries of the "first world." However, only in the strongly social-democratic societies such as Sweden is there much long-term evidence of the weakening of the consequences of social class.

The increasing dissolution of the peasant-lord relationship, initially in the commercially active and industrialising countries, and then in the unindustrialised countries as well, has virtually eliminated the class of peasants. Poor rural labourers still exist, but their current relationship with production is predominantly as landless wage labourers or rural proletarians. The destruction of the peasantry, and its conversion into a rural proletariat, is largely a result of the general proletarianisation of all work. This process is today largely complete, although it was arguably incomplete in the 1960s and 1970s.

Dialectics, or Historical Materialism, in Marxist Class

Marx saw class categories as defined by continuing historical processes. Classes, in Marxism, are not static entities, but are regenerated daily through the productive process. Marxism views classes as human social relationships which change over time, with historical commonality created through shared productive processes. A 17th century farm labourer who worked for day wages shares a similar relationship to production as an average office worker of the 21st century. In this example, it is the shared structure of wage labour that makes both of these individuals "working class."

Marxism has a rather heavily defined dialectic between objective factors (i.e., material conditions, the social structure) and subjective factors (i.e. the conscious organization of class members). While most Marxism analyses people's class based on objective factors (class structure), major Marxist trends have made greater use of subjective factors in understanding the history of the working class. E.P. Thompson's *The Making of the English Working Class* is a definitive example of this "subjective" Marxist trend. Thompson analyses the English working class as a group of people with shared material conditions coming to a positive self-consciousness of their social position. This feature of social class is commonly termed class consciousness in Marxism, a concept which became famous with Georg Lukacs's *History and Class Consciousness* (1923). It is seen as the process of a "class in itself" moving in the direction of a "class for itself," a collective agent that changes history rather than simply being a victim of the historical process. In Lukacs' words, the proletariat was the "subject-object of history", and the first class which could separate false consciousness (inherent to the bourgeois's consciousness), which reified economic laws as universal (whereas they are only a consequence of historic capitalism).

Max Weber

The seminal sociological interpretation of class was advanced by Max Weber. Weber formulated a three-component theory of stratification, with class, status and party (or politics) as subordinate to the ownership of the means of production, but for Weber how they interact is a contingent question and one that will vary from society to society. Weber is also known for his six "American Dream" Values which are: 1) Hard work, 2) Universalism, 3) Individualism, 4) Wealth, 5) Activism, and 6) Rationality.

Academic Models

Schools of sociology differ in how they conceptualise class. A distinction can be drawn between *analytical* concepts of social class, such as the Marxian and Weberian traditions, and the more *empirical* traditions such as socio-economic status approach, which notes the correlation of income, education and wealth with social outcomes without necessarily implying a particular theory of social structure. The Warnerian approach can be considered *empirical* in the sense that it is more descriptive than analytical.

The traditional 'pigeon-holing' mainstay of much of the advertising industry used to be that of social class. Recently, however, as affluence has become more widespread, the process has become much less clear. It is now argued that the new 'opinion leaders' come from within the same social class. The class groupings that were traditionally used by advertising agencies (for example in the NRS social grade schema were: AB-Managerial and professional, C1-Supervisory and clerical, C2-Skilled manual, DE-Unskilled manual and unemployed.) have been reported to be of decreasing value in recent decades, especially in the distinction between clerical workers and manual workers in education and disposable income.

Whereas some four decades ago, when these groupings were first widely used, the numbers in each of the main categories (C, D and E) were reasonably well balanced, today the C group in total (although now usually split to give C1 and C2) forms such a large sector that it dominates the whole classification system and offers less in terms of usable concentration of marketing effort.

Middle Class

In about the 1770s, when the term "social class" first entered the English lexicon, the concept of a "middle class" within that structure was also becoming important. The Industrial Revolution was allowing a much greater portion of the population to have time for the kind of education and cultural pursuits once restricted to the European feudal division of aristocracy, bourgeoisie, and peasantry which in that period would have included what later became the industrial proletarians of the towns and cities.

Today, concepts of social class assume three general categories: an upper class of proprietors and senior managers; a middle class of people who may not exert power over others, but may earn a significant proportion of their income through commerce, land ownership, or professional employment; and a lower class, who rely on wages for their livelihood.

It is important, however, to highlight the distinction of such a class model from that of the British concept of class in which the terms upper, middle and working-class have different definitions. The chief difference relates to the association of inherited wealth and landed property as a defining characteristic of the upper class. This distinguishes its members from those of the middle class whose membership is more fluid and more reliant upon employment status and its income. This is a broad generalization as there are classes within the middle class, such as the upper middle class whose interest in culture, and whose manners and mores distinguish them from other ranks in the middle strata, but is nonetheless a useful marker by which to distinguish the British concept of class from that of the new world.

In the United States, the term "middle class" is applied very broadly and includes people who would elsewhere be considered working class. As the vast majority of Americans identify themselves as being middle class, there are multiple theories as to what constitutes the American middle class. The term has been used to describe people from all walks of life, from janitors to attorneys. The definition of middle class is also relevant to the perspective of the individual. Due to the high standard of living in wealthy countries such as the U.S., the term middle class is also relevant to the standard of living of the majority of people in the world.

From this perspective, the term middle class becomes more inclusive. As a result, the US middle class is often sub-divided into two or three groups. While one set of theories claim that the middle class is composed of those in the middle of the social strata, other theories maintain that professionals and managers who have a college degree make up most of the middle class. In 2005 roughly 35% of Americans worked in the professional/ professional support or managerial field and 27% had a college degree. Sociologists such as Dennis Gilbert or Joseph J. Hickey argue that the middle class is divided into two sub-groups. The upper middle class consists of white collar professionals with advanced educations and constitutes roughly 15% of the population. In 2005, the top 15% of income earners (age 25+) had incomes exceeding $62,500. The lower middle class (or middle-middle class for those who divide the middle class into three segments) consists of other mostly white collar employees with less autonomy in their work, lower educational attainment, lower personal income and less prestige than those of the upper middle class.

Sociologists such as Gilbert, Hickey, James Henslin, and William Thompson have brought forth class models in which the middle class is divided into two sections which combine to represent 47% to 49% of the population. Economist Michael Zweig defines class as power relationships among the members of a society, rather than as a lifestyle or by income. Zweig says that the middle class is only about 34% of the U.S. population, typically employed as managers, supervisors, small business owners and other professional people.

Class Structure in Various Societies

Although class can be discerned in any society, some cultures have published specific guidelines to rank. In some cases, the ideologies presented in these rankings may not concur with the mainstream power dialectic of social class as it is understood in modern English use.

Pre-capitalist Class Structures

Ancient Rome

Social class in ancient Rome played a major role in the lives of Romans. Ancient Roman society was hierarchical. Free-born adult male Roman citizens were divided into several classes, both by ancestry and by property. There were also several classes of non-citizens with different legal rights, along with married women, children, and slaves, who had no rights, and could be legally killed, ejected, or sold by the head of their household.

Renaissance Europe

The Mantegna Tarocchi, sets of cards made as an educational aid in Ferrara in the late 15th century, used the following hierarchy for the "Conditions of Man", largely ignoring the rural population:

- Beggar
- Servant (Fameio)
- Craftsman (Artixan)
- Merchant (Merchadante)-presumably living mostly off income as a landlord
- Gentleman (Zintilomo)
- Knight (Chavalier)
- Doge (Doxe)-ie a local ruler
- King (Re)

- Emperor (Imperator)
- Pope (Papa).

Aztec

Aztec society traditionally was divided into classes. The highest class were the *pîpiltin* or nobility. Originally this status was not hereditary, although the sons of *pillis* had access to better resources and education, so it was easier for them to become *pillis*. Later the class system took on hereditary aspects.

The second class were the *mâcehualtin* (people), originally peasants. Eduardo Noguera estimates that in later stages only 20% of the population was dedicated to agriculture and food production. The other 80% of society were warriors, artisans and traders.

Slaves or *tlacotin* also constituted an important class. Aztecs could become slaves because of debts, as a criminal punishment or as war captives. A slave could have possessions and even own other slaves.

Traveling merchants called *pochtecah* were a small, but important class as they not only facilitated commerce, but also communicated vital information across the empire and beyond its borders. They were often employed as spies.

Chinese

Confucian doctrine later minimized the importance of the nobles (except the emperor), abolished great men and scholars as noble classes, and further divided commoner workers based on the perceived usefulness of their work. Scholars (now not exclusively nobles) ranked the highest because the opportunity to conceive clear ideas in a state of leisure would lead them to wise laws (an idea that has much in common with Plato's ideal of a philosopher king). The scholars were mainly from the gentry, who owned land, and may be educated and wealthy but had no aristocratic titles. Under them were the farmers, who produced necessary food, and the artisans who produced useful objects. Merchants ranked at the bottom because they did not actually produce anything, while soldiers were sometimes ranked even lower because of their perceived expendability. The Confucian model is notably different from the modern European view of social class, since merchants could attain great wealth without reaching the social status accorded to a poor farmer. In practice, a rich merchant might purchase land to reach farmer status, or even buy a good education for his heirs in the hopes that they would attain scholar status and go into the imperial civil service. The Chinese model was widely disseminated throughout east Asia.

Pre-revolutionary French

France was an monarchy with a king and other princes at the top of the class structure. The French States-General, established in 1302 was an assembly whose members were ranked according to hereditary class. The First Estate was the clergy, all Roman Catholic, and by this time with the bishops and higher roles dominated by sons of the nobility. The Second Estate consisted of lay members of the nobility, who constituted approximately two percent of the total population. The Third Estate consisted, technically, of everyone else, but was represented by representatives elected by a complicated system, in practice dominated by the bourgeois lawyers who held offices in the various regional Parlements. The peasantry had no official status in this system. This may be contrasted with the ideologically high status of farmers in Confucian China. The rigidity of the French hereditary system has been suggested as a major cause of the French Revolution.

Inca

Indian

Traditionally, the Indian caste system was one of the oldest and most important systems of social class with peculiar rigidity (in the sense that it lacks upward or downward mobility between castes). It differs from Varnashrama Dharma found in Hinduism, which allowed people born into a certain Varna to move upward or downwards depending on their qualification. It divided society based on skill and qualifications. Briefly, the Brahmin varna was idealized as a leisurely priest class devoted to religious ceremonies, while the Kshatriya defended them as military princes. The modern concept of the middle class was represented by the Vaishya varna artisans, farmers, and merchants, and the lower varna were the

Shudra labourers. Within this basic framework were arranged a huge number of jatis, or subcastes. Despite being notorious for its rigidity, it should be recognised not as a religious system (as Varnashrama Dharma prescribed in Hinduism), but a social system, which evolved from Varnashrama Dharma. After, the end of British occupation in 1947, the Constitution of India introduced various affirmative action plans to abolish the caste system with limited success.

Iranian

Under the Qajar dynasty of Iran, the class structure was set up as follows:

- the permanent hereditary class of Qajar princes
- an upper class of "nobles and notables"
- religious leaders and students of theology
- merchants (note the difference from east Asian models)
- agricultural landowners
- master artisans and shopkeepers.

As in many official class structures, the labourers who made up the majority of the population but owned no land and relied on wages were not even considered part of the structure at all.

Japanese

The Japanese class structure, while influenced by the Chinese, was based on a much more feudal environment. The Emperor was not claimed to be a deity until pre-World War II military government did so but still was unquestionably at the pinnacle of the Japanese class structure (and still is, although no longer officially considered a god). However, for much of Japanese history the emperor was not allowed outside the palace grounds and his will was "interpreted" by a shogun, or military dictator. Beneath the shogun, daimyos or regional lords, administered the provinces through their samurai lieutenants. Perhaps through Chinese influence, and perhaps springing from a lack of arable land, the Japanese class structure also ranked farmers above merchants and other bourgeois.

Korean

The Korean ruling class, or Korean power elite, is the relatively small number of Korean people who through similar schools, education, family clans, upbringing, or corporate chaebol wealth and urban power control decision making and policy within either of the partitioned Koreas.

This group is placed within the historical tradition of Confucianism and yangban scholars whose creation can be dated towards the end of the Goryeo dynasty; and that continues through the republican post-1945 and contemporary period; and which is represented by a controlling benevolent stewardship of the politics and economy of Korea by seniors or the older urban-dwelling elements of the population which crosses class, religious, party, and political lines.

3

The State

The State in International Politics

Economic globalization would mean that the world economy, or at least the globalized portion of it, would be integrated and not merely interdependent. The difference between an interdependent and an integrated world is a qualitative one and not a mere matter of proportionately more trade and a greater and more rapid flow of capital. With integration, the world would look like one big state. Economic markets and economic interests cannot perform the functions of government. Integration requires or presumes a government to protect, direct, and control. Interdependence, in contrast to integration, is "the mere mutualism" of states, as Emile Durkheim put it.

It is not only less close than usually thought but also politically less consequential. Interdependence did not produce the world-shaking events of 1989-91. A political event, the failure of one of the world's two great powers, did that. Had the configuration of international politics not fundamentally changed, neither the unification of Germany nor the war against Saddam Hussein would have been possible. The most important events in international politics are explained by differences in the capabilities of states, not by economic forces operating across states or transcending them. Interdependers, and globalizers even more so, argue that the international economic interests of states work against their going to war. True, they do. Yet if one asks whether economic interests or nuclear weapons inhibit war more strongly, the answer obviously is nuclear weapons. European great powers prior to

World War I were tightly tied together economically. They nevertheless fought a long and bloody war. The United States and the Soviet Union were not even loosely connected economically. They coexisted peacefully through the four-and-a-half decades of the Cold War. The most important causes of peace, as of war, are found in international-political conditions, including the weaponry available to states. Events following the Cold War dramatically demonstrate the political weakness of economic forces. The integration (not just the interdependence) of the parts of the Soviet Union and of Yugoslavia, with all of their entangling economic interests, did not prevent their disintegration. Governments and people sacrifice welfare and even security to nationalism, ethnicity, and religion.

Political explanations weigh heavily in accounting for international-political events. National politics, not international markets, account for many international economic developments. A number of students of politics and of economics believe that blocs are becoming more common internationally. Economic interests and market forces do not create blocs; governments do. Without governmental decisions, the Coal and Steel Community, the European Economic Community, and the European Union would not have emerged. The representatives of states negotiate regulations in the European Commission. The Single-Market Act of 1985 provided that some types of directives would require less than a unanimous vote in the Council of Ministers. This political act cleared the way for passage of most of the harmonization standards for Europe (Dumez and Jeunemaitre 1996, 229). American governments forged NAFTA; Japan fashioned an East and Southeast Asian producing and trading area. The decisions and acts of a country, or a set of countries arriving at political agreements, shape international political and economic institutions. Governments now intervene much more in international economic matters than they did in the earlier era of interdependence. Before World War I, foreign-ministry officials were famed for their lack of knowledge of, or interest in, economic affairs. Because governments have become much more active in economic affairs at home and abroad, interdependence has become less of an autonomous force in international politics.

The many commentators who exaggerate the closeness of interdependence, and even more so those who write of globalization, think in unit rather than in systemic terms. Many small states import and export large shares of their gross domestic products. States with large GDPs do not. They are little dependent on others, while a number of other states heavily depend on them. The terms of political, economic, and military competition are set by the larger units of the international-political system. Through centuries of multipolarity, with five or so great powers of comparable size competing with one another, the international system was quite closely interdependent. Under bi-and unipolarity the degree of interdependence declined markedly.

States are differentiated from one another not by function but primarily by capability. For two reasons, inequalities across states have greater political impact than inequalities across income groups within states. First, the inequalities of states are larger and have been growing more rapidly. Rich countries have become richer while poor countries have remained poor. Second, in a system without central governance, the influence of the units of greater capability is disproportionately large because there are no effective laws and institutions to direct and constrain them. They are able to work the system to their advantage, as the petrodollar example showed. I argued in 1970 that what counts are states' capacity to adjust to external conditions and their ability to use their economic leverage for political advantage. The United States was then and is still doubly blessed. It remains highly important in the international economy, serving as a principal market for a number of countries and as a major supplier of goods and services, yet its dependence on others is quite low. Precisely because the United States is relatively little dependent on others, it has a wide range of policy choices and the ability both to bring pressure on others and to assist them. The "herd" with its capital may flee from countries when it collectively decides that they are politically and economically unworthy, but some countries abroad, like some firms at home, are so important that they cannot be allowed to fail. National governments and international agencies then come to the rescue. The United States is the country that most often has the ability and the will to step in. The agency that most often acts is the IMF, and most countries think of the IMF as the enforcement arm of the U.S. Treasury (Strange 1996, 192). Thomas Friedman believes that when the "herd" makes its decisions, there is no appeal; but often there is an appeal, and it is for a bail out organized by the United States.

The international economy, like national economies, operates within a set of rules and institutions. Rules and institutions have to be made and sustained. Britain, to a large extent, provided this service prior to World War I; no one did between the wars, and the United States has done so since. More than any other state, the United States makes the rules and maintains the institutions that shape the international political economy.

Economically, the United States is the world's most important country; militarily, it is not only the most important country, it is the decisive one. Thomas Friedman puts the point simply: The world is sustained by "the presence of American power and America's willingness to use that power against those who would threaten the system of globalization.... The hidden hand of the market will never work without a hidden fist" (1999, 373). But the hidden fist is in full view. On its military forces, the United States outspends the next six or seven big spenders combined. When force is needed to keep or to restore the peace, either the United States leads the way or the peace is not kept. The Cold War militarized international politics. Relations between the United States and the Soviet Union, and among some other countries as well, came to be defined largely in a single dimension, the military one. As the German sociologist Erich Weede has remarked, "National security decision making in some... democracies (most notably in West Germany) is actually penetrated by the United States" (1989, 225).

Oddly, the end of the Cold War has raised the importance of the American military to new heights. The United States continues to spend at a Cold War pace. In real terms, America's 1995 military budget approximately equaled the 1980 budget, and in 1980 the Cold War reached its peak. That other countries have reduced their budgets more than the United States has heightened the military dominance of one country. To say that the world is unipolar and that the world is becoming one through globalization is all too suggestive. Some say that the world is not really unipolar because the United States often needs, or at least wants, the help of others. The truth, however, remains: The stronger have many more ways of coping with adversities than the weak have, and the latter depend on the former much more than the other way around. The United States is the only country that can organize and lead a military coalition, as it did in Iraq and in the Balkans. Some states have little choice but to participate, partly because of the pressure the strong can bring to bear on the weak and partly because of the needs of the latter. Western European countries and Japan are more dependent on Middle Eastern oil than the United States, and Western European countries are more affected by what happens in Eastern Europe than the United States is.

As expected, the beneficiaries resent their benefactor, which leads to talk of righting the imbalance of power. Yet, when the imbalance between one and the rest is great, to catch up is difficult. French leaders, especially, bemoan the absence of multipolarity and call for greater European strength, but one cannot usefully will the end without willing the means. The uneven distribution of capabilities continues to be the key to understanding international politics.

To an increasing extent, American foreign policy relies on military means. America continues to garrison much of the world and to look for ways of keeping troops in foreign countries rather than ways to withdraw them as one might have expected at the Cold War's end. The 1992 draft of the Pentagon's Defence Planning Guidance advocated "discouraging the advanced industrialized nations from... even aspiring to a larger global or regional role." The United States may at times want help from others, but not too much help lest it lose its leading position in one part of the world or another. The document, when it was leaked, provoked criticism. In response, emphasis was placed on its being only a draft, but it continues to guide and describe America's policy.

William J. Perry and Ashton B. Carter, respectively the former secretary and assistant secretary of defence, have recently offered the concept of "preventive defence" as a guide to American policy. Preventive defence is conducted by American defence officials engaging in "security and military dialogue with regional states";

it calls for "a more robust defence to defence program" (1999, 9. 11; cf., Carter, Perry, and Steinbruner 1992). Bismarck tried to keep Germany's military officials away from their opposite numbers in foreign countries lest the military's military policy become the country's foreign policy. In part, World War I resulted from his successors' failure to do this. In the United States, Treasury and Defence now make as much or more foreign policy than State does.

Nation State

The nation-state is a certain form of state that derives its political legitimacy from serving as a sovereign entity for a nation as a sovereign territorial unit. The state is a political and geopolitical entity; the nation is a cultural and/or ethnic entity. The term "nation-state" implies that the two geographically coincide, and this distinguishes the nation state from the other types of state, which historically preceded it.

Due to ambiguities in the word state, for instance in the United States, the term nation-state is also used to mean any sovereign state, whether or not its political boundaries coincide with ethnic and cultural ones. Ambiguities in the usage of terms such as *nation, international, state*, and *country*, are discussed at *nation*.

History and Origins

The origins and early history of nation-states are disputed. A major theoretical issue is: "which came first— the nation or the nation state?" For nationalists themselves, the answer is that the nation existed first, nationalist movements arose to present its legitimate demand for sovereignty, and the nation-state met that demand. Some "modernisation theories" of nationalism see the national identity largely as a product of government policy, to unify and modernise an already existing state. Most theories see the nation state as a 19th-century European phenomenon, facilitated by developments such as mass literacy and the early mass media. However, historians also note the early emergence of a relatively unified state, and a sense of common identity, in Portugal and the Dutch Republic. In France, Eric Hobsbawm argues, the French state preceded the formation of the French people. Hobsbawm considers that the state made the French nation, and not French nationalism, which emerged at the end of the 19th century, the time of the Dreyfus Affair. At the time of the 1789 French Revolution, only half of the French people spoke some French, and between 12% to 13% spoke it "fairly", according to Hobsbawm. During Italian unification, the number of people speaking the Italian language was even lower. The French state promoted the unification of various dialects and languages into the French language. The introduction of conscription, and the Third Republic's 1880s laws on public instruction, facilitated the creation of a national identity, under this theory.

The theorist Benedict Anderson argues that nations are "imagined communities" (the members cannot possibly know each other), and that the main causes of nationalism and the creation of an imagined community are the reduction of privileged access to particular script languages (e.g. Latin), the movement to abolish the ideas of divine rule and monarchy, as well as the emergence of the printing press under a system of capitalism (or, as Anderson calls it, "print-capitalism"). The "state-driven" theories of the origin of nation-states tend to emphasise a few specific states, such as France and its rival England. These states expanded from core regions, and developed a national consciousness and sense of national identity ("Frenchness" and "Englishness"). Both assimilated peripheral regions (Wales, Brittany, Aquitaine and Occitania); these areas experienced a revival of interest in the regional culture in the 19th century, leading to the creation of autonomist movements in the 20th century.

Some nation-states, such as Germany or Italy, came into existence at least partly as a result of political campaigns by nationalists, during the nineteenth century. In both cases, the territory was previously divided among other states, some of them very small. The sense of common identity was at first a cultural movement, such as in the *Völkisch movement* in German-speaking states, which rapidly acquired a political significance. In these cases, the nationalist sentiment and the nationalist movement clearly precede the unification of the German and Italian nation-states. Historians Hans Kohn, Liah Greenfeld, Philip White, and others have classified nations such as Germany or Italy-where cultural unification preceded state unification-as *ethnic nations*, or *ethnic nationalities*. Whereas 'state-driven' national unifications, such as in France, England, or China, are more likely to flourish in multiethnic societies, producing a traditional national heritage of *civic nations*, or *territory-based nationalities*.

The idea of a nation-state is associated with the rise of the modern system of states— often called the "Westphalian system" in reference to the Treaty of Westphalia (1648). The balance of power, which characterises that system, depends for its effectiveness upon clearly defined, centrally controlled, independent entities, whether empires or nation states, which recognise each other's sovereignty and territory. The Westphalian system did not create the nation state, but the nation state meets the criteria for its component states (assuming that there is no disputed territory).

The nation-state received a philosophical underpinning in the era of Romanticism, at first as the 'natural' expression of the individual peoples (romantic nationalism — see Fichte's conception of the Volk, which would be later opposed by Ernest Renan). The increasing emphasis during the 19th century, on the ethnic and racial origins of the nation, led to a redefinition of the nation-state in these terms. Racism, which in Boulainvilliers's theories was inherently antipatriotic and antinationalist, joined itself with colonialist imperialism and "continental imperialism", most notably in pan-Germanic and pan-Slavic movements. This relation between racism and ethnic nationalism reached its height in the fascist and Nazi movements of the 20th century. The specific combination of 'nation' ('people') and 'state' expressed in such terms as the *Völkische Staat* and implemented in laws such as the 1935 Nuremberg laws made fascist states such as early Nazi Germany qualitatively different from non-fascist nation-states. Obviously, minorities, who are not part of the *Volk*, have no authentic or legitimate role in such a state. In Germany, neither Jews nor the Roma were considered part of the *Volk*, and specifically targeted for persecution. However German nationality law defined 'German' on the basis of German ancestry, excluding *all* non-Germans from the 'Volk'.

In recent years, the nation-state's claim to absolute sovereignty within its borders has been much criticised. A global political system based on international agreements, and supernational blocs characterized the postwar era. Non-state actors, such as international corporations and non-governmental organizations, are widely seen as eroding the economic and political power of nation-states, potentially leading to their eventual disappearance.

Before Nation-states

In Europe, in the eighteenth century, the classic non-national states were the *multi-ethnic* empires, (the Austro-Hungarian Empire, the Russian Empire, the Ottoman Empire, the French Empire, the British Empire), and smaller states at what would now be called sub-national level. The multi-ethnic empire was a monarchy ruled by a king, emperor, or Sultan. The population belonged to many ethnic groups, and they spoke many languages. The empire was dominated by one ethnic group, and their language was usually the language of public administration. The ruling dynasty was usually, but not always, from that group. This type of state is not specifically European: such empires existed on all continents. Some of the smaller European states were not so ethnically diverse, but were also dynastic states, ruled by a royal house. Their territory could expand by royal intermarriage, or merge with another state when the dynasty merged. In some parts of Europe, notably Germany, very small territorial units existed. They were recognised by their neighbours as independent, and had their own government and laws. Some were ruled by princes or other hereditary rulers, some were governed by bishops or abbots. Because they were so small, however, they had no separate language or culture: the inhabitants shared the language of the surrounding region.

In some cases these states were simply overthrown by nationalist uprisings in the 19th century. Some older nation-states, such as England and France seem to have grown by accretion of smaller entities, such as city states, before the 19th century, or chiefdoms earlier in history. Liberal ideas of free trade played a role in German unification, which was preceded by a customs union, the Zollverein. However, the Austro-Prussian War, and the German alliances in the Franco-Prussian War, were decisive in the unification. The Austro-Hungarian Empire and the Ottoman Empire broke up after the First World War, the Russian Empire became the Soviet Union, after the long Russian Civil War.

Some of the smaller states survived: the independent principalities of Liechtenstein, Andorra, and Monaco, and the republic of San Marino. The Vatican City is not a survival, although there was a larger Papal State. In its present form, it was created by the 1929 Lateran treaties between Italy and the Roman Catholic Church.

Characteristics of the Nation-state

Nation states have their own characteristics, differing from those of the pre-national states. For a start, they have a different attitude to their territory, compared to the dynastic monarchies: it is semi-sacred, and non-transferable. No nation would swap territory with other states simply, for example, because the king's daughter got married. They have a different type of border, in principle defined only by the area of settlement of the national group, although many nation states also sought natural borders (rivers, mountain ranges).

The most noticeable characteristic is the degree to which nation-states use the state as an instrument of national unity, in economic, social and cultural life.

The nation-state promoted economic unity, first by abolishing internal customs and tolls. In Germany this process-the creation of the Zollverein-preceded formal national unity. Nation states typically have a policy to create and maintain a national transportation infrastructure, facilitating trade and travel. In 19th century Europe, the expansion of the rail transport networks was at first largely a matter for private railway companies, but gradually came under control of the national governments. The French rail network, with its main lines radiating from Paris to all corners of France, is often seen as a reflection of the centralised French nation-state, which directed its construction. Nation states continue to build, for instance, specifically national motorway networks. Specifically trans-national infrastructure programmes, such as the Trans-European Networks, are a recent innovation.

The nation-states typically had a more centralised and uniform public administration than its imperial predecessors: they were smaller, and the population less diverse. (The internal diversity of, for instance, the Ottoman Empire was very great). After the

19th century triumph of the nation-state in Europe, regional identity was subordinate to national identity, in regions such as Alsace-Lorraine, Catalonia, Brittany, Sicily, Sardinia and Corsica. In many cases, the regional administration was also subordinated to central (national) government. This process was partially reversed from the 1970s onward, with the introduction of various forms of regional autonomy, in formerly centralised states such as France.

However, the most obvious impact of the nation-state, as compared to its non-national predecessors, is the creation of a uniform national culture, through state policy. The model of the nation-state implies that its population constitutes a nation, united by a common descent, a common language, and many forms of shared culture. When the implied unity was absent, the nation-state often tried to create it. It promoted a uniform national language, through language policy. The creation of national systems of compulsory primary education and a relatively uniform curriculum in secondary schools, was the most effective instrument in the spread of the national languages. The schools also taught the national history, often in a propagandistic and mythologised version, and (especially during conflicts) some nation-states still teach this kind of history.

Language and cultural policy was sometimes negative, aimed at the suppression of non-national elements. Language prohibitions were sometimes used to accelerate the adoption of national languages, and the decline of minority languages.

In some cases these policies triggered bitter conflicts and further ethnic separatism. But where it worked, the cultural uniformity and homogeneity of the population increased. Conversely, the cultural divergence at the border became sharper: in theory, a uniform French identity extends from the Atlantic coast to the Rhine, and on the other bank of the Rhine, a uniform German identity begins. To enforce that model, both sides have divergent language policy and educational systems, although the linguistic boundary is in fact well inside France, and the Alsace region changed hands four times between 1870 and 1945.

The Nation-state in Practice

In some cases, the geographic boundaries of an ethnic

population and a political state largely coincide. In these cases, there is little immigration or emigration, few members of ethnic minorities, and few members of the "home" ethnicity living in other countries.

Clear examples of nation states include:

- Albania: The vast majority of the population is ethnically Albanian at about 98.6% of the population, with the remainder consisting of a few small ethnic minorities.
- Armenia: The vast majority of Armenia's population consists of ethnic Armenians at about 98% of the population, with the remainder consisting of a few small ethnic minorities.
- Bangladesh: The vast majority ethnic group of Bangladesh are the Bengali people, comprising 98% of the population, with the remainder consisting of mostly Bihari migrants and indigenous tribal groups. Therefore, Bangladeshi society is to a great extent linguistically and culturally homogeneous, with very small populations of foreign expatriates and workers, although there is a substantial number of Bengali workers living abroad.
- Egypt: The vast majority of Egypt's population consists of ethnic Egyptians at about 99% of the population, with the remainder consisting of a few small ethnic minorities, as well as refugees or asylum seekers. Modern Egyptian identity is closely tied to the geography of Egypt and its long history, its development over the centuries saw overlapping or conflicting ideologies. Though today an Arabic-speaking people, that aspect constitutes for Egyptians a cultural dimension of their identity, not a necessary attribute of or prop for their national political being. Today most Egyptians see themselves, their history, culture and language as specifically Egyptian and not "Arab."
- Finland: Finns including Swedish-speaking Finns make up about 97% of the population.
- Hungary: Native Hungarians or the Magyar people consist of about 95% of the population, with a small Rome and German minority.

- Iceland: although the inhabitants are ethnically related to other Scandinavian groups, the national culture and language are found only in Iceland. There are no cross-border minorities — the nearest land is too far away.
- Japan: Japan is also traditionally seen as an example of a nation-state and also the largest of a nation state with population in excess of 120 million. It should be noted that Japan has a small number of minorities such as Ryûkyû peoples, Koreans, and Chinese, and on the northern island of Hokkaidô, the indigenous Ainu minority. However, they are either numerically insignificant (Ainu), their difference is not as pronounced (though Ryukyuan culture is closely related to Japanese culture, it is nonetheless distinctive in that it historically received much more influence from China and has separate political and non poliitical and religious traditions) or well assimilated (Zainichi population is collapsing due to assimilation/ naturalisation).
- Lesotho: Lesotho's ethno-linguistic structure consists almost entirely of the Basotho (singular Mosotho), a Bantu-speaking people; about 99.7% of the population are Basotho.
- North and South Korea, are one of the most ethnically and linguistically homogeneous in the world. Particularly in reclusive North Korea, there are very few ethnic minority groups and expatriate foreigners.
- Poland, after World War II (After the Expulsion of Germans after World War II) and the extermination of the Jews executed by the invading German Nazis.
- Several Polynesian countries such as Tonga, Samoa, Tuvalu, etc.
- Portugal: Although surrounded by other lands and people, the Portuguese nation has occupied the same territory for almost 800 years. The modern Portuguese nation is a very old amalgam of formerly distinct historical populations that passed through and settled in the territory of modern Portugal: native Iberian peoples, Celts, ancient Mediterraneans (Greeks, Phoenicians, Romans, Jews), and invading Germanic peoples like the Suebi and the Visigoths, and Berbers and Arabs.

- Somalia: The Somali people consist of about 95% of the population, with small Bantu and Arab minorities.
- Swaziland: The vast majority of the population is ethnically Swazi at about 98.6% of the population, with the remainder consisting of a few small ethnic minorities.

The notion of a unifying "national identity" also extends to countries which host multiple ethnic or language groups, such as India & China. For example, Switzerland is constitutionally a confederation of cantons, and has four official languages, but it has also a 'Swiss' national identity, a national history, and a classic national hero, Wilhelm Tell.

Innumerable conflicts have arisen where political boundaries did not correspond with ethnic or cultural boundaries. For one example, the Hatay Province was transferred to Turkey from Syria after the majority-Turkey population complained of mistreatment. The traditional homeland of the Kurdish people extends between northern Iraq and southeastern Turkey, and western Iran. Some of its inhabitants call for the creation of an independent Kurdistan, citing mistreatment by the Turkish and Iraqi governments. An armed conflict between the Kurdistan Workers Party and the Turkish government over this issue has been ongoing since 1984.

After WWII in the Tito era, nationalism was appealed to for uniting South Slav peoples. Later in the 20th century, after the break-up of the Soviet Union, leaders appealed to ancient ethnic feuds or tensions that ignited conflict between the Serbs, Croats and Slovenes, as well Bosnians, Montenegrins and Macedonians, eventually breaking up the long collaboration of peoples and ethnic cleansing was carried out in the Balkans, resulting in the destruction of the formerly communist republic and produced the civil wars in Bosnia-Herzegovina in 1992-95, resulted in mass population displacements and segregation that radically altered what was once a highly diverse and intermixed ethnic makeup of the region. These conflicts were largely about creating a new political framework of states, each of which would be ethnically and politically homogeneous. Serbians, Croatians and Bosnians insisted they were ethnically distinct although many communities had a long history of intermarriage. All could speak the common Serbo-Croatian Language.

Belgium is a classic example of a disputed nation-state. The state was formed by secession from the United Kingdom of the Netherlands in 1830, protected by the Treaty of London 1839; the Flemish population in the north speaks Dutch. The Flemish identity is also ethnic and cultural, and there is a strong separatist movement, *Vlaams Belang*. The Francophone Walloon identity of Belgium is linguistically distinct and regionalist. There is also a unitary Belgian nationalism, several versions of a Greater Netherlands ideal, and a German-speaking community of Belgium annexed from Prussia in 1920, and re-annexed by Germany in 1940–1944.

China covers a large geographic area and uses the concept of "Zhonghua minzu" — "Chinese peoples", in the sense of ethnic groups — although it also officially recognizes the majority Han ethnic group, and no fewer than 55 ethnic national minorities. In practice, however, the Han majority represents over 92 percent of the population, and the process of sinicization has continued under the People's Republic.

The United Kingdom

The United Kingdom is a difficult state to classify: it was formed initially by the merger of two independent kingdoms, (the Kingdom of England and the Kingdom of Scotland), but the Treaty of Union that set out the agreed terms has ensured the continuation of distinct features of each state, including separate legal systems and separate national churches. 300 years later, some regard the UK as a nation state but others regard it as a multinational state. The current British Government itself describes the United Kingdom as "countries within a country."

Minorities

The most obvious deviation from the ideal of 'one nation, one state', is the presence of minorities, especially ethnic minorities, which are clearly not members of the majority nation. An ethnic nationalist definition of a nation is necessarily exclusive: ethnic nations typically do not have open membership. In most cases, there is a clear idea that surrounding nations are different, and that includes members of those nations who live on the 'wrong side' of the border. Historical examples of groups, who have been specifically singled out as *outsiders*, are the Roma and Jews in Europe.

Negative responses to minorities within the nation-state have ranged from state-enforced cultural assimilation, to expulsion, persecution, violence, and extermination. The assimilation policies are usually state-enforced, but violence against minorities is not always state initiated: it can occur in the form of mob violence such as lynching or pogroms. Nation-states are responsible for some of the worst historical examples of violence against minorities—that is, minorities which were not considered part of the nation.

However, many nation-states do accept specific minorities as being part of the nation, and the term *national minority* is often used in this sense. The Sorbs in Germany are an example: for centuries they have lived in German-speaking states, surrounded by a much larger ethnic German population, and they have no other historical territory. They are now generally considered to be part of the German nation, and are accepted as such by the Federal Republic of Germany, which constitutionally guarantees their cultural rights. Of the thousands of ethnic and cultural minorities in nation states across the world, only a few have this level of acceptance and protection.

Multiculturalism is an official policy in many states, establishing the ideal of peaceful existence among multiple ethnic, cultural, and linguistic groups. Many nations have laws protecting minority rights.

Irredentism

Ideally, the border of a nation-state extends far enough to include all the members of the nation, and all of the national homeland. Again, in practice some of them always live on the 'wrong side' of the border. Part of the national homeland may be there too, and it may be inhabited by the 'wrong' nation. The response to the non-inclusion of territory and population may take the form of irredentism-demands to annex *unredeemed* territory and incorporate it into the nation-state. *Irredentist* claims are usually based on the fact that an identifiable part of the national group lives across the border. However, they can include claims to territory where no members of that nation live at present, either because they lived there in the past, or because the national language is spoken in that region, or because the national culture has influenced it, or because of geographical unity with the existing territory, or for a wide variety of other reasons. Past grievances are usually involved. It is sometimes difficult to distinguish irredentism from pan-nationalism, since both claim that all members of an ethnic and cultural nation belong in one specific state. Pan-nationalism is less likely to ethnically specify the nation. For instance, variants of Pan-Germanism have different ideas about what constituted Greater Germany, including the confusing term *Grossdeutschland*- which in fact implied the inclusion of huge Slavic minorities from the Austro-Hungarian Empire.

Typically, irredentist demands are at first made by members of non-state nationalist movements. When they are adopted by a state, they typically result in tensions, and actual attempts at annexation are always considered a *casus belli*, a cause for war. In many cases, such claims result in long-term hostile relations between neighbouring states. Irredentist movements typically circulate maps of the claimed national territory, the *greater* nation-state. That territory, which is often much larger than the existing state, plays a central role in their propaganda.

Irredentism should not be confused with claims to overseas colonies, which are not generally considered part of the national homeland. Some French overseas colonies would be an exception: French rule in Algeria did indeed treat the colony legally as a *département* of France, unsuccessfully.

Future

It has been speculated by both proponents of globalization and various future fiction writers that the concept of a nation-state may disappear with the ever-increasingly interconnected nature of the world. Such ideas are sometimes expressed around concepts of a world government.

This falls into line with the concept of Internationalism, which states that sovereignty is an outdated concept and a barrier to achieving peace and harmony in the world, thus also stating that nation-states are also a similar outdated concept.

If the nation-state does begin to disappear, then it may well be the direct or indirect result of globalization and Internationalism. The two concepts state that sovereignty is an outdated concept and, as the concept and existence of a nation-state depends on 'untouchable' sovereignty, it is therefore reasonable to assume that.

Globalization especially has helped to bring about the discussion about the disappearance of nation states, as global trade and the rise of the concepts of a 'global citizen' and a common identity have helped to reduce differences and 'distances' between individual nation states, especially with regards to the internet.

"Clash of Civilizations"

In direct contrast to cosmopolitan theories about an ever more connected world that no longer requires nation-states, is the Clash of Civilizations theory. The proposal by political scientist Samuel P. Huntington is that people's cultural and religious identities will be the primary source of conflict in the post-Cold War world.

The theory was originally formulated in a 1992 lecture at the American Enterprise Institute, which was then developed in a 1993 *Foreign Affairs* article titled "The Clash of Civilizations?", in response to Francis Fukuyama's 1992 book, *The End of History and the Last Man*. Huntington later expanded his thesis in a 1996 book *The Clash of Civilizations and the Remaking of World Order*.

Huntington began his thinking by surveying the diverse theories about the nature of global politics in the post-Cold War period. Some theorists and writers argued that human rights, liberal democracy and capitalist free market economics had become the only remaining ideological alternative for nations in the post-Cold War world. Specifically, Francis Fukuyama argued that the world had reached the 'end of history' in a Hegelian sense.

Huntington believed that while the age of ideology had ended, the world had only reverted to a normal state of affairs characterized by cultural conflict. In his thesis, he argued that the primary axis of conflict in the future will be along cultural and religious lines.

As an extension, he posits that the concept of different civilizations, as the highest rank of cultural identity, will become increasingly useful in analyzing the potential for conflict.

In the 1993 *Foreign Affairs* article, Huntington writes:

It is my hypothesis that the fundamental source of conflict in this new world will not be primarily ideological or primarily economic. The great divisions among humankind and the dominating source of conflict will be cultural. Nation states will remain the most powerful actors in world affairs, but the principal conflicts of global politics will occur between nations and groups of different civilizations. The clash of civilizations will dominate global politics. The fault lines between civilizations will be the battle lines of the future.

Huntington seems to fall in the primordialist school, believing that culturally defined groups are ancient and natural, however his early work suggests he is a Structural Functionalist. His view that nation states will remain the most powerful actors aligns with realism. Finally, his warning that the Western civilization may decline is inspired by Arnold J. Toynbee, Carroll Quigley, and Oswald Spengler.

State Sovereignty

State sovereignty has, for the past several hundred years, been a defining principle of interstate relations and a foundation of world order. The concept lies at the heart of both customary international law and the United Nations (UN) Charter and remains both an essential component of the maintenance of international peace and security and a defence of weak states against the strong. At the same time, the concept has never been as inviolable, either in law or in practice, as a formal legal definition might imply. According to former Secretary-General Boutros Boutros-Ghali, "The time of absolute sovereignty ... has passed; its theory was never matched by reality."

Empirically, sovereignty has routinely been violated by the powerful. In today's globalizing world, it is generally recognized that cultural, environmental, and economic influences neither respect borders nor require an entry visa. The concept of state sovereignty is well entrenched in legal and political discourse. At the same time, territorial boundaries have come under stress and have diminished in significance as a result of contemporary international relations. Not only have technology and communications made borders permeable, but the political dimensions of internal disorder and suffering have also often resulted in greater international disorder. Consequently, perspectives on the range and role of state sovereignty have, particularly over the past decade, evolved quickly and substantially.

The purpose of this essay is to set out the scope and significance of state sovereignty as a foundation on which to explore contemporary debates on intervention. Students and scholars are aware of the enormous and contentious literature on this subject. As one scholar has summarized,

> Few subjects in international law and international relations are as sensitive as the notion of sovereignty. Steinberger refers to it in the *Encyclopedia of Public International Law* as "the most glittering and controversial notion in the history, doctrine and practice of international law." On the other hand, Henkin seeks to banish it from out vocabulary and Lauterpacth calls it a "word which has an emotive quality lacking meaningful specific content," while Verzijl notes that any discussion on this subject risks degenerating into a Tower of Babel. More affirmatively, Brownlie sees sovereignty as "the basic constitutional doctrine of the law of nations" and Alan James sees it as "the one and only organising principle in respect of the dry surface of the globe, all that surface now ... being divided among single entities of a sovereign, or constitutionally independent kind." As noted by Falk, "There is little neutral ground when it comes to sovereignty."

Nevertheless, a quick review of the basics is useful for less specialized readers. The analysis begins with a review of the origins of the concept and its role in the evolution of state practice. This is followed by a discussion of the legal meaning of sovereignty and of its counterpart principle, nonintervention in domestic affairs. Together they comprise the fundamental bedrock of the contemporary international order. The widely acknowledged limits of state sovereignty are then examined, before turning to four contemporary challenges.

Meaning and Purpose of Sovereignty

State sovereignty denotes the competence, independence, and legal equality of states. The concept is normally used to encompass all matters in which each state is permitted by international law to decide and act without intrusions from other sovereign states. These matters include the choice of political, economic, social, and cultural systems and the formulation of foreign policy. The scope of the freedom of choice of states in these matters is not unlimited; it depends on developments in international law (including agreements made voluntarily) and international relations.

The concept of sovereign rule dates back centuries in the context of regulated relationships and legal traditions among such disparate territorial entities as Egypt, China, and the Holy Roman Empire. However, the present foundations of international law with regard to sovereignty were shaped by agreements concluded by European states as part of the Treaties of Westphalia in 1648. After almost 30 years of war, the supremacy of the sovereign authority of the state was established within a system of independent and equal units, as a way of establishing peace and order in Europe. The core elements of state sovereignty were codified in the 1933 Montevideo Convention on the Rights and Duties of States. They include three main requirements: a permanent population, a defined territory, and a functioning government. An important component of sovereignty has always been an adequate display of the authority of states to act over their territory to the exclusion of other states.

The post-1945 system of international order enshrined in the UN Charter inherited this basic model. Following decolonization, what had been a restrictive and eurocentric (that is, Western) order became global. There were no longer "insiders" and "outsiders" because virtually every person on Earth lived within a sovereign state. At the same time, the multiplication of numbers did not diminish the controversial character of sovereignty.

In accordance with Article 2 (1) of the UN Charter, the world organization is based on the principle of the sovereign equality of all member states. While they are equal in relation to one another, their status of legal equality as a mark of sovereignty is also the basis on which intergovernmental organizations are established and endowed with capacity to act between and within states to the extent permitted by the framework of an organization. In 1949 the International Court of Justice (ICJ) observed that "between independent States, respect for territorial sovereignty is an essential foundation of international relations." Thirty years later, the ICJ referred to "the fundamental principle of state sovereignty on which the whole of international law rests."

As a hallmark of statehood, territorial sovereignty underlies the system of international order in relations among states. An act of aggression is unlawful, not only because it undermines international order, but also because states have exercised their sovereignty to outlaw war. In addition, the failure or weakening of state capacity that brings about a political vacuum within states leads to human tragedies and international and regional insecurity. Repressive, aggressive, or collapsed states may result in threats to international peace and security.

The principle of noninterference in affairs that are within the domestic jurisdiction of states is the anchor to state sovereignty within the system of international relations and obligations. Jurisdiction broadly refers to the power, authority, and competence of a state to govern persons and property within its territory. It is labelled "prescriptive" and "enforcement." Prescriptive jurisdiction relates to the power of a state to make or prescribe law within and outside its territory, and enforcement jurisdiction is about the power of the state to implement the law within its territory. Jurisdiction exercised by states is then the corollary of their sovereignty. Jurisdiction is clearly founded on territorial sovereignty but extends beyond it. Jurisdiction is *prima facie* exclusive over a state's territory and population, and the general duty of nonintervention in domestic affairs protects both the territorial sovereignty and the domestic jurisdiction of states on an equal basis.

Within the Charter of the UN, there is an explicit prohibition on the world organization from interfering in the domestic affairs of member states. What may be the Charter's most frequently cited provision, Article 2 (7), provides that "[n]othing contained in the present Charter shall authorise the United Nations to intervene in matters that are essentially within the domestic jurisdiction of any State or shall require the Members to submit such matters to settlement under the present Charter."

In sum, sovereignty is a key constitutional safeguard of international order. Despite the pluralization of international relations through the proliferation of nonstate actors — evidenced by an accelerated rate of economic globalization, democratization, and privatization worldwide — the state remains the fundamental guarantor of human rights locally, as well as the building block for collectively ensuring international order.

The equality in legal status of sovereignty also offers protection for weaker states in the face of pressure from the more powerful. This sentiment was captured by Algerian President Boueteflika, who, as President of the Organization for African Unity (OAU), addressed the UN General Assembly in 1999, immediately after the Secretary-General, and called sovereignty "our final defence against the rules of an unjust world."

Limits of Sovereignty

There are important and widely accepted limits to state sovereignty and to domestic jurisdiction in international law. First, the Charter highlights the tension between the sovereignty, independence, and equality of individual states, on the one hand, and collective international obligations for the maintenance of international peace and security, on the other. Sovereignty is not a barrier to action taken by the Security Council as part of measures in response to "a threat to the peace, a breach of the peace or an act of aggression." In other words, the sovereignty of states, as recognized in the UN Charter, yields to the demands of international peace and security. And the status of sovereign equality only holds effectively for each state when there is stability, peace, and order among states.

Second, state sovereignty may be limited by customary and treaty obligations in international relations and law. States are legally responsible for the performance of their international obligations, and state sovereignty therefore cannot be an excuse for their nonperformance. Obligations assumed by states by virtue of their membership in the UN and the corresponding powers of the world organization presuppose a restriction of the sovereignty of member states to the extent of their obligations under the Charter.

Specifically, Article 1 (2) stipulates that "[a]ll Members, in order to ensure to all of them the rights and benefits resulting from membership, shall fulfil in good faith the obligations assumed by them in accordance with the present Charter."

Furthermore, under "Purposes and Principles," this same article obliges member states to achieve international cooperation in solving problems of an economic, social, cultural, or humanitarian character and in promoting and encouraging respect for human rights and for fundamental freedoms for all, without distinction as to race, sex, language, or religion. This article further recognizes the UN as a centre for harmonizing the actions of states in the attainment of these common ends. Thus, the Charter elevates the solution of economic, social, cultural, and humanitarian problems, as well as human rights, to the international sphere. By definition, these matters cannot be said to be exclusively domestic, and solutions cannot be located exclusively within the sovereignty of states.

Sovereignty therefore carries with it primary responsibilities for states to protect persons and property and to discharge the functions of government adequately within their territories. The quality and range of responsibilities for governance have brought about significant changes in state sovereignty since 1945. In particular, since the signing of the UN Charter, there has been an expanding network of obligations in the field of human rights. These create a dense set of state obligations to protect persons and property, as well as to regulate political and economic affairs. Sovereignty is incapable, then, of completely shielding internal violations of human rights that contradict international obligations.

Similarly, Article 2 (7) of the Charter is also subject to widely accepted limits. In the first place, this article is concerned chiefly with the limits of the UN as an organization. In the second place, the words "*essentially* within the domestic jurisdiction of States" refer to those matters that are not regulated by international law. As the ICJ has concluded, "[T]he question whether a certain matter is or is not solely within the domestic jurisdiction of a State is an essentially relative question; it depends on the development of international relations." The ICJ has further concluded that it hardly seems conceivable that terms like "domestic jurisdiction" were intended to have a fixed content, regardless of the subsequent evolution of international law.

Sovereignty has been eroded by contemporary economic, cultural, and environmental factors. Interference in what would previously have been regarded as internal affairs — by other states, the private sector, and nonstate actors — has become routine. However, the preoccupation here is not these routine matters but the potential tension when the norm of state sovereignty and egregious human suffering coexist. As Kofi Annan suggested, in his opening remarks at the 1999 General Assembly, "States bent on criminal behaviour [should] know that frontiers are not the absolute defence." In this respect, events in the last decade have broken new ground.

Emerging Challenges to Sovereignty

The limits on sovereignty discussed above are widely accepted. They originate in the Charter itself, in authoritative legal interpretations of that document, and in the broader body of international law that has been agreed on by states. In recent decades, and particularly since the end of the Cold War, four more radical challenges to the notion of state sovereignty have emerged: continuing demands for self-determination, a broadened conception of international peace and security, the collapse of state authority, and the increasing importance of popular sovereignty.

In many ways, a central contemporary difficulty arises from the softening of two norms that had been virtually unchallenged during the Cold War, the sanctity of borders and the illegitimacy of secession. For almost half a century, collective self-determination was limited to the initial process of decolonization. Existing borders were sacrosanct, and it was unthinkable that an area of a state would secede, even with the consent of the original state. The OAU's Charter was clear that colonial borders, although it is generally agreed that they were arbitrarily drawn, still had to be respected, or chaos would ensue. *Uti possidetis, ita possideatis* (as you possess, so may you possess) was accepted as the necessary trade-off for a modicum of international order.

At the end of the Cold War, however, these relatively clear waters became muddied. First, the Soviet Union became a "former superpower." Russia inherited the Soviet Union's legal status, including a permanent seat on the Security Council, but 14 other new states were created. Shortly thereafter, Yugoslavia broke up into 6 independent states. Later in the decade, Eritrea seceded from Ethiopia.

That weakening of the norms relating to borders and secessions is creating new tensions. Contemporary politics in developing countries is deeply conditioned by the legacy of colonialism. As European states ruled so many Asian and African countries without their consent, respect for state sovereignty is the preemptive norm *par excellence* of ex-colonial states. In light of history, it is difficult for representatives of developing countries to take at face value altruistic claims by the West. What may appear as narrow legalism — for instance, that Security Council authorization is a prerequisite for intervention — often appears in the South as a necessary buttress against new forms of imperialism.

The second challenge is the broadening interpretation of threats to international peace and security, the Charter-enshrined licence to override the principle of nonintervention. It arises from the fact that the Charter's collective system of international peace and security was crafted on the experience of the Second World War, some of which is of doubtful contemporary relevance. The focus was principally on the external unlawful use of sovereignty by states in committing acts of aggression. Collective efforts by the UN to deal with internal problems of peace and security, and gross violations of human rights, including genocide, have therefore run against the grain of the claim to sovereign status as set out in the Charter. State actions approved or authorized after the Cold War's end by the Security Council have routinely broadened the notion of what is considered a threat to international peace and security. This process actually began during the Cold War with the Security Council's coercive decisions in the form of economic sanctions and arms and oil embargoes against apartheid in Southern Rhodesia and South Africa. However, what clearly motivated state decision making was the human costs resulting from aberrant domestic human rights policies of white-minority regimes. An affront to civilization was packaged as a threat to international peace and security in order to permit action.

The evolution of the definition of a threat to international peace and security accelerated in the 1990s. For instance, while recalling Article 2 (7) of the Charter, the Security Council, in Resolution 688 (1991), nonetheless condemned "the repression of the Iraqi civilian population in many parts of Iraq, including most recently in Kurdish populated areas." The Security Council has repeatedly condemned attacks on civilians, in Bosnia and Herzegovina, in Sierra Leone, and in Kosovo, which constitute grave violations of international law. It has reaffirmed that persons who commit or order the commission of grave breaches of the Geneva Conventions and the Additional Protocols are individually responsible in respect of such breaches. Similarly, the establishment of international tribunals with criminal jurisdiction and the negotiation of the Rome Statute on the International Criminal Court signal that atrocities committed against human beings by their own governments — including war crimes, crimes against humanity, and the perpetration of genocide — may trump claims of sovereignty.

The main interventions of the 1990s were justified, at least in part, on humanitarian grounds, though again the humanitarian dimensions were framed as threats to international peace and security. In most cases, the dire humanitarian situation was explicitly mentioned in the Security Council's authorization — the most extreme case being Somalia, where "humanitarian" appeared 18 times in Resolution 794 (1992). In a session devoted to Africa in January 2000, the AIDS pandemic was also framed as falling within the Security Council's mandate. In short, the range of interpretations of international peace and security — the concept that defines the Security Council's mandate — has been substantially broadened, albeit not without controversy.

The third challenge to traditional interpretations of state sovereignty has arisen because of the incapacity of certain states to effectively exercise authority over their territories and populations. In some cases, sovereignty is a legal fiction not matched by an actual political capacity. They are, in the words of one analyst, "quasi-states." And as mentioned earlier, the display of actual control over territory is a prominent dimension of sovereign status. Some commentators have even argued that failed states violate the substantive UN membership requirement in Charter Article 4 that they "are able to carry out" their obligations.

This perspective is important in light of the growing awareness that state capacity and authority are essential conditions for the protection of fundamental rights. These conditions do not invoke nostalgia for repressive national-security states, but they recognize that a modicum of state authority and capacity is a prerequisite for the maintenance of domestic and international order and justice.

The absence or disappearance of a functioning government can lead to the same kinds of human catastrophe as the presence of a repressive state or the outbreak of a deadly civil war. Resounding features of these so-called failed states are anarchy, chronic disorder, and civil war waged without regard for the laws of armed conflict. These features, individually or collectively, inhibit or prevent a state from acting with authority over its entire territory. The failure of state sovereignty is most obviously evidenced by the lack of control where territorial sovereignty is effectively contested by force internally. In this situation, insurgents may occupy and control large portions of the territory, inhibiting the state from carrying out its responsibility to protect lives and property and maintain public security.

The political vacuum resulting from these circumstances leads to nonstate actors' taking matters into their own hands, the massive flight of refugees, and the forced displacement of populations. These issues also create consequences of concern to other states, international organizations, and civil society. In lending support to the intervention by the Economic Community of West African States in Liberia, Zimbabwe went so far as to take the position that "when there is no government in being and there is just chaos in the country," domestic affairs should be qualified as meaning "affairs within a peaceful environment."

The grave humanitarian consequences of the failure of state capacity has led the Security Council to override state sovereignty by determining that internal disorder may pose a threat to international peace and security. In one case in particular, Somalia, the complete absence of state capacity prompted the Security Council to authorize.

The fourth challenge to traditional state sovereignty emerges from the changing balance between states and people as the source of legitimacy and authority. The older version of the rule of the law of states is being tempered by the rule of law based on the rights of individuals. And a broader concept of sovereignty, encompassing both the rights and the responsibilities of states, is now being more widely advocated.

One formulation has been proposed by Kofi Annan in his widely cited article in *The Economist* on the "two concepts of sovereignty," which helped launch the intense debate on the legitimacy of intervention on humanitarian grounds. In it he argued that one concept of sovereignty is oriented around states and the other around people:

State sovereignty, in its most basic sense, is being redefined—not least by the forces of globalization and international cooperation. States are now widely understood to be instruments at the service of their peoples, and not vice versa. At the same time individual sovereignty — by which I mean the fundamental freedom of each individual, enshrined in the Charter of the UN and subsequent international treaties — has been enhanced by a renewed and spreading consciousness of individual rights. When we read the Charter today, we are more than ever conscious that its aim is to protect individual human beings, not to protect those who abuse them.

For Annan and others, sovereignty is not becoming less relevant; it remains the ordering principle of international affairs. However, "it is the peoples' sovereignty rather than the sovereign's sovereignty."

Another way of approaching the increasing importance of popular sovereignty is the notion of "sovereignty as responsibility," most explicitly formulated by Francis M. Deng, the Representative of the Secretary-General on Internally Displaced Persons. This doctrine stipulates that when states are unable to provide life-supporting protection and assistance for their citizens, they are expected to request and accept outside offers of aid. Should they refuse or deliberately obstruct access to their displaced or other affected populations and thereby put large numbers at risk, there is an international responsibility to respond. Sovereignty then means accountability to two separate constituencies: internally, to one's own population; and internationally, to the community of responsible states and in the form of compliance with human rights and humanitarian agreements. Proponents of this view argue that sovereignty is not absolute but contingent. When a government massively abuses the fundamental rights of its citizens, its sovereignty is temporarily suspended.

A third variant on this theme revolves around the concept of human security. Security has traditionally been conceived in terms of the relations between states, but for a growing number of states the security of individuals is becoming a foreign policy priority in its own right. According to a group of states participating in the Human Security Network, "[H]uman security means freedom from pervasive threats to people's rights, their safety or even their lives." Though the state remains the principal provider of security, it is seen in instrumental terms — as a means to an end, rather than an end in itself. In the face of repressive or weak states, advocates of human security argue that international actors have a responsibility to come to the aid of populations at risk. Ultimately, "peace and security — national, regional and international — are possible only if they are derived from peoples' security."

These approaches all see the basis for sovereignty shifting from the absolute rights of state leaders to respect for the popular will and internal forms of governance based on international standards of democracy and human rights. Their advocates suggest that on a scale of values the sovereignty of a state does not stand higher than the human rights of its inhabitants.

Some observers charge that humanitarian intervention is simply the latest phase of Euro-centric domination. Human rights are the contemporary Western values being imposed in place of Christianity and the "standard of civilization" in the 19th and early 20th century. Nevertheless, from many quarters the view is emerging that sovereignty is no longer sacrosanct. Sovereignty as the supreme power of a state has always been limited, originally by divine law, respect for religious practices, and natural law; and subsequently, limitations have resulted from the consent-based system of the law of nations. "The doctrine of national sovereignty in its absolute and unqualified form, which gave rulers protection against attack from without while engaged within in the most brutal assault on their own citizens," writes Ramesh Thakur, "has gone with the wind."

State Citizenship

State citizenship usually refers to citizenship of one of the states of the United States of America. Citizenship was initially defined by Article 4 of the United States Constitution, and later clarified by the 14th Amendment, which states: "All persons born or naturalized in the United States, and subject to the jurisdiction thereof, are citizens of the United States and of the State wherein they reside."

Definition

In matters of international law, a citizen of one of the several States is frequently considered a United States citizen. Passports issued by the U.S. State Department refer to the "citizen/national," since the document is used by both classes. While being a citizen of the United States arises out of birth or naturalization, state Citizenship is based on birth and domicile. In an American court, however, State Citizenship is separate and distinct from U.S. citizenship. State laws (more frequently of states admitted to the Union before 1866 than after) also make this distinction.

A person is subject to the jurisdiction of a state simply by being physically present in that state. Any person, whether citizen, foreign national, corporation or other legal entity, is subject to the jurisdiction of both the laws of the state in which that person resides and the federal laws that apply to all the states. There are exceptions, such as for diplomats with immunity. Such persons also enjoy certain legal rights under both systems. For example, a UK Citizen accused of a crime in New Jersey can be found guilty and punished, but only after a trial conducted according to the standards of the United States and New Jersey legal systems.

As a practical matter, states may restrict certain privileges of citizenship to those who are long-term or permanent residents. Some states distinguish different pains and penalties for the same offense depending on whether the accused is a state Citizen or resident person.

Another more common example of this is in the public university system, where state residents pay substantially reduced tuition compared to persons who live outside the state. The definition of this "in-state" status varies from state to state. Citizens might be required to live in the state for a minimum of 1 year, or they might be required to pay state income or property taxes at least once.

Citizenship

Citizenship status, under social contract theory, carries with it both rights and responsibilities. "Active citizenship" is the philosophy that citizens should work towards the betterment of their community through economic participation, public service, volunteer work, and other such efforts to improve life for all citizens. In this vein, schools in some countries provide citizenship education.

National Citizenship

Generally citizenship is seen as the relation between an individual and a particular nation. In ancient Greece, the main political entity was the city-state, and citizens were members of particular city-states. In the past five hundred years, with the rise of the nation-state, citizenship is most closely identified with being a member of a particular nation. To some extent, certain entities cross national boundaries such as trade organizations, non-governmental organizations as well as multinational corporations, and sometimes the term "citizen of the world" applies in the sense of people having less ties to a particular nation and more of a sense of belonging to the world in general.

Supranational Citizenship

In recent years, some intergovernmental organizations have extended the concept and terminology associated with citizenship to the international level, where it is applied to the totality of the citizens of their constituent countries combined. Citizenship at this level is a secondary concept, with rights deriving from national citizenship.

European Union (EU) Citizenship

The Maastricht Treaty introduced the concept of citizenship of the European Union. Article 17 (1) of the amended EC Treaty states that Citizenship of the Union is hereby established. Every person holding the nationality of a Member State shall be a citizen of the Union. Citizenship of the Union shall complement and not replace national citizenship.

The amended EC Treaty establishes certain minimal rights for EU citizens. Article 12 of the amended EC Treaty guarantees a general right of non-discrimination within the scope of the Treaty. Article 18 provides a limited right to free movement and residence in Member States other than that of which the EU citizen is a national. Articles 18-21 and 225 provide certain political rights.

Union citizens have also extensive rights to move in order to exercise economic activity in any of the Member States (Articles 39, 43, 49 EC), which predate the introduction of Union citizenship.

Polis Citizenship

The first form of citizenship was based on the way people lived in the ancient Greek times, in small-scale organic communities of the polis. In those days citizenship was not seen as a public matter, separated from the private life of the individual person. The obligations of citizenship were deeply connected into one's everyday life in the polis. To be truly human, one had to be an active citizen to the community, which Aristotle famously expressed: "To take no part in the running of the community's affairs is to be either a beast or a god!" This form of citizenship was based on obligations of citizens towards the community, rather than rights given to the citizens of the community. This was not a problem because they all had a strong affinity with the polis; their own destiny and the destiny of the community were strongly linked. Also, citizens of the polis saw obligations to the community as an opportunity to be virtuous, it was a source of honour and respect. In Athens, citizens were both ruler and ruled, important political and judicial offices were rotated and all citizens had the right to speak and vote in the political assembly.

However, an important aspect of polis citizenship was exclusivity. Citizenship in ancient Greece and Rome, as well as Medieval cities that practiced polis citizenship, was exclusive and inequality of status was widely accepted. Citizens had a much higher status than non-citizens: Women, slaves or 'barbarians'. For example, women were seen to be irrational and incapable of political participation (although some, most notably Plato, disagreed). Methods used to determine whether someone could be a citizen or not could be based on wealth (the amount of taxes one paid), political participation, or heritage (both parents had to be born in the polis)..

In the Roman Empire, polis citizenship changed form: Citizenship was expanded from small scale communities to the entire empire. Romans realised that granting citizenship to people from all over the empire legitimized Roman rule over conquered areas. Citizenship in the Roman era was no longer a status of political agency; it had been reduced to a judicial safeguard and the expression of rule and law.

Honorary Citizenship

Some countries extend "honorary citizenship" to those whom they consider to be especially admirable or worthy of the distinction.

By act of United States Congress and presidential assent, honorary United States citizenship has been awarded to only seven individuals. Honorary Canadian citizenship requires the unanimous approval of Parliament. The only people to ever receive honorary Canadian citizenship are Raoul Wallenberg posthumously in 1985, Nelson Mandela in 2001, the 14th Dalai Lama Tenzin Gyatso in 2006, and Aung San Suu Kyi in 2007. In 2002 South Korea awarded honorary citizenship to Dutch football (soccer) coach Guus Hiddink who successfully and unexpectedly took the national team to the semi-finals of the 2002 FIFA World Cup. Honorary citizenship was also awarded to Hines Ward, a black Korean American football player, in 2006 for his efforts to minimize discrimination in Korea against half-Koreans.

American actress Angelina Jolie received an honorary Cambodian citizenship in 2005 due to her humanitarian efforts. Cricketers Matthew Hayden and Herschelle Gibbs were awarded honorary citizenship of St. Kitts and Nevis in March 2007 due to their record-breaking innings in the 2007 Cricket World Cup.

In Germany the honorary citizenship is awarded by cities, towns and sometimes federal states. The honorary citizenship ends with the death of the honoured, or, in exceptional cases, when it is taken away by the council or parliament of the city, town, or state. In the case of war criminals, all such honours were taken away by "Article VIII, section II, letter i of the directive 38 of the Allied Control Council for Germany" on October 12, 1946 In some cases, honorary citizenship was taken away from members of the former GDR regime, e.g. Erich Honecker, after the collapse of the GDR in 1989/90.

In Ireland, "honorary citizenship" bestowed on a foreigner is in fact full legal citizenship including the right to reside in Ireland, to vote etc.

Historically, many states limited citizenship to only a proportion of their population, thereby creating a citizen class with political rights superior to other sections of the population, but equal with each other. The classical example of a limited citizenry was Athens where slaves, women, and resident foreigners (called metics) were excluded from political rights. The Roman Republic forms another example, and, more recently, the nobility of the Polish-Lithuanian Commonwealth had some of the same characteristics.

School Subject

Citizenship has been introduced as a compulsory subject of the National Curriculum in state-run schools in England. Some state schools offer an examination in this subject, all state schools have a statutory requirement to report student's progress in Citizenship.

Citizenship is not offered as a normal General Certificate of Secondary Education (GCSE) course in many schools. Only some schools offer this subject as a GCSE course, and this is usually not a compulsory subject. Some schools may even give students an option, whether to study Citizenship or not at GCSE. All 14-16 year-olds must study Citizenship, but there are no exams, few assessments and is quite a different subject.Most advanced students may also study citizenship at the age of 11-12.

In Wales the model used is Personal and Social Education.

Citizenship is not taught as a subject in Scottish schools, however they do teach a subject called "Modern Studies" which covers the social, political and economic study of local, national and international issues.

It is taught in the Republic of Ireland as an exam subject for the Junior Certificate. It is known as Civic, Social and Political Education (CSPE).

Responsibilities or Duties of Citizenship

The legally enforceable duties of citizenship vary depending on one's country, and may include such items as:

- paying taxes
- serving on a jury
- Voting
- serving in the country's armed forces when called upon
- obeying the criminal laws enacted by one's government, even while abroad.

States' Rights

States' rights in U.S. politics refers to the political powers that U.S. states possess in relation to the federal government, as guaranteed by the Tenth Amendment of the Bill of Rights.

Background

The balance of federal powers and those powers held by the states as defined in the Supremacy Clause of the U.S. Constitution was first addressed in the case of McCulloch v. Maryland. Chief Justice John Marshall asserted that the laws adopted by the federal government, when exercising its constitutional powers, are generally paramount over any conflicting laws adopted by state governments. After *McCulloch*, the primary legal issues in this area concerned the scope of Congress' constitutional powers, and whether the states possess certain powers to the exclusion of the federal government, even if the Constitution does not explicitly limit them to the States.

Controversy to 1865

In the period between the American Revolution and the ratification of the United States Constitution, the states had united under a much weaker federal government, pursuant to the Articles of Confederation. The Articles gave the central government very little, if any, authority to overrule individual state actions. The

Constitution subsequently strengthened the central government, authorizing it to exercise powers deemed necessary to exercise its authority, with an ambiguous boundary between the two co-existing levels of government. In the event of any conflict between state and federal law, the Constitution resolved the conflict via the Supremacy Clause of Article VI in favour of the federal government, which declares federal law the "supreme Law of the Land" and provides that "the Judges in every State shall be bound thereby, any Thing in the Constitution or Laws of any State to the Contrary notwithstanding." However, the Supremacy Clause only applies if the federal government is acting in pursuit of its constitutionally authorized powers.

Alien and Sedition Acts

When the Federalists passed the Alien and Sedition Acts in 1798, Thomas Jefferson and James Madison secretly wrote the Kentucky and Virginia Resolutions, which provide a classic statement in support of states' rights. According to this theory, the federal Union is a voluntary association of states, and if the central government goes too far each state has the right to nullify that law. As Jefferson said in the Kentucky Resolutions:

Resolved, that the several States composing the United States of America, are not united on the principle of unlimited submission to their general government; but that by compact under the style and title of a Constitution for the United States and of amendments thereto, they constituted a general government for special purposes, delegated to that government certain definite powers, reserving each State to itself, the residuary mass of right to their own self-government; and that whensoever the general government assumes undelegated powers, its acts are unauthoritative, void, and of no force: That to this compact each State acceded as a State, and is an integral party, its co-States forming, as to itself, the other party....each party has an equal right to judge for itself, as well of infractions as of the mode and measure of redress.

The Kentucky and Virginia Resolutions, along with the supporting Report of 1800 by Madison, became bedrock documents of Jefferson's Democratic-Republican Party. The most vociferous supporters of states' rights, such as John Randolph of Roanoke, were called "Old Republicans" into the 1820s and 1830s. Another states' rights dispute occurred over the War of 1812. At the Hartford Convention, New England states voiced opposition to President James Madison and the war, and discussed secession from the Union.

Nullification Crisis of 1832

One major and continuous strain on the union, from roughly 1820 through the Civil War, was the issue of trade and tariffs. Heavily dependent upon trade, the almost entirely agricultural and export-oriented South imported most of its manufactured goods from Europe or obtained them from the North. The North, by contrast, had a growing domestic industrial economy that viewed foreign trade as competition. Trade barriers, especially protective tariffs, were viewed as harmful to the Southern economy, which depended on exports.

In 1828, the Congress passed protective tariffs to benefit trade in the northern states, but that were detrimental to the South. Southerners vocally expressed their tariff opposition in documents such as the South Carolina Exposition and Protest in 1828, written in response to the "Tariff of Abominations." *Exposition and Protest* was the work of South Carolina senator and former vice president John C. Calhoun, formerly an advocate of protective tariffs and internal improvements at federal expense.

South Carolina's Nullification Ordinance declared both the tariff of 1828 and the 1832 null and void within the state borders of South Carolina. This action initiated the Nullification Crisis. Passed by a state convention on November 24, 1832, it led, on December 10, to President Andrew Jackson's proclamation against South Carolina, which sent a naval flotilla and a threat of sending federal troops to enforce the tariffs.

Civil War

Over the following decades, another central dispute over states' rights moved to the fore. The issue of slavery polarized the union, with the Jeffersonian principles often being used by both sides—anti-slavery Northerners, and Southern slaveholders and secessionists—in debates that ultimately led to the American Civil

War. Supporters of slavery often argued that one of the rights of the states was the protection of slave property wherever it went, a position endorsed by the U.S. Supreme Court in the 1857 Dred Scott decision. In contrast, opponents of slavery argued that the non-slave-states' rights were violated both by that decision and by the Fugitive Slave Law of 1850. Exactly *which*—and *whose*—states' rights were the casus belli in the Civil War remain in controversy.

Southern Arguments

Jefferson Davis used the following argument in favour of the equal rights of states:

Resolved, That the union of these States rests on the equality of rights and privileges among its members, and that it is especially the duty of the Senate, which represents the States in their sovereign capacity, to resist all attempts to discriminate either in relation to person or property, so as, in the Territories—which are the common possession of the United States—to give advantages to the citizens of one State which are not equally secured to those of every other State.

The Preamble to the Confederate States Constitution begins: "We, the people of the Confederate States, each State acting in its sovereign and independent character..."

Northern Arguments

The historian McPherson noted that Southerners were inconsistent on the states' rights issue, and that Northern states tried to protect the rights of their states against the South during the Gag Rule and fugitive slave law controversies. The historian Freehling noted that the South's argument for a states' rights to secede was different from Thomas Jefferson's, in that Jefferson based such a right on the unalianable equal rights of man. The South's version of such a right was modified to be consistent with slavery, and with the South's blend of democracy and authoritarianism. Various historians and commentators, including Adams, Sinha, and Richards, among others, are of the opinion that the States' Rights argument made by supporters of the Confederacy was in fact a thinly disguised justification of continued slavery in the southern states, and/or moves by the Southern states to violate the states' rights of Northern states. Historian Henry Brooks Adams explains that the anti-slavery North took a consistent and principled stand on states' rights against Federal encroachment throughout its history, while the Southern states, whenever they saw an opportunity to expand slavery and the reach of the slave power, often conveniently forgot the principle of states' rights—and fought in favour of Federal centralization:

> Between the slave power and states' rights there was no necessary connection. The slave power, when in control, was a centralizing influence, and all the most considerable encroachments on states' rights were its acts. The acquisition and admission of Louisiana; the Embargo; the War of 1812; the annexation of Texas "by joint resolution" [rather than treaty]; the war with Mexico, declared by the mere announcement of President Polk; the Fugitive Slave Law; the Dred Scott decision — all triumphs of the slave power — did far more than either tariffs or internal improvements, which in their origin were also southern measures, to destroy the very memory of states' rights as they existed in 1789. Whenever a question arose of extending or protecting slavery, the slaveholders became friends of centralized power, and used that dangerous weapon with a kind of frenzy. Slavery in fact required centralization in order to maintain and protect itself, but it required to control the centralized machine; it needed despotic principles of government, but it needed them exclusively for its own use. Thus, in truth, states' rights were the protection of the free states, and as a matter of fact, during the domination of the slave power, Massachusetts appealed to this protecting principle as often and almost as loudly as South Carolina.

Sinha and Richards both argue that the *states' rights* that the Southern states claimed were actually:

- States' rights to engage in slavery;
- States' rights to suppress the freedom of speech of those opposed to slavery or its expansion, by seizing abolitionist literature from the mail;
- States' rights to violate the sovereignty of the non-slave States by sending slave-catchers into their territory to enforce the Fugitive Slave Law of 1850, to seize supposed runaway slaves by force of arms.

- States' rights to send armed Border Ruffians into the territories of the United States such as Kansas to engage in massive vote fraud and acts of violence;
- States' rights to deem portions of their population *"beings of an inferior order, and altogether unfit to associate with the white race, either in social or political relations, and so far inferior that they had no rights which the white man was bound to respect"*, by means of the Dred Scott decision;
- States' rights to secede from the United States after an election whose result they disagreed with, the election in 1860 of Abraham Lincoln;
- States' rights to seize forts and arsenals of the United States following their purported secession;
- States' rights to have a less democratic form of government; Sinha, in particular, argues this point, illustrating that the state of South Carolina, home of John Calhoun, the ideological godfather of the Slave Power, had a far less democratic order than the several other United States. Although all white male residents were allowed to vote, property restrictions for office holders were higher in South Carolina than in any other state. South Carolina had the only state legislature where slave owners had the majority of seats. It was the only state where the legislature elected the governor, all judges and state electors. The state's chief executive was a figurehead who had no authority to veto legislative law.
- States' rights to overturn the ideal expressed in the Declaration of Independence — that "We hold these truths to be self-evident, that all men are created equal, that they are endowed by their Creator with certain unalienable Rights, that among these are Life, Liberty and the pursuit of Happiness".

Sinha and Richards conclude their cases by arguing that the Civil War had nothing to do with *"states' rights"*, democracy, or resistance to arbitrary power. They argue that it was instead the result of the increasing cognitive dissonance in the minds of Northerners and (some) Southern non-slaveowners between the ideals that the United States was founded upon and identified itself as standing for, as expressed in the Declaration of Independence, the Constitution of the United States, and the Bill of Rights, and the reality that the slave-power represented, as what they describe as an anti-democratic, counter-republican, oligarchic, despotic, authoritarian, if not totalitarian, movement for ownership of human beings as the personal chattels of the slaver. As this cognitive dissonance increased, the people of the Northern states, and the Northern states themselves, became increasingly inclined to resist the encroachments of the slave power upon their states' rights and encroachments of the slave power by and upon the Federal Government of the United States. The slave power, having failed to maintain its dominance of the Federal Government through democratic means, sought other means of maintaining its dominance of the Federal Government, by means of military aggression, by right of force and coercion, and thus, the Civil War occurred.

Since 1865

A series of Supreme Court decisions developed the state action constraint on the Equal Protection Clause. The state action theory weakened the effect of the Equal Protection Clause against state governments, in that the clause was held not to apply to unequal protection of the laws caused in part by complete lack of state action in specific cases, even if state actions in other instances form an overall pattern of segregation and other discrimination. The separate but equal theory further weakened the effect of the Equal Protection Clause against state governments.

In Case Law

With United States v. Cruikshank (1876), a case which arose out of the Colfax Massacre of blacks contesting the results of a Reconstruction era election, the Fourteenth Amendment, First Amendment and Second Amendment were held by the Supreme Court to apply only to state actions, not private acts of violence.

United States v. Harris (1883) held that the Equal Protection Clause did not apply to an 1883 prison lynching since the Fourteenth Amendment applied only to states, not to individual criminal matters.

The Civil Rights Cases (1883) allowed segregation by striking down the Civil Rights Act of 1875, a statute that prohibited racial discrimination in public accommodations. There, the Supreme Court held that the Equal Protection Clause applied only to acts done by states, not to those done by private individuals; because the Civil Rights Act of 1875 applied to private establishments, the Court said, it exceeded congressional power under Section Five of the Fourteenth Amendment.

Plessy v. Ferguson (1896) held that the separate but equal doctrine complied with the Equal Protection Clause, and marked the beginning of Jim Crow laws by approving the de jure segregation. The Fourteenth and Fifteenth Amendments would be largely inactive until the American Civil Rights Movement. Some modern courts up to and including the U.S. Supreme Court still interpret the *Civil Rights Cases* as limiting the scope of the Fourteenth Amendment.

Direct Election of Senators

Under the original constitutional system, while federal Representatives were popularly elected, federal Senators were appointed by State legislatures, thus ensuring a balance between Federal and State interests at the Federal level. The Seventeenth Amendment significantly altered the relationship of State and Federal powers, weakening pro-state-autonomy influence at the Federal level.

Later Progressive Era and World War II

By the beginning of the 20th century, greater cooperation began to grow between the State and federal governments. Soon, the federal government began to accumulate more power. It was early in this period that a federal income tax was implemented, first during the Civil War and then permanently with the Sixteenth Amendment in 1913. Before this, the states played a larger role in government.

States's rights were affected by the fundamental alteration of the federal government resulting from the Seventeenth Amendment, depriving state governments of an avenue of control over the federal government via the representation of each state's legislature in the U.S. Senate. This change has been described by legal critics as the loss of a check and balance on the federal government by the states.

Following the Great Depression, the New Deal and then World War II continued the growth of the federal government, its authority, and its responsibilities. The case of Wickard v. Filburn allowed the federal government to enforce the Agricultural Adjustment Act, providing subsidies to farmers for limiting their crop yields, arguing agriculture affected interstate commerce and came under the jurisdiction of the Commerce Clause even when a farmer grew his crops not to be sold, but for his own private use.

After World War II, President Harry Truman supported a civil rights bill and desegregated the military. The reaction was a split in the Democratic Party that led to the formation of the "States' Rights Party"—better known as the Dixiecrats—led by Strom Thurmond. Thurmond ran as the States' Rights candidate for President in 1948, losing to Truman.

African-American Civil Rights Movement

During the African-American Civil Rights Movement of the 1950s and 1960s, the longstanding use of states' rights to maintain Southern racial politics was highlighted with proponents of racial segregation and Jim Crow laws denouncing federal interference in these state-level policies.

Brown v. Board of Education (1954) overruled the Plessy v. Ferguson (1896) decision, but the Fourteenth and Fifteenth amendments were largely inactive in the South until the Civil Rights Act of 1964 (42 U.S.C. § 21) and the Voting Rights Act of 1965. Several states passed Interposition Resolutions to declare that the Supreme Court's ruling in Brown usurped states' rights.

There was also states' rights opposition to voting rights at Edmund Pettus Bridge, which was part of the Selma to Montgomery marches that resulted in the Voting Rights Act of 1965.

Contemporary Debates

In 1964, the issue of fair housing in California involved the boundary between state laws and federalism. California Proposition 14 overturned the Rumsford Fair Housing Act and allowed discrimination in any type of home sale. Martin Luther King, Jr. and others saw this as a backlash against civil rights. Actor Ronald Reagan gained popularity by supporting Proposition 14, and was later elected governor of California. The U.S. Supreme Court's Reitman v. Mulkey decision overturned Proposition 14 in 1967 in favour of the Equal Protection Clause of the Fourteenth Amendment.

Another concern is the fact that on more than one occasion, the federal government has threatened to withhold highway funds from states which did not pass certain articles of legislation. Any state which lost highway funding for any extended period would face financial impoverishment, infrastructure collapse or both. Although the first such action (the enactment of a national speed limit) was directly related to highways and done in the face of a fuel shortage, most subsequent actions have had little or nothing to do with highways and have not been done in the face of any compelling national crisis. An example of this would be the federally mandated drinking age of 21. Critics of such actions feel that when the federal government does this they upset the traditional balance between the states and the federal government.

More recently, the issue of states' rights has come to a head when the Base Realignment and Closure Commission (BRAC) recommended that Congress and the Department of Defence implement sweeping changes to the National Guard by consolidating some Guard installations and closing others. These recommendations in 2005 drew strong criticism from many states, and several states sued the federal government on the basis that Congress and the Pentagon would be violating states' rights should they force the realignment and closure of Guard bases without the prior approval of the governors from the affected states. After Pennsylvania won a federal lawsuit to block the deactivation of the 111th Fighter Wing of the Pennsylvania Air National Guard, defence and Congressional leaders chose to try to settle the remaining BRAC lawsuits out of court, reaching compromises with the plaintiff states.

Current states' rights issues include the death penalty, assisted suicide, gay marriage and the medicinal use of marijuana, the last of which is in violation of federal law. In Gonzales v. Raich, the

Supreme Court ruled in favour of the federal government, permitting the Drug Enforcement Administration (DEA) to arrest medical marijuana patients and caregivers. In Gonzales v. Oregon, the Supreme court ruled the practice of physician-assisted suicide in Oregon is legal.

States' Rights as "Code Word"

The term "states' rights," some have argued, was used as a code word by defenders of segregation. It was the official name of the "Dixiecrat" party led by white supremacist presidential candidate Strom Thurmond. George Wallace, the Alabama governor—who famously declared in his inaugural address, "Segregation now! Segregation tomorrow! Segregation forever!"—later remarked that he should have said, "States' rights now! States' rights tomorrow! States' rights forever!" Wallace, however, claimed that segregation was but one issue symbolic of a larger struggle for states' rights; in that view, which some historians dispute, his replacement of *segregation* with *states' rights* would be more of a clarification than a euphemism.

States' Rights and the Rehnquist Court

The Supreme Court's University of Alabama v. Garrett (2001) and Kimel v. Florida Board of Regents (2000) decisions allowed states to use a rational basis review for discrimination against the aged and disabled, arguing that these types of discrimination were rationally related to a legitimate state interest, and that no "razorlike precision" was needed." The Supreme Court's United States v. Morrison (2000) decision limited the ability of rape victims to sue their attackers in federal court. Chief Justice William H. Rehnquist explained that "States historically have been sovereign" in the area of law enforcement, which in the Court's opinion required narrow interpretations of the Commerce Clause and Fourteenth Amendment.

Kimel, *Garrett* and *Morrison* indicated that the Court's previous decisions in favour of enumerated powers and limits on Congressional power over the states, such as United States v. Lopez (1995), Seminole Tribe v. Florida (1996) and City of Boerne v. Flores (1997) were more than one time flukes. In the past, Congress relied on the Commerce Clause and the Equal Protection

Clause for passing civil rights bills, including the Civil Rights Act of 1964.

Lopez limited the Commerce Clause to things that directly affect interstate commerce, which excludes issues like gun control laws, hate crimes, and other crimes that affect commerce but are not directly related to commerce. *Seminole* reinforced the "sovereign immunity of states" doctrine, which makes it difficult to sue states for many things, especially civil rights violations. The *Flores* "congruence and proportionality" requirement prevents Congress from going too far in requiring states to comply with the Equal Protection Clause, which replaced the ratchet theory advanced in Katzenbach v. Morgan (1966). The ratchet theory held that Congress could ratchet up civil rights beyond what the Court had recognized, but that Congress could not ratchet down judicially recognized rights. An important precedent for *Morrison* was United States v. Harris (1883), which ruled that the Equal Protection Clause did not apply to a prison lynching because the state action doctrine applies Equal Protection only to state action, not private criminal acts. Since the ratchet principle was replaced with the "congruence and proportionality" principle by *Flores*, it was easier to revive older precedents for preventing Congress from going beyond what Court interpretations would allow. Critics such as Associate Justice John Paul Stevens accused the Court of judicial activism (i.e., interpreting law to reach a desired conclusion). The tide against federal power in the Rehnquist court was stopped in the case of Gonzales v. Raich, in which the court upheld the federal power to prohibit medicinal use of cannabis even if states have permitted it. Rehnquist himself was a dissenter in the *Raich* case.

Sovereign State

A sovereign state, commonly simply referred to as a state, is a political association with effective internal and external sovereignty over a geographic area and population which is not dependent on, or subject to any other power or state. While in abstract terms a sovereign state can exist without being recognised by other sovereign states, unrecognised states will often find it hard to exercise full treaty-making powers and engage in diplomatic relations with other sovereign states.

Definition

Although the term often includes broadly all institutions of government or rule—ancient and modern—the modern state system bears a number of characteristics that were first consolidated beginning in earnest in the 15th century, when the term "state" also acquired its current meaning. Thus the word is often used in a strict sense to refer only to modern political systems.

In casual usage, the terms "country", "nation", and "state" are often used as if they were synonymous; but in a more strict usage they can be distinguished:

- *Nation* denotes a people who are believed to or deemed to share common customs, origins, and history. However, the adjectives *national* and *international* also refer to matters pertaining to what are strictly *sovereign states,* as in *national capital, international law.*
- *State* refers to the set of governing and supportive institutions that have sovereignty over a definite territory and population.

Because terminology has changed over time and past writers often used the word "state" in a different ways it is difficult to accurately define the concept of state. Mikhail Bakunin used the term simply to mean a governing organization. Other writers used the term "state" to mean any law-making or law-enforcement agency. Karl Marx defined the state as the institution used by the ruling class of a country to maintain the conditions of its rule. According to Max Weber, the state is an organization with an effective monopoly on the use of force in a particular geographic area. Fascist and some nationalist ideologies view the state as an organic body synonymous with the cultural construct of the nation.

Constitutive Theory of Statehood

In 1815 at the Congress of Vienna the Final Act only recognised 39 sovereign states in the European diplomatic system, and as a result it was firmly established that in future new states would have to be recognised by other states, and that meant in practice recognition by one or more of the great powers.

The constitutive theory was developed in the 19th century to define what is and is not a state. With this theory, the obligation to obey international law depends on a entity's recognition by other countries. Because of this, new states could not immediately become part of the international community or be bound by international law, and recognized nations did not have to respect international law in their dealings with them.

One of the major criticisms of this law is the confusion caused when some states recognize a new entity, but other states do not, a situation the theory does not deal with. Hersch Lauterpacht, one of the theory's main proponents, suggested that it is a state's duty to grant recognition as a possible solution. However, a state may use any criteria when judging if they should give recognition and they have no obligation to use such criteria. Many countries may only recognize a state if it is to their advantage.

Declarative Theory of Statehood

One of the criteria most commonly cited by micronations with regard to difficulty getting international recognition is the Montevideo Convention. The Montevideo Convention was signed on December 26 1933 by the United States, Honduras, El Salvador, Dominican Republic, Haiti, Argentina, Venezuela, Uruguay, Paraguay, Mexico, Panama, Bolivia, Guatemala, Brazil, Ecuador, Nicaragua, Colombia, Chile, Peru and Cuba but it never received international consensus. The Montevideo Convention has four conditions that an entity must meet to become a country:

- a permanent population
- defined territory
- Government
- capacity to enter into relations with other states.

De facto and de jure States

Most sovereign states are states *de jure* and *de facto* (ie they exist both in law and in reality). However sometimes states exist only as *de jure* states in that an organisation is recognised as having sovereignty over and being the legitimate government of a territory over which they have no actual control. Many continental European countries maintained governments-in-exile during the Second World War which continued to enjoy diplomatic relations with the Allies, notwithstanding that their countries were under Nazi occupation. Other states may have sovereignty over a territory but as they lack international recognition, are *de facto* states only. Somaliland is commonly considered to be such a state, as well as Taiwan.

State (Polity)

A state is a set of institutions that possess the authority to make the rules that govern the people in one or more societies, having internal and external sovereignty over a definite territory. In Max Weber's influential definition, it is that organization that has a "monopoly on the legitimate use of physical force within a given territory." It thus includes such institutions as the armed forces, civil service or state bureaucracy, courts, and police.

Although the term often refers broadly to all institutions of government or rule—ancient and modern—the modern state system bears a number of characteristics that were first consolidated in western Europe, beginning in earnest in the 15th century, when the term "state" also acquired its current meaning. Thus the word is often used in a strict sense to refer only to modern political systems.

Within a federal system, the term state also refers to political units, not sovereign themselves, but subject to the authority of the larger state, or federal union, such as the "states and territories of Australia" and the "states" in the United States. Within a monarchy, two or more states may share personal union under the same monarch, but retain an individual identity, even unto a separate legislature and/or government.

In casual usage, the terms "country," "nation," and "state" are often used as if they were synonymous; but in a more strict usage they can be distinguished:

- *Country* denotes a geographical area
- *Nation* denotes a people who share common customs, origins, and history. However, the adjectives *national* and *international* also refer to matters pertaining to what are strictly *states,* as in *national capital, international law*
- *State* refers to set of governing institutions that has sovereignty over a definite territory.

Etymology

The word *state* and its cognates in other European languages (*stato* in Italian, *état* in French, *Staat* in German) ultimately derive from the Latin *status*, meaning "condition" or "status." With the revival of the Roman law in the 14th century in Europe, this Latin term was used to refer to the legal standing of persons (such as the various "estates of the realm"-noble, common, and clerical), and in particular the special status of the king. The word was also associated with Roman ideas (dating back to Cicero) about the "status rei publicae", the "condition of public matters". In time, the word lost its reference to particular social groups and became associated with the legal order of the entire society and the apparatus of its enforcement.

It has also been claimed that the word "state" originates from the medieval *state* or regal chair upon which the head of state (usually a monarch) would sit. Two quotations which reference these different meanings, both commonly, though probably apocryphally, attributed to King Louis XIV of France, are "L'État, c'est moi" ("I am the State") and "Je m'en vais, mais l'État demeurera toujours." ("I am going away, but the State will always remain"). A similar association of terms can today be seen in the practice of referring to government buildings as having authority, for example *"The White House today released a press statement..."*.

Empirical and Juridical Senses of the Word State

The word 'state' has both an empirical and a juridical sense, i.e., entities can be states either de facto or de jure or both.

Empirically (or de facto), an entity is a state if, as in Max Weber's influential definition, it is that organization that has a 'monopoly on legitimate violence' over a specific territory. Such an entity imposes its own legal order over a territory, even if it is not legally recognized as a state by other states (e.g., the Somali region of Somaliland). Juridically (or de jure), an entity is a state in international law if it is recognized as such by other states, even if it does not actually have a monopoly on the legitimate use of force over a territory. Only an entity juridically recognized as a state can enter into many kinds international agreements and be represented in a variety of legal forums, such as the United Nations.

States, Government Types, and Political Systems

The concept of the state can be distinguished from two related concepts with which it is sometimes confused: the concept of a form of government or regime, such as democracy or dictatorship, and the concept of a political system. The form of government identifies only one aspect of the state, namely, the way in which the highest political offices are filled and their relationship to each other and to society. It does not include other aspects of the state that may be very important in its everyday functioning, such as the quality of its bureaucracy. For example, two democratic states may be quite different if one has a capable, well-trained bureaucracy while the other does not. Thus generally speaking the term "state" refers to the instruments of political power, while the term regime or form of government refers more to the way in which such instruments can be accessed and employed.

Some scholars have suggested that the term "state" is too imprecise and loaded to be used productively in sociology and political science, and ought to be substituted by the more comprehensive term "political system." The "political system" refers to the ensemble of all social structures that function to produce collectively binding decisions in a society. In modern times, these would include the political regime, political parties, and various sorts of organizations. The term "political system" thus denotes a broader concept than the state.

The Historical Development of the State

The earliest forms of the state emerged whenever it became possible to centralize power in a durable way. Agriculture and writing are almost everywhere associated with this process: agriculture because it allowed for the emergence of a class of people who did not have to spend most of their time providing for their own subsistence, and writing (or the equivalent of writing, like Inca quipus) because it made possible the centralization of vital information.

The State in Classical Antiquity

The history of the state in the West usually begins with classical antiquity. During that period, the state took a variety of forms, none of them very much like the modern state. There were monarchies whose power (like that of the Egyptian Pharaoh) was based on the religious function of the king and his control of a centralized army. There were also large, quasi-bureaucratized empires, like the Roman empire, which depended less on the religious function of the ruler and more on effective military and legal organizations and the cohesiveness of an aristocracy.

Perhaps the most important political innovations of classical antiquity came from the Greek city-states and the Roman Republic. The Greek city-states before the 4th century granted citizenship rights to their free population, and in Athens these rights were combined with a directly democratic form of government that was to have a long afterlife in political thought and history.

In contrast, Rome developed from a monarchy into a republic, governed by a senate dominated by the Roman aristocracy. The Roman political system contributed to the development of law, constitutionalism and to the distinction between the private and the public spheres.

From the Feudal State to the Modern State in the West

The story of the development of the specifically modern state in the West typically begins with the dissolution of the western Roman empire. This led to the fragmentation of the imperial state into the hands of private lords whose political, judicial, and military roles corresponded to the organization of economic production. In these conditions, according to Marxists, economic unit of society—was the state.

The state-system of feudal Europe was an unstable configuration of suzerains and anointed kings. A monarch, formally at the head of a hierarchy of sovereigns, was not an absolute power who could rule at will; instead, relations between lords and monarchs were mediated by varying degrees of mutual dependence, which was ensured by the absence of a centralized system of taxation. This reality ensured that each ruler needed to obtain the 'consent' of each estate in the realm. This was not quite a 'state' in the Weberian sense of the term, since the king did not monopolize either the power of lawmaking (which was shared with the church) or the means of violence (which were shared with the nobles). The formalization of the struggles over taxation between the monarch and other elements of society (especially the nobility and the cities) gave rise to what is now called the Standestaat, or the state of Estates, characterized by parliaments in which key social groups negotiated with the king about legal and economic matters. These estates of the realm sometimes evolved in the direction of fully-fledged parliaments, but sometimes lost out in their struggles with the monarch, leading to greater centralization of lawmaking and coercive (chiefly military) power in his hands. Beginning in the 15th century, this centralizing process gives rise to the absolutist state.

The Modern State

The rise of the "modern state" as a public power constituting the supreme political authority within a defined territory is associated with western Europe's gradual institutional development beginning in earnest in the late 15th century, culminating in the rise of absolutism and capitalism.

As Europe's dynastic states—England under the Tudors, Spain under the Habsburgs, and France under the Bourbons—embarked on a variety of programs designed to increase centralized political and economic control, they increasingly exhibited many of the institutional features that characterize the "modern state." This centralization of power involved the delineation of political boundaries, as European monarchs gradually defeated or co-opted other sources of power, such as the Church and lesser nobility. In place of the fragmented system of feudal rule, with its often-indistinct territorial claims, large, unitary states with extensive control over definite territories emerged. This process gave rise to the highly centralized and increasingly bureaucratic forms of absolute monarchical rule of the 17th and 18th centuries, when the principal features of the contemporary state system took form, including the introduction of a standing army, a central taxation system, diplomatic relations with permanent embassies, and the development of state economic policy—mercantilism.

Cultural and national homogenization figured prominently in the rise of the modern state system. Since the absolutist period, states have largely been organized on a national basis. The concept of a national state, however, is not synonymous with nation-state. Even in the most ethnically homogeneous societies there is not always a complete correspondence between state and nation, hence the active role often taken by the state to promote nationalism through emphasis on shared symbols and national identity.

It is in this period that the term "the state" is first introduced into political discourse in more or less its current meaning. Although Niccolò Machiavelli is often credited with first using the term to refer to a territorial sovereign government in the modern sense in *The Prince*, published in 1532, it is not until the time of the British thinkers Thomas Hobbes and John Locke and the French thinker Jean Bodin that the concept in its current meaning is fully developed.

Today, most Western states more or less fit the influential definition of the state in Max Weber's *Politics as a Vocation*. According to Weber, the modern state monopolizes the means of legitimate physical violence over a well-defined territory. Moreover, the legitimacy of this monopoly itself is of a very special kind, "rational-legal" legitimacy, based on impersonal rules that constrain the power of state elites.

However, in some other parts of the world states do not fit Weber's definition as well. They may not have a complete monopoly over the means of legitimate physical violence over a definite territory, or their legitimacy may not be adequately described as rational-legal. But they are still recognizably distinct from feudal and absolutist states in the extent of their bureaucratization and their reliance on nationalism as a principle of legitimation.

Since Weber, an extensive literature on the processes by which the "modern state" emerged from the feudal state has been generated. Marxist scholars, for example, assert that the formation of modern states can be explained primarily in terms of the interests and struggles of social classes.

Scholars working in the broad Weberian tradition, by contrast, have often emphasized the institution-building effects of war. For example, Charles Tilly has argued that the revenue-gathering imperatives forced on nascent states by geopolitical competition and constant warfare were mostly responsible for the development of the centralized, territorial bureaucracies that characterize modern states in Europe. States that were able to develop centralized tax-gathering bureaucracies and to field mass armies survived into the modern era; states that were not able to do so did not.

State and Civil Society

The modern state is both separate from and connected to civil society. The nature of this connection has been the subject of considerable attention in both analyses of state development and normative theories of the state. Classical thinkers, such as Thomas Hobbes, J. J. Rousseau, Immanuel Kant emphasized the identity of the state and society, while modern thinkers, by contrast, beginning with G. W. F. Hegel and Alexis de Tocqueville, started to emphasize the relations between them as independent entities. Following Karl Marx, Jürgen Habermas, has argued that civil society may form an economic base for a public sphere, as a placed in political superstructure domain of extra-institutional engagement with matters of public interest trying to influence the state and yet necessarily connected with it.

Some Marxist theorists, such as Antonio Gramsci, have questioned the distinction between the state and civil society altogether, arguing that the former is integrated into many parts of the latter. Others, such as Louis Althusser, maintain that civil organizations such as church, schools, and even trade unions are part of an 'ideological state apparatus.' In this sense, the state can fund a number of groups within society that, while autonomous in principle, are dependent on state support.

Given the role that many social groups have in in the development of public policy and the extensive connections between state bureaucracies and other institutions, it has become increasingly difficult to identify the boundaries of the state. Privatization, nationalization, and the creation of new regulatory bodies also change the boundaries of the state in relation to society. Often the nature of quasi-autonomous organizations is unclear, generating debate among political scientists on whether they are part of the state or civil society. Some political scientists thus prefer to speak of policy networks and decentralized governance in modern societies rather than of state bureaucracies and direct state control over policy.

The State and the International System

Since the late 19th century, virtually the entirety of the world's inhabitable land has been parceled up into areas with more or less definite borders claimed by various states. Earlier, quite large land areas had been either unclaimed or uninhabited, or inhabited by nomadic peoples who were not organized as states.

However, even within present-day states there are vast areas of wilderness, like the Amazon Rainforest, which are uninhabited or inhabited solely or mostly by indigenous people. Also, there are states which do not hold de facto control over all of their claimed territory or where this control is challenged (as in the 2006 civil war in Somalia).

Currently more than 200 states comprise the international community, with the vast majority of them represented in the United Nations. These states form what International relations theorists call a system, where each state takes into account the behaviour of other states when making their own calculations. From this point of view, states embedded in an international system face internal and external security and legitimation dilemmas.

Recently the notion of an 'international community' has been developed to refer to a group of states who have established rules, procedures, and institutions for the conduct of their relations. In this way the foundation has been laid for international law, diplomacy, formal regimes, and organizations.

The State and Supranationalism

In the late 20th century, the globalization of the world economy, the mobility of people and capital, and the rise of many international institutions all combined to circumscribe the freedom of action of states. These constraints on the state's freedom of action are accompanied in some areas, notably Western Europe, with projects for interstate integration such as the European Union. Sovereignty to a large degree is reduced voluntarily by national states themselves. However, the state remains the basic political unit of the world, as it has been since the 16th century. The state is therefore considered the most central concept in the study of politics, and its definition is the subject of intense scholarly debate.

The State and International Law

By modern practice and the law of international relations, a state's sovereignty is conditional upon the diplomatic recognition of the state's claim to statehood. Degrees of recognition and sovereignty may vary. However any degree of recognition, even recognition by a majority of the states in the international system, is not binding on third-party states.

The legal criteria for statehood are not obvious. Often, the laws are surpassed by political circumstances. However, one of the documents often quoted on the matter is the Montevideo Convention from 1933, the first article of which states:

The state as a person of international law should possess the following qualifications: (a) a permanent population; (b) a defined territory; (c) government; and (d) capacity to enter into relations with the other states.

Contemporary Approaches to the Study of the State

There are three main traditions within political science and sociology that shape 'theories of the state': the Marxist, the pluralist, and the institutionalist. Each of these theories has been employed to gain understanding on the state, while recognizing its complexity. Several issues underlie this complexity. First, the boundaries of the state are not closely defined, but constantly changing. Second, the state is not only the site of conflict between different organizations, but also internal conflict and conflict within organizations. Some scholars speak of the 'state's interest,' but there are often various interests within different parts of the state that are neither solely state-centred nor solely society-centred, but develop between different groups in civil society and different state actors.

Marxism

For Marxist theorists, the role of modern states is determined or related to their position in capitalist societies. Many contemporary Marxists offer a liberal interpretation of Marx's comment in *The Communist Manifesto* that the state is but the executive committee for managing the common affairs of the whole bourgeoisie. Ralph Miliband argued that the ruling class uses the state as its instrument to dominate society by virtue of the interpersonal ties between state officials and economic elites. For Miliband, the state is dominated by an elite that comes from the same background as the capitalist class. State officials therefore share the same interests as owners of capital and are linked to them through a wide array of interpersonal and political ties.

By contrast, other Marxist theorists argue that the question of who controls the state is irrelevant. Heavily influenced by Gramsci, Nicos Poulantzas, a Greek neo-Marxist theorist argued that capitalist states do not always act on behalf of the ruling class, and when they do, it is not necessarily the case because state officials consciously strive to do so, but because the 'structural' position of the state is configured in such a way to ensure that the long-term interests of capital are always dominant. Poulantzas' main contribution to the Marxist literature on the state was the concept of 'relative autonomy' of the state. While Poulantzas' work on 'state autonomy' has served to sharpen and specify a great deal of Marxist literature on the state, his own framework came under criticism for its 'structural functionalism.'

Pluralism

While neo-Marxist theories of the state were relatively influential in continental Europe in the 1960s and 1970s, pluralism, a contending approach, gained greater adherence in the United States. Within the pluralist tradition, Robert Dahl developed the theory of the state as a neutral arena for contending interests or its agencies as simply another set of interest groups. With power competitively arranged in society, state policy is a product of recurrent bargaining. Although pluralism recognizes the existence of inequality, it asserts that all groups have an opportunity to pressure the state. The pluralist approach suggests that the modern democratic state's actions are the result of pressures applied by a variety of organized interests. Dahl called this kind of state a polyarchy.

Institutionalism

Both the Marxist and pluralist approaches view the state as reacting to the activities of groups within society, such as classes or interest groups. In this sense, they have both come under criticism for their 'society-centred' understanding of the state by scholars who emphasize the autonomy of the state with respect to social forces.

In particular, the "new institutionalism," an approach to politics that holds that behaviour is fundamentally molded by the institutions in which it is embedded, asserts that the state is not an 'instrument' or an 'arena' and does not 'function' in the interests of a single class. Scholars working within this approach stress the importance of interposing civil society between the economy and the state to explain variation in state forms.

"New institutionalist" writings on the state, such as the works of Theda Skocpol, suggest that state actors are to an important degree autonomous. In other words, state personnel have interests of their own, which they can and do pursue independently (at times in conflict with) actors in society. Since the state controls the means of coercion, and given the dependence of many groups in civil society on the state for achieving any goals they may espouse, state personnel can to some extent impose their own preferences on civil society.

'New institutionalist' writers, claiming allegiance to Weber, often utilize the distinction between 'strong states' and 'weak states,' claiming that the degree of 'relative autonomy' of the state from pressures in society determines the power of the state—a position that has found favour in the field of international political economy.

The State in Modern Political Thought

The rise of the modern state system was closely related to changes in political thought, especially concerning the changing understanding of legitimate state power. Early modern defenders of absolutism such as Thomas Hobbes and Jean Bodin undermined the doctrine of the divine right of kings by arguing that the power of kings should be justified by reference to the people. Hobbes in particular went further and argued that political power should be justified with reference to the individual, not just to the people understood collectively. Both Hobbes and Bodin thought they were defending the power of kings, not advocating democracy, but their arguments about the nature of sovereignty were fiercely resisted by more traditional defenders of the power of kings, like

Sir Robert Filmer in England, who thought that such defenses ultimately opened the way to more democratic claims.

These and other early thinkers introduced two important concepts in order to justify sovereign power: the idea of a state of nature and the idea of a social contract. The first concept describes an imagined situation in which the state-understood as a centralized, coercive power-does not exist, and human beings have all their natural rights and powers; the second describes the conditions under which a voluntary agreement could take human beings out of the state of nature and into a state of civil society. Depending on what they understood human nature to be and the natural rights they thought human beings had in that state, various writers were able to justify more or less extensive forms of the state as a remedy for the problems of the state of nature. Thus, for example, Hobbes, who described the state of nature as a "war of every man, against every man," argued that sovereign power should be almost absolute since almost all sovereign power would be better than such a war, whereas John Locke, who understood the state of nature in more positive terms, thought that state power should be strictly limited. Both of them nevertheless understood the powers of the state to be limited by what rational individuals would agree to in a hypothetical or actual social contract.

The idea of the social contract lent itself to more democratic interpretations than Hobbes or Locke would have wanted. Jean-Jacques Rousseau, for example, argued that the only valid social contract would be one were individuals would be subject to laws that only themselves had made and assented to, as in a small direct democracy. Today the tradition of social contract reasoning is alive in the work of John Rawls and his intellectual heirs, though in a very abstract form. Rawls argued that rational individuals would only agree to social institutions specifying a set of inviolable basic liberties and a certain amount of redistribution to alleviate inequalities for the benefit of the worst off. Lockean state of nature reasoning, by contrast, is more common in the libertarian tradition of political thought represented by the work of Robert Nozick. Nozick argued that given the natural rights that human beings would have in a state of nature, the only state that could be justified would be a minimal state whose sole functions would be to provide protection and enforce agreements. Murray Rothbard, another prominent libertarian, suggests that these protection and enforcement functions of government lead to a definition of the state as any entity that has a monopoly on crime in a given area.

Some contemporary thinkers, such as Michel Foucault, have argued that political theory needs to get away from the notion of the state: "We need to cut off the king's head. In political theory that has still to be done." By this he meant that power in the modern world is much more decentralized and uses different instruments than power in the early modern era, so that the notion of a sovereign, centralized state is increasingly out of date.

Alternatives to the Notion of State

There are those who believe that the state is not necessarily required to the management of social affairs. Karl Marx, for example, believed that under communism the state would eventually "wither away."

Also, anarchist political thought has argued that, a group of people, imbued with a sort of commonality and common sense as well as understanding and respect for one-another are able to live in liberty, free from the oppression of any state government and yet manage to tackle all aspects of life on their own.

Throughout history, there have been a number of anarchist communities, spanning a wide ranging of surfaces of land (some of them just a few sq. kilometres) and with lifespans from as little as several months to 1000 years. Some of them, such as the Whiteway Colony, still exist today.

4

The Concept of Freedom, Liberty and Equality

Political Freedom

Political freedom is the absence of interference with the sovereignty of an individual by the use of coercion or aggression.

The opposite of a free society is a totalitarian state, which highly restricts political freedom in order to regulate almost every aspect of behaviour. In this sense 'freedom' refers solely to the relation of humans to other humans, and the only infringement on it is coercion by humans.

Types

The concept of political freedom is very closely allied with the concepts of civil liberties and individual rights, which in most democratic societies is characterized by various freedoms which are afforded the legal protection from the state. Some of these freedoms may include (in alphabetical order):

- Freedom of assembly
- Freedom of association
- Freedom of movement
- Freedom of religion
- Freedom of speech
- Freedom of the press
- Freedom of thought
- Freedom from unreasonable searches and seizures, which is related to freedom of privacy

- Freedom to bear arms
- Suffrage
- Scientific freedom
- Academic freedom.

Views

Various groups along the political spectrum naturally differ on what they believe constitutes "true" political freedom. Left wing political philosophy generally couples the notion of freedom with that of positive liberty, or the enabling of an individual to realize his or her own potential. Freedom, in this sense, may include freedom from poverty, starvation, treatable disease, and oppression, as well as freedom from force and coercion, from whomever they may issue.

However Friedrich Hayek, a well-known classical liberal, criticized this as a misconception of freedom: the use of 'liberty' to describe the physical 'ability to do what I want', the power to satisfy our wishes, or the extent of the choice of alternatives open to us...has been deliberately fostered as part of the socialist argument... Once this identification of freedom with power is admitted, there is no limit to the sophisms by which the attractions of the word 'liberty' can be used to support measures which destroy individual liberty, no end to the tricks by which people can be exhorted in the name of liberty to give up their liberty. It has been with the help of this equivocation that the notion of collective power over circumstances has been substituted for that of individual liberty and that in totalitarian states liberty has been suppressed in the name of liberty.

Hayek also famously noted that "liberty" and "freedom" have probably been the most abused words in recent history.

Milton Friedman, another classical liberal, strongly incorporated the absence from coercion into his description of political freedom.

The essence of political freedom is the absence of coercion of one man by his fellow men. The fundamental danger to political freedom is the concentration of power. The existence of a large measure of power in the hands of a relatively few individuals enables them to use it to coerce their fellow men. Preservation of freedom requires either the elimination of power where that is possible or its dispersal where it cannot be eliminated.

Many social anarchists see negative and positive liberty as complementary concepts of freedom. They describe the negative liberty-centric view endorsed by capitalists as "selfish freedom". According to Anarchism FAQ:

The right-libertarian does not address or even acknowledge that the (absolute) right of private property may lead to extensive control by property owners over those who use, but do not own, property (such as workers and tenants). Thus a free-market capitalist system leads to a very selective and class-based protection of "rights" and "freedoms." For example, under capitalism, the "freedom" of employers inevitably conflicts with the "freedom" of employees. When stockholders or their managers exercise their "freedom of enterprise" to decide how their company will operate, they violate their employee's right to decide how their labouring capacities will be utilised. In other words, under capitalism, the "property rights" of employers will conflict with and restrict the "human right" of employees to manage themselves. Capitalism allows the right of self-management only to the few, not to all. Or, alternatively, capitalism does not recognise certain human rights as universal which anarchism does.

Some people treat freedom as if it were almost synonymous with democracy, while other people see conflicts or even opposition between the two concepts. For example, some people argue that Iraq was free under Paul Bremer on the grounds that it was a rational, humanist, non-subjugating government, long before elections were held. Others have argued that Iraq was free under Saddam Hussein because Iraq was not a colony, while a third one's claim is that neither dictatorial nor colonial rule in Iraq are examples of political freedom.

Environmentalists often argue that political freedoms should include some constraint on use of ecosystems. They maintain there is no such thing, for instance, as "freedom to pollute" or "freedom to deforest" given that such activities create negative externalities. The popularity of SUVs, golf, and urban sprawl has been used as evidence that some ideas of freedom and ecological conservation can clash. This leads at times to serious confrontations and clashes of values reflected in advertising campaigns, e.g. that of PETA regarding fur.

There have been numerous philosophical debates over the nature of freedom, the claimed differences between various types of freedom, and the extent to which freedom is desirable. Determinists argue that all human actions are pre-determined and thus freedom is an illusion. Isaiah Berlin saw a distinction between negative liberty and positive liberty.

In jurisprudence, freedom is the right to determine one's own actions autonomously; generally it is granted in those fields in which the subject has no obligations to fulfil or laws to obey, according to the interpretation that the hypothetical natural unlimited freedom is limited by the law for some matters.

Liberty

Liberty is a concept of political philosophy and identifies the condition in which an individual has the right to act according to his or her own will. In feudal times, a liberty was an area of allodial land in which regalian rights had been waived. Individualist and classical liberal conceptions of liberty relate to the freedom of the individual from outside compulsion or coercion.

Philosophy

Opinions on what constitute liberty can vary widely, but can be generally classified as positive liberty and negative liberty. Positive liberty asserts that freedom is the ability of society to achieve an end. For example, Puritans such as Cotton Mather often referred to liberty in their writings, but focused on the liberty from sin (e.g. sexual urges) even at the expense of liberty from the government. In the negative sense, one is considered free to the extent to which no person interferes with his or her activity. According to Thomas Hobbes, for example, "a free man is he that... is not hindered to do what he hath the will to do."

John Stuart Mill, in his work, *On Liberty*, was the first to recognize the difference between liberty as the freedorr to act and liberty as the absence of coercion. In his book, *Two Concepts of Liberty*, Isaiah Berlin formally framed the differences between these two perspectives as the distinction between two opposite concepts of liberty: positive liberty and negative liberty. The latter designates a negative condition in which an individual is protected from tyranny and the arbitrary exercise of authority, while the former refers to having the means or opportunity, rather than the lack of restraint, to do things.

Mill offered insight into the notions of *soft tyranny* and *mutual liberty* with his *harm principle*. It can be seen as important to understand these concepts when discussing liberty since they all represent little pieces of the greater puzzle known as freedom. In a philosophical sense, it can be said that morality must supersede tyranny in any legitimate form of government. Otherwise, people are left with a societal system rooted in backwardness, disorder, and regression.

The concept of negative liberty has several noteworthy aspects. First, negative liberty defines a realm or "zone" of freedom (in the "silence of law"). In Berlin's words, "liberty in the negative sense involves an answer to the question 'What is the area within which the subject — a person or group of persons — is or should be left to do or be what he is able to do or be, without interference by other persons." Some philosophers have disagreed on the extent of this realm while accepting the main point that liberty defines that realm in which one may act unobstructed by others. Second, the restriction (on the freedom to act) implicit in negative liberty is imposed by a person or persons and not due to causes such as nature, lack, or incapacity. Helvetius expresses this point clearly: "The free man is the man who is not in irons, nor imprisoned in a gaol (jail), nor terrorized like a slave by the fear of punishment... it is not lack of freedom not to fly like an eagle or swim like a whale."

The dichotomy of positive and negative liberty is considered specious by political philosophers in traditions such as socialism, social democracy, libertarian socialism, and Marxism. Some of them argue that positive and negative liberty are indistinguishable in practice, while others claim that one kind of liberty cannot exist independently of the other. A common argument is that the preservation of negative liberty requires positive action on the part of the government or society to prevent some individuals from taking away the liberty of others. A socialist defines liberty as being connected to the reasonably equitable distribution of wealth, arguing that the unrestrained concentration of wealth (the means of production) into only a few hands negates liberty. In other words, without relatively equal ownership, the subsequent concentration of power and influence into a small portion of the population inevitably results in the domination of the wealthy and the subjugation of the poor. Thus, freedom and material equality are seen as intrinsically connected. On the other hand, the classical liberal argues that wealth cannot be evenly distributed without force being used against individuals which reduces individual liberty.

Freedom as a Triadic Relation

In 1967, Gerald MacCallum argued that proponents of positive and negative liberty converge on a single definition of liberty, but simply have different approaches in establishing it. According to McCallum, freedom is a triadic relationship: "x is/is not free from y to do/not to do or become/not become z". In this way, rather than defining liberty in terms of two separate paradigms, positive and negative liberty, he defined liberty as a single, complete formula.

The question is whether this formula fully captures what positive liberty means. Positive liberty, understood as "internal forces which determine how a person shall act" is saying more than 'x is free to do z.' One is free when one *becomes* the ideal of oneself, which includes MacCallum's triadic relation; but the latter alone is insufficient to fully capture what positive liberty means.

Liberty and Political Thought

Meaning of Liberty

The first known use of the word *freedom* in a political context dates back to the 24th century BC, in a text describing the restoration of social and economic liberty in Lagash, a Sumerian city-state. Urukagina, the king of Lagash, established the first known legal code to protect citizens from the rich and powerful. Known as a great reformer, Urukagina established laws that forbade compelling the sale of property and required the charges against the accused to be stated before any man accused of a crime could be punished.

This is the first known example of any form of due process in the history of humanity.

Like Urukagina, most ancient freedoms focused on *negative liberty*, protecting the less fortunate from harassment or imposition. Other ancient legal codes, such as the Code of Hammurabi, similarly forbade compulsion in economic matters, like the sale of land, and made it clear that when a rich man murders a poor one, it is still murder. Still, these codes relied on a certain virtuousness of kings and ministers, which was far from reliable.

In the Persian Empire, citizens of all religions and ethnic groups were given the same rights and had the same freedom of religion, women had the same rights as men, and slavery was abolished. All the palaces of the kings of Persia were built by paid workers in an era where slaves typically did such work.

In the Maurya Empire of ancient India, citizens of all religions and ethnic groups had rights to freedom, tolerance, and equality. The need for tolerance on an egalitarian basis can be found in the Edicts of Ashoka the Great, which emphasize the importance of tolerance in public policy by the government. The slaughter or capture of prisoners of war was also condemned by Ashoka. Slavery was also non-existent in ancient India.

Roman law also embraced certain limited forms of liberty, even under the rule of the Roman Emperors. However, these liberties were accorded only to Roman citizens. Still, the Roman citizen enjoyed a combination of positive liberty (the right to a trial, a right of appeal, law and contract enforcement) and negative liberty (unhindered right to contract and the right to not be tortured). Many of the liberties enjoyed under Roman law endured through the Middle Ages, but were enjoyed solely by the nobility, never by the common man. The idea of unalienable and universal liberties had to wait until the Age of Enlightenment.

Social Contract

The social contract theory, invented by Hobbes, John Locke and Rousseau, were among the first to provide a political classification of rights, in particular through the notion of sovereignty and of natural rights. The thinkers of the Enlightenment reasoned the assertion that law governed both heavenly and human affairs, and that law gave the king his power, rather than the king's power giving force to law. The divine right of kings was thus opposed to the sovereign's unchecked *auctoritas*. This conception of law would find its culmination in Montesquieu's thought. The conception of law as a relationship between individuals, rather than families, came to the fore, and with it the increasing focus on individual liberty as a fundamental reality, given by "Nature and Nature's God," which, in the ideal state, would be as expansive as possible. The Enlightenment created then, among other ideas, *liberty*: that is, of a free individual being most free within the context of a state which provides stability of the laws. Later, more radical philosophies such as socialism articulated themselves in the course of the French Revolution and in the 19th century.

Modern Perspectives

The modern conceptions of democracy, whether representative democracies or other types of democracies, are all found on the Rousseauist idea of popular sovereignty. However, liberalism distinguishes itsef from socialism and communism in that it advocates for a form of representative democracy, while socialism claims to work for a direct democracy.

Liberalism is a political current embracing several historical and present-day ideologies that claim defence of individual liberty as the purpose of government. Two main strands are apparent, although both are founded on an individualist ideology. In continental Europe the term usually refers to economic liberalism, that is the right of individual to contract, trade and operate in a market free of constraint. In the United States it often refers to social liberalism, including the right to dissent from orthodox tenets or established authorities in political or religious matters. Both are core political issues, and highly contentious. In the United States Supreme Court decision Griswold v. Connecticut, Justice William O. Douglas argued that liberties relating to personal relationships,such as marriage, have a unique primacy of place in the hierarchy of freedoms. Professor Jacob M. Appel has summarized this principle as follows:

I am grateful that I have rights in the proverbial public square—

but, as a practical matter, my most cherished rights are those that I possess in my bedroom and hospital room and death chamber. Most people are far more concerned that they can control their own bodies than they are about petitioning Congress.

A school of thought popular among US libertarians holds that there is no tenable distinction between the two sorts of liberty — that they are, indeed, one and the same, to be protected (or opposed) together. In the context of U.S. constitutional law, for example, they point out that the constitution twice lists "life, liberty, and property" without making any distinctions within that troika.

Anarcho-Individualists, such as Max Stirner, demanded the utmost respect for the liberty of the individual. From a very similar perspective from North America, primitivists like John Zerzan proclaimed that civilization *not just the state* (as in socialist thought) would need to be abolished to foster liberty. Some in the US see protecting the ideal of liberty as a conservative policy, because this would conform to the spirit of individual liberty that they consider is at the heart of the American constitution. Some think liberty is almost synonymous with democracy, at least in one sense of that word, while others see conflicts or even opposition between the two concepts, with democracy being nothing more than the tyranny of the majority.

Social Equality

Social equality is a social state of affairs in which all people within a specific society or isolated group have the same status in a certain respect. At the very least, social equality includes equal rights under the law, such as security, voting rights, freedom of speech and assembly, and the extent of property rights. However, it also includes access to education, health care and other social securities. It also includes equal opportunities and obligations, and so involves the whole society.

Social equality requires the lack of legally enforced social class or caste boundaries and the lack of unjustified discrimination motivated by an inalienable part of a person's identity. For example, gender, age, sexual orientation, origin, caste or class, income or property, language, religion, convictions, opinions, health or disability must not result in unequal treatment under the law and should not reduce opportunities unjustifiably.

Social equality refers to social, rather than economic, or income equality. "Equal opportunities" is interpreted as being judged by ability, which is compatible with a free-market economy. A problem is horizontal inequality, the inequality of two persons of *same* origin and ability.

Perfect social equality is an ideal situation that, for various reasons, does not exist in any society in the world today. The reasons for this are widely debated. Reasons cited for social inequality include commonly economics, immigration/emigration, foreign politics and national politics. Also, in complexity economics, it has been found that horizontal inequality arises in complex systems.

A counterexample to social equality was the social inequality of medieval Europe, where a person's estate, which was usually inherited, determined the legal and social rights the person had. For example, clergy could claim the benefit of clergy to receive a more lenient punishment for a crime. Likewise, women have historically been and still are in some countries formally denied access to higher education—even if they could pay the tuition. In 19th century Europe, if female enrollment was even permitted, women had to apply for an "exemption from gender" to enroll in a university.

In apartheid-era South Africa, both blacks and whites had formal access to health care and similar public services. However, the segregated health care arranged for blacks did not meet the same standards as those for whites. That is, there was enforced social inequality. Currently, in North Korea, certain groups are officially considered "disloyal" to the regime; the "disloyalty" is inherited, prevents advancement in society, and results in harsher punishments for crimes.

5

Theories of Property

Labor Theory of Property

The labor theory of property or labor theory of appropriation is a natural law theory that holds that property originally comes about by the exertion of labor upon natural resources. (This is not to be confused with a labor theory of value). In his *Second Treatise on Government*, the philosopher John Locke asked by what right an individual can claim to own one part of the world, when, according to the Bible, God gave the world to all humanity in common. He answered that persons own themselves and therefore their own labor. When a person works, that labor enters into the object. Thus, the object becomes the property of that person.

Locke argued in support of individual property rights as "natural rights". Following the argument the fruits of one's labor are "his" because he had worked for it. Furthermore the labourer must also hold a natural property right in the resource itself because-as Locke believes-exclusive ownership was immediately necessary for production. Jean-Jacques Rousseau later criticized this second step in Discourse on Inequality, where he effectively argues that the natural right argument does not extend to resources that one did not create. Both philosophers hold that the relation between labor and ownership pertains only to property that was unowned before such labor took place.

Land in its original state would be considered unowned by anyone, but if an individual applied his labor to the land by farming it, for example, it becomes his property. Merely placing a fence around land rather than using the land enclosed would not bring property into being according to most natural law theorists. For instance, economist Murray Rothbard stated:

> If Columbus lands on a new continent, is it legitimate for him to proclaim all the new continent his own, or even that sector 'as far as his eye can see'? Clearly, this would not be the case in the free society that we are postulating. Columbus or Crusoe would have to use the land, to 'cultivate' it in some way, before he could be asserted to own it.... If there is more land than can be used by a limited labor supply, then the unused land must simply remain unowned until a first user arrives on the scene. Any attempt to claim a new resource that someone does not use would have to be considered invasive of the property right of whoever the first user will turn out to be.

The labor theory of property does not only apply to land itself, but to any application of labor to nature. For example, natural-rightist Lysander Spooner, says that an apple taken from an unowned tree would become the property of the person who plucked it, as he has labored to acquire it. He says the "only way, in which ["the wealth of nature"] can be made useful to mankind, is by their taking possession of it individually, and thus making it private property." However, some, such as Benjamin Tucker have not seen this as creating property in all things. Tucker argued that "in the case of land, or of any other material the supply of which is so limited that all cannot hold it in unlimited quantities," these should only be considered owned while the individual is in the act of using or occupying these things.

Property

Property is any physical or intangible entity that is owned by a person or jointly by a group of persons. Depending on the nature of the property, an owner of property has the right to consume, sell, rent, mortgage, transfer, exchange or destroy their property, and/or to exclude others from doing these things. Important widely-recognized types of property include real property (land), personal property (physical possessions belonging to a person), private property (property owned by legal persons or business entities), public property (state owned or publicly owned and available possessions) and intellectual property (exclusive rights over artistic creations, inventions, etc.), although the latter is not always as widely recognized or enforced. A title, or a right of ownership, is associated with property that establishes the relation between the goods/services and other persons, assuring the owner the right to dispense with the property as they see fit. Some philosophers assert that property rights arise from social convention. Others find origins for them in morality or natural law.

Use of the Term

Various scholarly communities (e.g., law, economics, anthropology, sociology) may treat the concept more systematically, but definitions vary within and between fields. Scholars in the social sciences frequently conceive of property as a bundle of rights. They stress that property is not a relationship between people and things, but a relationship between people *with regard to* things.

Public property is any property that is controlled by a state or by a whole community. *Private property* is any property that is not public property. Private property may be under the control of a single person or by a group of persons jointly.

General Characteristics

Modern property rights conceive of ownership and possession as belonging to legal persons, even if the legal person is not a natural person. Corporations, for example, have legal rights similar to American citizens, including many of their constitutional rights. Therefore, the corporation is a juristic person or artificial legal entity, which some refer to as "corporate personhood".

Property rights are protected in the current laws of states usually found in the form of a constitution or a bill of rights. The United States Constitution provides explicitly for the protection of private property in the Fifth Amendment and Fourteenth Amendment:

The Fifth Amendment states: Nor be deprived of life liberty, or property, without due process of law; nor shall private property be taken for public use, without just compensation.

The Fourteenth Amendment states: No State shall make or enforce any law which shall abridge the privileges or immunities of citizens of the United States; nor shall any State deprive any person of life, liberty, or property, without due process of law.

Protection is also found in the United Nations's Universal Declaration of Human Rights, Article 17, and in the French Declaration of the Rights of Man and of the Citizen, Article XVII, and in the European Convention on Human Rights (ECHR), Protocol 1.

Property is usually thought of in terms of a bundle of rights as defined and protected by the local sovereignty. Ownership, however, does not necessarily equate with sovereignty. If ownership gave supreme authority, it would be sovereignty, not ownership. These are two different concepts.

Traditional principles of property rights includes:

1. control of the use of the property
2. the right to any benefit from the property (examples: mining rights and rent)
3. a right to transfer or sell the property
4. a right to exclude others from the property.

Traditional property rights do not include:

1. uses that unreasonably interfere with the property rights of another private party (the right of quiet enjoyment).
2. uses that unreasonably interfere with public property rights, including uses that interfere with public health, safety, peace or convenience.

Legal systems have evolved to cover transactions and disputes that arise over the possession, use, transfer, and disposal of property, most particularly involving contracts. Positive law defines such rights, and a judiciary is used to adjudicate and to enforce.

In his classic text, "The Common Law", Oliver Wendell Holmes describes property as having two fundamental aspects. The first is possession, which can be defined as control over a resource based on the practical inability of another to contradict the ends of the possessor. The second is title, which is the expectation that others will recognize rights to control resource, even when it is not in possession. He elaborates the differences between these two concepts, and proposes a history of how they came to be attached to persons, as opposed to families or entities such as the church.

According to Adam Smith, the expectation of profit from "improving one's stock of capital" rests on private property rights. It is a belief central to capitalism that property rights encourage the property holders to develop the property, generate wealth, and efficiently allocate resources based on the operation of the market. From this evolved the modern conception of property as a right enforced by positive law, in the expectation that this would produce more wealth and better standards of living.

Classical Liberals, Objectivists and Related Traditions

"Just as man can't exist without his body, so no rights can exist without the right to translate one's rights into reality, to think, to work and keep the results, which means: the right of property." (Ayn Rand, *Atlas Shrugged*)

Most thinkers from these traditions subscribe to the labor theory of property. They hold that you own your own life, and it follows that you must own the products of that life, and that those products can be traded in free exchange with others.

"Every man has a property in his own person. This nobody has a right to, but himself." (John Locke, *Second Treatise on Civil Government*)

"Life, liberty, and property do not exist because men have made laws. On the contrary, it was the fact that life, liberty, and property existed beforehand that caused men to make laws in the first place."

"The reason why men enter into society is the preservation of their property." (John Locke, *Second Treatise on Civil Government*)

- Socialism's fundamental principles are centred on a critique of this concept, stating, among other things, that the cost of defending property is higher than the returns from private property ownership, and that even when property rights encourage the property-holder to develop his property, generate wealth, etc., he will only do so for his own benefit, which may not coincide with the benefit of other people or society at large.
- Libertarian socialism generally accepts property rights, but with a short abandonment time period. In other words,

a person must make (more or less) continuous use of the item or else he loses ownership rights. This is usually referred to as "possession property" or "usufruct." Thus, in this usufruct system, absentee ownership is illegitimate, and workers own the machines they work with.

- Communism argues that only collective ownership of the means of production through a polity (though not necessarilý a state) will assure the minimization of unequal or unjust outcomes and the maximization of benefits, and that therefore private property (which in communist theory is limited to capital) should be abolished.

Both communism and some kinds of socialism have also upheld the notion that private property is inherently illegitimate. This argument centeres mainly on the idea that creation of private property always benefits one class over another, giving way to domination through the use of this private property. Communists are naturally not opposed to personal property that is "Hard-won, self-acquired, self-earned" (Communist Manifesto), by members of the proletariat.

Not every person, or entity, with an interest in a given piece of property may be able to exercise all of the rights mentioned a few paragraphs above.

For example, as a lessee of a particular piece of property, you may not sell the property, because a tenant is only in possession, and does not have title to transfer. Similarly, while you are a lessee, the owner cannot use their right to exclude to keep you from the property. (Or, if they does, you may be entitled to stop paying rent or sue for access.)

Further, property may be held in a number of forms, e.g., joint ownership, community property, sole ownership, lease, etc. These different types of ownership may complicate an owner's ability to exercise property rights unilaterally.

For example if two people own a single piece of land as joint tenants then, depending on the law in the jurisdiction, each may have limited recourse for the actions of the other. For example, one of the owners might sell their interest in the property to a stranger that the other owner does not particularly like.

Theories of Property

There exist many theories. One is the relatively rare first possession theory of property, where ownership of something is seen as justified simply by someone seizing something before someone else does. Perhaps one of the most popular, is the natural rights definition of property rights as advanced by John Locke. Locke advanced the theory that when one mixes one's labor with nature, one gains a relationship with that part of nature with which the labor is mixed, subject to the limitation that there should be "enough, and as good, left in common for others."

From the RERUM NOVARUM, Pope Leo XIII wrote "It is surely undeniable that, when a man engages in remunerative labor, the impelling reason and motive of his work is to obtain property, and thereafter to hold it as his very own."

Anthropology studies the diverse systems of ownership, rights of use and transfer, and possession under the term "theories of property." Western legal theory is based, as mentioned, on the owner of property being a legal person. However, not all property systems are founded on this basis.

In every culture studied ownership and possession are the subject of custom and regulation, and "law" where the term can meaningfully be applied. Many tribal cultures balance individual ownership with the laws of collective groups: tribes, families, associations and nations. For example the 1839 Cherokee Constitution frames the issue in these terms:

Sec. 2. The lands of the Cherokee Nation shall remain common property; but the improvements made thereon, and in the possession of the citizens respectively who made, or may rightfully be in possession of them: Provided, that the citizens of the Nation possessing exclusive and indefeasible right to their improvements, as expressed in this article, shall possess no right or power to dispose of their improvements, in any manner whatever, to the United States, individual States, or to individual citizens thereof; and that, whenever any citizen shall remove with his effects out of the limits of this Nation, and become a citizen of any other government, all his rights and privileges as a citizen of this Nation shall cease: Provided, nevertheless, That the National Council shall have power to re-admit, by law, to all the rights of citizenship, any such person or persons who may, at any time, desire to return to the Nation, on memorializing the National Council for such readmission.

Communal property systems describe ownership as belonging to the entire social and political unit, while corporate systems describe ownership as being attached to an identifiable group with an identifiable responsible individual. The Roman property law was based on such a corporate system.

Different societies may have different theories of property for differing types of ownership. Pauline Peters argued that property systems are not isolable from the social fabric, and notions of property may not be stated as such, but instead may be framed in negative terms: for example the taboo system among Polynesian peoples.

Property in Philosophy

In medieval and Renaissance Europe the term "property" essentially referred to land. Much rethinking has come to be regarded as only a special case of the property genus. This rethinking was inspired by at least three broad features of early modern Europe: the surge of commerce, the breakdown of efforts to prohibit interest (then called "usury"), and the development of centralized national monarchies.

Ancient Philosophy

Urukagina, the king of the Sumerian city-state Lagash, established the first laws that forbade compelling the sale of property.

The Ten Commandments shown in Exodus 20:2-17 and Deuteronomy 5:6-21 stated that the Israelites were not to steal. These texts, written in approximately 1300 B.C. by modern dating, or 2000 B.C. by traditional dating (assuming Mosaic authorship), were a blanket early protection of private property.

Aristotle, in *Politics,* advocates "private prope.ty." In one of the first known expositions of tragedy of the commons he says, "that which is common to the greatest number has the least care bestowed upon it. Every one thinks chiefly of his own, hardly at all of the common interest; and only when he is himself concerned as an individual." In addition he says that when property is common, there are natural problems that arise due to differences in labor: "If they do not share equally enjoyments and toils, those who labor much and get little will necessarily complain of those who labor little and receive or consume much. But indeed there is always a difficulty in men living together and having all human relations in common, but especially in their having common property." (*Politics, 1261b34*)

Pre-industrial English Philosophy

Thomas Hobbes (1600s)

The principal writings of Thomas Hobbes appeared between 1640 and 1651—during and immediately following the war between forces loyal to King Charles I and those loyal to Parliament. In his own words, Hobbes' reflection began with the idea of "giving to every man his own," a phrase he drew from the writings of Cicero. But he wondered: How can anybody call anything his own? He concluded: My own can only truly be mine if there is one unambiguously strongest power in the realm, and that power treats it as mine, protecting its status as such.

James Harrington (1600s)

A contemporary of Hobbes, James Harrington, reacted differently to the same tumult; he considered property natural but not inevitable. The author of *Oceana*, he may have been the first political theorist to postulate that political power is a consequence, not the cause, of the distribution of. He said that the worst possible situation is one in which the commoners have half a nation's property, with crown and nobility holding the other half—a circumstance fraught with instability and violence. A much better situation (a stable republic) will exist once the commoners own most property, he suggested.

In later years, the ranks of Harrington's admirers included American revolutionary and founder John Adams.

Robert Filmer (1600s)

Another member of the Hobbes/Harrington generation, Sir

Robert Filmer, reached conclusions much like Hobbes', but through Biblical exegesis. Filmer said that the institution of kingship is analogous to that of fatherhood, that subjects are but children, whether obedient or unruly, and that property rights are akin to the household goods that a father may dole out among his children—his to take back and dispose of according to his pleasure.

John Locke (1600s)

In the following generation, John Locke sought to answer Filmer, creating a rationale for a balanced constitution in which the monarch had a part to play, but not an overwhelming part. Since Filmer's views essentially require that the Stuart family be uniquely descended from the patriarchs of the Bible, and since even in the late seventeenth century that was a difficult view to uphold, Locke attacked Filmer's views in his First Treatise on Government, freeing him to set out his own views in the Second Treatise on Civil Government. Therein, Locke imagined a pre-social world, the unhappy residents of which create a social contract. They would, he allowed, create a monarchy, but its task would be to execute the will of an elected legislature.

"To this end" he wrote, meaning the end of their own long life and peace, "it is that men give up all their natural power to the society they enter into, and the community put the legislative power into such hands as they think fit, with this trust, that they shall be governed by declared laws, or else their peace, quiet, and property will still be at the same uncertainty as it was in the state of nature."

Even when it keeps to proper legislative form, though, Locke held that there are limits to what a government established by such a contract might rightly do.

"It cannot be supposed that [the hypothetical contractors] they should intend, had they a power so to do, to give any one or more an absolute arbitrary power over their persons and estates, and put a force into the magistrate's hand to execute his unlimited will arbitrarily upon them; this were to put themselves into a worse condition than the state of nature, wherein they had a liberty to defend their right against the injuries of others, and were upon equal terms of force to maintain it, whether invaded by a single man or many in combination. Whereas by supposing they have given up themselves to the absolute arbitrary power and will of a legislator, they have disarmed themselves, and armed him to make a prey of them when he pleases..."

Note that both "persons *and* estates" are to be protected from the arbitrary power of any magistrate, inclusive of the "power and will of a legislator." In Lockean terms, depredations against an estate are just as plausible a justification for resistance and revolution as are those against persons. In neither case are subjects required to allow themselves to become prey.

To explain the ownership of property Locke advanced a labor theory of property.

William Blackstone (1700s)

In the 1760s, William Blackstone sought to codify the English common law. In his famous *Commentaries on the Laws of England* he wrote that "every wanton and causeless restraint of the will of the subject, whether produced by a monarch, a nobility, or a popular assembly is a degree of tyranny."

How should such tyranny be prevented or resisted? Through property rights, Blackstone thought, which is why he emphasized that indemnification must be awarded a non-consenting owner whose property is taken by eminent domain, and that a property owner is protected against physical invasion of his property by the laws of trespass and nuisance. Indeed, he wrote that a landowner is free to kill any stranger on his property between dusk and dawn, even an agent of the King, since it isn't reasonable to expect him to recognize the King's agents in the dark.

David Hume (1700s)

In contrast to the figures discussed in this section thus far, David Hume lived a relatively quiet life that had settled down to a relatively stable social and political structure. He lived the life of a solitary writer until 1763 when, at 52 years of age, he went off to Paris to work at the British embassy.

In contrast, one might think, to his outrage-generating works on religion and his skeptical views in epistemology, Hume's views on law and property were quite conservative.

He did not believe in hypothetical contracts, or in the love of mankind in general, and sought to ground politics upon actual human beings as one knows them. "In general," he wrote, "it may be affirmed that there is no such passion in human mind, as the love of mankind, merely as such, independent of personal qualities, or services, or of relation to ourselves." Existing customs should not lightly be disregarded, because they have come to be what they are as a result of human nature. With this endorsement of custom comes an endorsement of existing governments, because he conceived of the two as complementary: "A regard for liberty, though a laudable passion, ought commonly to be subordinate to a reverence for established government."

These views led to a view on property rights that might today be described as legal positivism. There are property rights because of and to the extent that the existing law, supported by social customs, secure them. He offered some practical home-spun advice on the general subject, though, as when he referred to avarice as "the spur of industry," and expressed concern about excessive levels of taxation, which "destroy industry, by engendering despair."

Critique and Response

By the mid 19th century, the industrial revolution had transformed England and had begun in France. The established conception of what constitutes property expanded beyond land to encompass scarce goods in general. In France, the revolution of the 1790s had led to large-scale confiscation of land formerly owned by church and king. The restoration of the monarchy led to claims by those dispossessed to have their former lands returned. Furthermore, the labor theory of value popularized by classical economists such as Adam Smith and David Ricardo were utilized by a new ideology called socialism to critique the relations of property to other economic issues, such as profit, rent, interest, and wage-labor. Thus, property was no longer an esoteric philosophical question, but a political issue of substantial concern.

Charles Comte-Legitimate Origin of Property

Charles Comte, in *Traité de la propriété* (1834), attempted to justify the legitimacy of private property in response to the Bourbon

Restoration. According to David Hart, Comte had three main points: "firstly, that interference by the state over the centuries in property ownership has had dire consequences for justice as well as for economic productivity; secondly, that property is legitimate when it emerges in such a way as not to harm anyone; and thirdly, that historically some, but by no means all, property which has evolved has done so legitimately, with the implication that the present distribution of property is a complex mixture of legitimately and illegitimately held titles." (*The Radical Liberalism of Charles Comte and Charles Dunoyer*

Comte, as Proudhon later did, rejected Roman legal tradition with its toleration of slavery. He posited a communal "national" property consisting of non-scarce goods, such as land in ancient hunter-gatherer societies. Since agriculture was so much more efficient than hunting and gathering, private property appropriated by someone for farming left remaining hunter-gatherers with more land per person, and hence did not harm them. Thus this type of land appropriation did not violate the Lockean proviso-there was "still enough, and as good left." Comte's analysis would be used by later theorists in response to the socialist critique on property.

Pierre Proudhon-Property is Theft

In his 1849 treatise *What is Property?*, Pierre Proudhon answers with "Property is theft!" In natural resources, he sees two types of property, *de jure* property (legal title) and *de facto* property (physical possession), and argues that the former is illegitimate. Proudhon's conclusion is that "property, to be just and possible, must necessarily have equality for its condition."

His analysis of the product of labor upon natural resources as property (usufruct) is more announced. He asserts that land itself cannot be property, yet it should be held by individual possessors as stewards of mankind with the product of labor being the property of the producer. Proudhon reasoned that any wealth gained without labor was stolen from those who labored to create that wealth. Even a voluntary contract to surrender the product of labor to an employer was theft, according to Proudhon, since the controller of natural resources had no moral right to charge others for the use of that which he did not labor to create and therefore did not own. Proudhon's theory of property greatly influenced the budding socialist movement, inspiring anarchist theorists such as Mikhail Bakunin who modified Proudhon's ideas, as well as antagonizing theorists like Karl Marx.

Frédéric Bastiat-Property is Value

In a radical departure from traditional property theory, he defines property not as a physical object, but rather as a relationship between people with respect to an object. Thus, saying one owns a glass of water is merely verbal shorthand for *I may justly gift or trade this water to another person*. In essence, what one owns is not the object but the value of the object. By "value," Bastiat apparently means *market value*; he emphasizes that this is quite different from utility. *"In our relations with one another, we are not owners of the utility of things, but of their value, and value is the appraisal made of reciprocal services."*

Strongly disputing Proudhon's equality-based argument, Bastiat theorizes that, as a result of technological progress and the division of labor, the stock of communal wealth increases over time; that the hours of work an unskilled labourer expends to buy e.g. 100 liters of wheat decreases over time, thus amounting to "gratis" satisfaction. Thus, private property continually destroys itself, becoming transformed into communal wealth. The increasing proportion of communal wealth to private property results in a tendency toward equality of mankind. *"Since the human race started from the point of greatest poverty, that is, from the point where there were the most obstacles to be overcome, it is clear that all that has been gained from one era to the next has been due to the spirit of property."*

This transformation of private property into the communal domain, Bastiat points out, does not imply that private property will ever totally disappear. This is because man, as he progresses, continually invents new and more sophisticated needs and desires.

Contemporary Views

Among contemporary political thinkers who believe that natural persons enjoy rights to own property and to enter into contracts, there are two views about John Locke. On the one hand there are ardent Locke admirers, such as W.H. Hutt (1956), who praised Locke for laying down the "quintessence of individualism."

On the other hand, there are those such as Richard Pipes who think that Locke's arguments are weak, and that undue reliance thereon has weakened the cause of individualism in recent times. Pipes has written that Locke's work "marked a regression because it rested on the concept of Natural Law" rather than upon Harrington's sociological framework.

Hernando de Soto has argued that an important characteristic of capitalist market economy is the functioning state protection of property rights in a formal property system where ownership and transactions are clearly recorded. These property rights and the whole formal system of property make possible:

- Greater independence for individuals from local community arrangements to protect their assets;
- Clear, provable, and protectable ownership;
- The standardization and integration of property rules and property information in the country as a whole;
- Increased trust arising from a greater certainty of punishment for cheating in economic transactions;
- More formal and complex written statements of ownership that permit the easier assumption of shared risk and ownership in companies, and insurance against risk;
- Greater availability of loans for new projects, since more things could be used as collateral for the loans;
- Easier access to and more reliable information regarding such things as credit history and the worth of assets;
- Increased fungibility, standardization and transferability of statements documenting the ownership of property, which paves the way for structures such as national markets for companies and the easy transportation of property through complex networks of individuals and other entities;
- Greater protection of biodiversity due to minimizing of shifting agriculture practices.

All of the above enhance economic growth.

Types of Property

Most legal systems distinguish different types (immovable property, estate in land, real estate, real property) of property, especially between land and all other forms of property-goods and chattels, movable property or personal property. They often distinguish tangible and intangible property.

One categorization scheme specifies three species of property: land, improvements (immovable man made things) and personal property (movable man made things).

In common law, real property (immovable property) is the combination of interests in land and improvements thereto and personal property is interest in movable property.

'Real property' rights are rights relating to the land. These rights include ownership and usage. Owners can grant rights to persons and entities in the form of leases, licenses and easements.

Later, with the development of more complex forms of non-tangible property, personal property was divided into tangible property (such as cars, clothing, etc.) and intangible property (such as financial instruments, including stocks and bonds, etc.), and intellectual property, including (patents, copyrights, and trademarks).

What can be Property?

The two major justifications given for original property, or homesteading, are effort and scarcity. John Locke emphasized effort, "mixing your labor" with an object, or clearing and cultivating virgin land. Benjamin Tucker preferred to look at the telos of property, i.e. What is the purpose of property? His answer: to solve the scarcity problem. Only when items are relatively scarce with respect to people's desires do they become property. For example, hunter-gatherers did not consider land to be property, since there was no shortage of land. Agrarian societies later made arable land property, as it was scarce. For something to be economically scarce, it must necessarily have the *exclusivity property*-that use by one person excludes others from using it. These two justifications lead to different conclusions on what can be property. Intellectual property-non-corporeal things like ideas, plans, orderings and arrangements (musical compositions, novels, computer programs)-are generally considered valid property to those who support an effort justification, but invalid to those who support a scarcity justification, since they don't have the exclusivity property (however they may still support other 'intellectual property'-laws such as Copyright, as long as these are a subject of contract instead of government arbitration). Thus even ardent propertarians may disagree about IP. By either standard, one's body is one's property.

From some anarchist points of view, the validity of property depends on whether the "property right" requires enforcement by the state. Different forms of "property" require different amounts of enforcement: intellectual property requires a great deal of state intervention to enforce, ownership of distant physical property requires quite a lot, ownership of carried objects requires very little, while ownership of one's own body requires absolutely no state intervention.

Many things have existed that did not have an owner, sometimes called the commons. The term "commons," however, is also often used to mean something quite different: "general collective ownership"-i.e. common ownership. Also, the same term is sometimes used by statists to mean government-owned property that the general public is allowed to access. Law in all societies has tended to develop towards reducing the number of things not having clear owners. Supporters of property rights argue that this enables better protection of scarce resources, due to the tragedy of the commons, while critics argue that it leads to the 'exploitation' of those resources for personal gain and that it hinders taking advantage of potential network effects. These arguments have differing validity for different types of "property"—things that are not scarce are, for instance, not subject to the tragedy of the commons. Some apparent critics advocate general collective ownership rather than ownerlessness.

Things that do not have owners include: ideas (except for intellectual property), seawater (which is, however, protected by anti-pollution laws), parts of the seafloor, gasses in Earth's atmosphere, animals in the wild (though there may be restrictions on hunting etc. — and in some legal systems, such as that of New York, they are actually treated as government property), celestial bodies and outer space, and land in Antarctica.

The nature of children under the age of majority is another contested issue here. In ancient societies children were generally considered the property of their parents. Children in most modern societies theoretically own their own bodies—but they are considered incompetent to exercise their rights, and their parents or guardians are given most of the actual rights of control over them.

Questions regarding the nature of ownership of the body also come up in the issue of abortion and drugs.

In many ancient legal systems (e.g. early Roman law), religious sites (e.g. temples) were considered property of the God or gods they were devoted to. However, religious pluralism makes it more convenient to have religious sites owned by the religious body that runs them.

Intellectual property and air (airspace, no-fly zone, pollution laws, which can include tradeable emissions rights) can be property in some senses of the word.

Rights of use as Property

Ownership of land can be held separately from the ownership of rights over that land, including sporting rights, mineral rights, development rights, air rights, and such other rights as may be worth segregating from simple land ownership.

Who can be an Owner?

Ownership laws may vary widely among countries depending on the nature of the property of interest (e.g. firearms, real property, personal property, animals). Persons can own property directly. In most societies legal entities, such as corporations, trusts and nations (or governments) own property.

In the Inca empire, the dead emperors, who were considered gods, still controlled property after death..

Whether and to what extent the State may interfere with property: Under United States law the principal limitations on whether and the extent to which the State may interfere with property rights are set by the Constitution. The "Takings" clause requires that the government (whether state or federal——for the 14th Amendment's due process clause imposes the 5th Amendment's takings clause on state governments) may take private property only for a public purpose, after exercising due process of law, and upon making "just compensation." If an interest is not deemed a "property" right, or the conduct is merely an intentional tort, these limitations do not apply and the doctrine of sovereign immunity precludes relief. Moreover, if the interference does not almost completely make the property valueless, the interference will not be deemed a taking but instead a mere regulation of use. On the other hand, some governmental regulations of property use have been deemed so severe that they have been considered "regulatory takings." Moreover, conduct sometimes deemed only a nuisance or other tort has been held a taking of property where the conduct was sufficiently persistent and severe.

A Radical Theory of Property

Intellectual property is the least respected form of property in our society. I think that's because it jars with some people's traditional sense of what property is. They live in the physical world and the non-physical is counter to the intuitions that life engenders.

When you steal a car, the former owner loses the car. The reasons for property here seem clear to all but the most communist of thinkers. But when you copy a copyrighted work, the original owner still has their copy. Nothing physical is stolen, so it seems very different.

And indeed for many people, that difference is enough to treat intellectual property (IP) with disrespect. Many people who would return a Rolex they found lying on the ground — or be racked with guilt if they didn't — will happily make illicit copies of software.

Yet IP is becoming vastly important in the modern world, and the foundation of a growing chunk of the world's economy. This growth has led for all sorts of diverse movements. Some feel we should just abandon most concepts if IP. Some want to strengthen them to deal with the disrespect they receive. Some wish to try technological approaches of various sorts.

I want to put forward two notions; one straightforward and one radical. The first is that to understand IP, one must realize that property is about control, not possession. The second is the notion that perhaps intellectual property is the "real" property and physical property the illusion.

Intellectual Property as the True Property

Philosophers argue about what property is, why we should have it and how it should be allocated, owned and protected. Of course, in some philosophies property is viewed as inappropriate. Early socialists like Prudhon felt that "Property is theft," because one person's control of property deprived the rest of the world of it.

For various reasons, most people hold different views. However, one of Marx's concepts, the labour theory of value, holds the germ of a different understanding of intellectual property.

We must first ask ourselves, when something is valuable as a piece of property, why is it valuable? I will assert that while the raw materials that comprise it hold some value, the true value comes from how those raw materials have been arranged. This derives both from the work to arrange them, and the design of how they are arranged.

We value a new car far more than the squashed cube it can become in the wrecking yard, yet materially it is the same stuff. Two meals, made from the same raw ingredients, by the very same person in the same amount of time — but with two different recipes, may differ vastly in value. The value is partly from the materials and labour but most of it comes from the recipe.

Indeed the bulk of the true value of almost everything artificial resides in its design and the ideas behind it. Natural property (such as "real" estate) is another matter as you'll see later.

With intellectual property, like books and films, this becomes even more clear. Physically, and from a labour standpoint, two cd-roms or video tapes are identical. The intellectual property, represented as magnetic ghosts on the tape, makes all the difference. With the internet we're now used to receiving IP without any physical storage medium at all, and it becomes even clearer where what we value is.

It's also worth considering that in the end, all matter is composed of just a very small number of absolutely identical fundamental particles — protons, electrons and neutrons. What really makes one thing different from another is just the numbers of these particles and how they are arranged with respect to one another. What's valuable or meaningful is not the particles themselves, but the information about how they are arranged. Some feel that in the future we will possess a technology of "molecular assembly" — vaguely analogous to the *replicators* on the TV show "Star Trek: The Next Generation." In that world, the concept that the true value of things is mostly in the information, and not the matter, becomes crystal clear.

Now these theories of value derive from a basic principle that most people agree with. You own your own self. This concept sits at the base of not just property and liberty, but also most civil rights. The law chips away at it, but few argue that whatever ownership means, it starts with ownership — control — of one's own body and mind.

To own yourself is to own your thoughts, at least while they are inside your head. And thus we come to the first insight of IP as the "true" property. The relationship between a person and the thoughts they create is the most real relationship in the world. Unlike all the other forms of property, especially real estate, my ownership of the creative thoughts in my own head exists without law, without society, without philosophy. Even solipsists accept this relationship between creator and creation!

My ownership of my land, my so called "real" estate is much more dubious. I just paid money for it, down through a chain to somebody who got assigned it by a government, which conquered the region it's in from tribal groups who, while they had it in their "territory" were using it marginally if at all. I need have no intrinsic relationship to my land. I get to claim it as property because there is a document down at the County which society will accept and back up with police.

The thoughts in my head are mine without police, without documents, without society.

Sharing Thoughts

Of course, if I reveal my thoughts to others, they can have them in their heads too. And, unlike physical objects, in some cases they can come up with very similar thoughts of their own independently of me. So while the relationship is intrinsic, we do need to create philosophy and laws to govern just what control of shared thoughts means.

When it comes to complex creative works, like stories, or software, the odds of somebody else thinking up exactly the same novel are so slim that it's safe to reflect the creator-creation relationship in law, and that law is copyright.

Simpler concepts which can be thought up by multiple parties-inventions-are harder to deal with, so patent law must be more complex. In a fair system two people who thought up an idea on their own would both have rights to it. But since there is no way to safely determine that, society has instead put rules on what can be patented and simply arbitrarily granted the right to the first to invent or the first to file a patent.

Indeed, this theory of intellectual property as the "true" property doesn't greatly affect how we try to build our property laws. We still live in society constrained by pragmatism. The difference comes in how we think of things, and decide what's moral.

Why don't we steal? For most of us, it's not the police or the law or the fear of getting caught. It's because we were taught the basic ethical principles of our society on our mother's knee, and perhaps later in life came to see why they are good for ourselves. Most aren't taught as children to respect intellectual property as the true property, and so we don't. The current generation isn't being taught this either, but this may change. In the end that's the only way the rights of others ever get respected.

Napster tells us, however, that when presented with no risk, and a good user interface, and particularly with more convenient access to material that otherwise is locked up and hard to use, large numbers of people have little interest in obeying the wishes of the creators of music and their control over who gets copies.

Anti-Property

Of course, many feel that there should be no such rights, and would bristle at the idea of working to teach children to respect them. The issue is far from simple. Because information can be trivially copied, the economics of intellectual property differ greatly from those of traditional property. The world still hasn't figured out the rules.

Even the most rabid opponents of intellectual property, however, seem to support some element of creator's rights. Most feel that creators have a firm right to credit for their work, and view plagiarism, or even stripping the creator's name off the work as pretty nasty sins.

Some people — myself included — have made good money from intellectual property, without any need to file lawsuits or put technical protections on the material. This leads some to think that perhaps we should not bother with protections at all. After all, if value resides in information, and information can be duplicated without limit, the whole world can immediately be rich.

It is not, however that simple. In spite of claims that "information wants to be free" the fact remains that proprietary information gets far more distributed and far more widely used than free information. Microsoft Windows still is vastly more deployed than Linux. It's rare to find free software that doesn't have a more widely used commercial counterpart. Tom Clancy sells more books than Shakespeare. And this is all because the proprietary information is allowed to make money to promote its own distribution. Like a bacterium, it needs food to grow and replicate, and money is that food.

There are some exceptions. The bible and other religious books certainly are well distributed, but there are clear other factors that led to this, and those who distributed these books actually did well materially from them. There are a few free software packages without commercial counterparts. But these are the exception, not the rule. People who make their software free "so more people can use it" often end up getting fewer users than those who charge for their software.

Indeed, while the principle above was very solid until the 1990s, the internet made distribution so easy and cheap that the balance is shifting, and making something copyright-free is no longer the counter-intuitive shackle on its wide distribution that it used to be. I don't think the balance has shifted entirely the other way, but the trend is evident. There are some areas where copyright-free materials are surpassing their more controlled counterparts, and these areas may grow.

In addition, a philosophy of support for the ability of creators to control their creations doesn't imply that that control can or should be absolute, since once information is in my hands, such control implies control over me and my thoughts. And in particular, defending the rights of the creator does not imply that all information should be locked up in an encryption Alcatraz with the tools that manipulate the content made illegal.

6

Justice and the Common Good

Justice

Justice is the concept of moral rightness based on ethics, rationality, law, natural law, fairness, or equity.

Concept of Justice

Justice concerns itself with the proper ordering of things and persons within a society. As a concept it has been subject to philosophical, legal, and theological reflection and debate throughout our history. A number of important questions surrounding justice have been fiercely debated over the course of western history: What is justice? What does it demand of individuals and societies? What is the proper distribution of wealth and resources in society: equal, meritocratic, according to status, or some other arrangement? There are myriad possible answers to these questions from divergent perspectives on the political and philosophical spectrum.

According to most theories of justice, it is overwhelmingly important: John Rawls, for instance, claims that "Justice is the first virtue of social institutions, as truth is of systems of thought.": Justice can be thought of as distinct from and more fundamental than benevolence, charity, mercy, generosity or compassion. Justice has traditionally been associated with concepts of fate, reincarnation or Divine Providence, i.e. with a life in accordance with the cosmic plan. The association of justice with fairness has thus been historically and culturally rare and is perhaps chiefly a modern innovation.

Studies at UCLA in 2008 have indicated that reactions to fairness are "wired" into the brain and that, "Fairness is activating the same part of the brain that responds to food in rats... This is consistent with the notion that being treated fairly satisfies a basic need". Research conducted in 2003 at Emory University, Georgia, involving Capuchin Monkeys demonstrated that other cooperative animals also possess such a sense and that "inequality aversion may not be uniquely human." indicating that ideas of fairness and justice may be instinctual in nature.

Variations of Justice

Utilitarianism is a form of consequentialism, where punishment is forward-looking. Justified by the ability to achieve future social benefits resulting in crime reduction, the moral worth of an action is determined by its outcome.

Retributive justice regulates proportionate response to crime proven by lawful evidence, so that punishment is justly imposed and considered as morally-correct and fully deserved. The law of *retaliation* (lex talionis) is a military theory of retributive justice, which says that reciprocity should be equal to the wrong suffered; "life for life, wound for wound, stripe for stripe."

Restorative justice is concerned not so much with retribution and punishment as with (a) making the victim whole and (b) reintegrating the offender into society. This approach frequently brings an offender and a victim together, so that the offender can better understand the effect his/her offense had on the victim.

Distributive justice is directed at the proper allocation of things — wealth, power, reward, respect — between different people.

Oppressive Law exercises an authoritarian approach to legislation which is "totally unrelated to justice", a tyrannical interpretation of law is one in which the population lives under restriction from unlawful legislation.

Some theorists, such as the classical Greeks and Romans, conceive of justice as a virtue—a property of people, and only derivatively of their actions and the institutions they create. Others emphasize actions or institutions, and only derivatively the people who bring them about. The source of justice has variously been attributed to harmony, divine command, natural law, or human creation.

Distributive Justice

After outlining the scope of this entry and the role of distributive principles, the first relatively simple principle of distributive justice examined is strict egalitarianism, which advocates the allocation of equal material goods to all members of society.

John Rawls' alternative distributive principle, which he calls the Difference Principle, is then examined. The Difference Principle allows allocation that does not conform to strict equality so long as the inequality has the effect that the least advantaged in society are materially better off than they would be under strict equality. However, some have thought that Rawls' Difference Principle is not sensitive to the responsibility people have for their economic choices. Resource-based distributive principles, and principles based on what people deserve because of their work, endeavor to incorporate this idea of economic responsibility.

Advocates of Welfare-based principles do not believe the primary distributive concern should be material goods and services. They argue that material goods and services have no intrinsic value and are valuable only in so far as they increase welfare. Hence, they argue, the distributive principles should be designed and assessed according to how they affect welfare. Advocates of Libertarian principles, on the other hand, generally criticize any patterned distributive ideal, whether it is welfare or material goods that are the subjects of the pattern.

They generally argue that such distributive principles conflict with more important moral demands such as those of liberty or respecting self-ownership. Finally, feminist critiques of existing distributive principles note that they tend to ignore the particular circumstances of women, especially the fact that women often have primary responsibility for child-rearing. Some feminists therefore are developing and/or modifying distributive principles to make them sensitive to the circumstances of women and to the fact that, on average, women spend less of their lifetimes in the market economy than men.

Scope and Role of Distributive Principles

Distributive principles may vary in numerous dimensions. They can vary in what is subject to distribution (income, wealth, opportunities, jobs, welfare, utility, etc.); in the nature of the subjects of the distribution (natural persons, groups of persons, reference classes, etc.); and on what basis distribution should be made (equality, maximization, according to individual characteristics, according to free transactions, etc.). This entry will focus on principles of distributive justice designed to cover the distribution of the benefits and burdens of economic activity among individuals in a society. Although principles of this kind have been the dominant source of Anglo-American debate about distributive justice over the last four decades, there are other important distributive justice questions, some of which are covered by other entries in the encyclopedia. These include questions of distributive justice at the global level rather than just at the national level, distributive justice across generations and how the topic of distributive justice can be approached, not as a set of principles but as a virtue.

Although the numerous proposed distributive principles vary along different dimensions, for simplicity, they are broadly grouped here. It is important to keep in mind though that this involves oversimplication, particularly with respect to the criticisms of each of the groups of principles. The criticisms may not apply to every principle in the group. The issue of how we are to understand and respond to criticisms of distributive principles is discussed briefly in the section on methodology at the end.

There has never been, and never will be, a purely libertarian society or Rawlsian society, or any society whose distribution conforms to one of the proposed principles. Some are misled by this fact to believe that discussions of distributive justice are exercises in ideal theory, which is unfortunate because, in the end, distributive justice theory is a practical enterprise.

Throughout most of history, people were born into, and largely stayed in a fairly rigid economic position. The distribution of economic benefits and burdens was seen as fixed, either by nature or by God. Only when people realized that the distribution of economic benefits and burdens could be affected by government did distributive justice become a live topic. Now the topic is unavoidable. Governments continuously make and change laws affecting the distribution of economic benefits and burdens in their societies. Almost all changes, from the standard tax and industry laws through to divorce laws have some distributive effect, and, as a result, different societies have different distributions. Every society then is always faced with a choice about whether to stay with the current laws and policies or to modify them. Distributive justice theory contributes practically by providing guidance for these unavoidable and constant choices. For instance, advocates of the difference principle are arguing that we should change our policies and laws to raise the position of the least advantaged in society. Others are arguing for changes to bring economic benefits and burdens more in accordance with what people deserve. Libertarians usually urge a reduction in government intervention in the economy. Sometimes a number of the theories will recommend the same change in policy; other times they will diverge. Contrary to a popular misconception, economics alone cannot decide what policy changes we should make. Economics, at its best, can tell us the effects of pursuing different policies; it cannot, without the guidance of normative principles, recommend which policy to pursue. The arguments and principles discussed in the present entry aim to supply this kind of guidance.

Strict Egalitarianism

One of the simplest principles of distributive justice is that of strict or radical equality. The principle says that every person should have the same level of material goods and services. The principle is most commonly justified on the grounds that people are owed equal respect and that equality in material goods and services is the best way to give effect to this ideal.

Even with this ostensibly simple principle some of the difficult specification problems of distributive principles can be seen. The two main problems are the construction of appropriate indices for measurement (the index problem), and the specification of time frames. Because there are numerous proposed solutions to these problems, the 'principle of strict equality' is not a single principle but a name for a group of closely related principles. This range of possible specifications occurs with all the common principles of distributive justice.

The index problem arises primarily because the goods to be distributed need to be measured if they are going to be distributed according to some pattern (such as equality). The strict equality principle stated above says that there should be 'the same *level* of material goods and services'. The problem is how to specify and measure levels. One way of solving the index problem in the strict equality case is to specify that everyone should have the same *bundle* of material goods and services rather than the same *level* (so everyone would have 4 oranges, 6 apples, 1 bike, etc.). The main problem with this solution is that there will be many other allocations of material goods and services which will make some people better off without making anybody else worse off. For instance, a person preferring apples to oranges will be better off if she swaps some of the oranges from her bundle for some of the apples belonging to a person preferring oranges to apples. Indeed, it is likely that everybody will have something they would wish to trade in order to make themselves better off. As a consequence, requiring identical bundles will make virtually everybody materially worse off than they would be under an alternative allocation. So specifying that everybody must have the same *bundle* of goods does not seem to be a satisfactory way of solving the index problem. Some index for measuring the value of goods and services is required.

Money is an index for the value of material goods and services. It is an imperfect index and its pitfalls are well-documented in most economics textbooks. Moreover, once the goods to be allocated are extended beyond material ones to include opportunities, etc. it needs to be combined with other indices. Nevertheless, using money as index for the value of material goods and services is the most practical response so far suggested to the index problem and is widely used in the specification and implementation of distributive principles.

The second main specification problem involves time frames. Many distributive principles identify and require that a particular pattern of distribution be achieved. But they also need to specify *when* the pattern is required. One version of the principle of strict equality requires that all people should have the same wealth at some initial point, after which people are free to use their wealth in whatever way they choose. Principles specifying initial distributions after which the pattern need not be preserved are commonly called 'starting-gate' principles.

Because 'starting-gate' forms of the strict equality principle may lead in time to very inegalitarian wealth distributions they are not common. The most common form of strict equality principle specifies that *income* (measured in terms of money) should be equal in *each* time-frame, though even this may lead to significant disparities in wealth if variations in savings are permitted. Hence, strict equality principles are commonly conjoined with some society-wide specification of just saving behaviour.

There are a number of direct moral criticisms made of strict equality principles: that they unduly restrict freedom, that they do not give best effect to equal respect for persons, that they conflict with what people deserve, etc. But the most common criticism is a welfare-based one: that everyone can be materially better off if incomes are not strictly equal. It is this fact which partly inspired the Difference Principle.

The Difference Principle

The wealth of an economy is not a fixed amount from one period to the next. More wealth can be produced and indeed this has been the experience of industrialized countries over the last few centuries. The most common way of producing more wealth is to have a system where those who are more productive earn greater incomes. This partly inspired the formulation of the Difference Principle.

The most widely discussed theory of distributive justice in the past three decades has been that proposed by John Rawls in *A Theory of Justice*, (Rawls 1971), and *Political Liberalism*, (Rawls 1993). Rawls proposes the following two principles of justice:

1. Each person has an equal claim to a fully adequate scheme of equal basic rights and liberties, which scheme is compatible with the same scheme for all; and in this scheme the equal political liberties, and only those liberties, are to be guaranteed their fair value.

2. Social and economic inequalities are to satisfy two conditions: (a) They are to be attached to positions and offices open to all under conditions of fair equality of opportunity; and (b), they are to be to the greatest benefit of the least advantaged members of society. (Rawls 1993, pp. 5-6. The principles are numbered as they were in Rawls' original *A Theory of Justice.*)

Under Rawls' proposed system Principle (1) has priority over Principle (2). In addition to (2b) it is possible to think of Principles (1) and (2a) as principles of distributive justice: (1) to govern the distribution of liberties, and (2a) the distribution of opportunities. Looking at the principles of justice in this way makes all principles of justice, principles of distributive justice (even principles of retributive justice will be included on the basis that they distribute negative goods). Keeping in line with the primary focus of this entry though, let us concentrate on (2b), known as the Difference Principle.

The main moral motivation for the Difference Principle is similar to that for strict equality: equal respect for persons. Indeed the Difference Principle materially collapses to a form of strict equality under empirical conditions where differences in income have no effect on the work incentive of people. The overwhelming opinion though is that in the foreseeable future the possibility of earning greater income will bring forth greater productive effort. This will increase the total wealth of the economy and, under the Difference Principle, the wealth of the least advantaged. Opinion divides on the size of the inequalities which would, as a matter of empirical fact, be allowed by the Difference Principle, and on how much better off the least advantaged would be under the Difference Principle than under a strict equality principle. Rawls' principle however gives fairly clear guidance on what type of arguments will count as justifications for inequality. Rawls is not opposed to the principle of strict equality *per se*, his concern is about the *absolute* position of the least advantaged group rather than their *relative* position. If a system of strict equality maximizes the absolute position of the least advantaged in society, then the Difference Principle advocates strict equality. If it is possible to raise the absolute position of the least advantaged further by having some inequalities of income and wealth, then the Difference Principle prescribes inequality up to that point where the absolute position of the least advantaged can no longer be raised.

Because there has been such extensive discussion of the Difference Principle in the last 30 years, there have been numerous criticisms of it from the perspective of all the other theories of distributive justice outlined here. Briefly, the main criticisms are as follows.

Advocates of strict equality argue that inequalities permitted by the Difference Principle are unacceptable even if they do benefit the least advantaged. The problem for these advocates is to explain in a satisfactory way why the relative position of the least advantaged is more important than their absolute position, and hence why society should be prevented from materially benefiting the least advantaged when this is possible. The most common explanation appeals to solidarity (Crocker): that being materially equal is an important expression of the equality of persons. Another common explanation appeals to the power some may have over others, if they are better off materially. Rawls' response to this latter criticism appeals to the priority of his first principle: The inequalities consistent with the Difference Principle are only permitted so long as they do not compromise the fair value of the political liberties. So, for instance, very large wealth differentials may make it practically impossible for poor people to be elected to political office or to have their political views represented. These inequalities of wealth, even if they increase the material position of the least advantaged group, may need to be reduced in order for the first principle to be implemented.

The Utilitarian objection to the Difference Principle is that it does not maximize utility. In *A Theory of Justice*, Rawls uses Utilitarianism as the main theory for comparison with his own, and hence he responds at length to this Utilitarian objection and argues for his own theory in preference to Utilitarianism (some of these arguments are outlined in the section on Welfare-Based Principles).

Libertarians object that the Difference Principle involves unacceptable infringements on liberty. For instance, the Difference Principle may require redistributive taxation to the poor, and

Libertarians commonly object that such taxation involves the immoral taking of just holdings.

The Difference Principle is also criticized as a primary distributive principle on the grounds that it mostly ignores claims that people *deserve* certain economic benefits in light of their actions. Advocates of Desert-Based Principles argue that some may deserve a higher level of material goods because of their hard work or contributions even if their unequal rewards do not also function to improve the position of the least advantaged. They also argue that the explanations of *how* people come to be in more or less advantaged positions is relevant to their fairness, yet the Difference Principle wrongly ignores these explanations.

Like desert theorists, advocates of Resource-based principles criticize the Difference Principle on the grounds that it is not 'ambition-sensitive' enough, i.e. it is not sensitive to the consequences of people's choices. They also argue that it is not adequately 'endowment-sensitive': it does not compensate people for natural inequalities (like handicaps or ill-health) over which people have no control.

Resource-Based Principles

Resource-based principles (also called Resource Egalitarianism) prescribe equality of resources. Interestingly, resource-based principles do not normally prescribe a patterned outcome — the idea being that the outcomes are determined by people's free use of their resources. Resource-theorists claim that the Difference Principle is insufficiently 'ambition-sensitive' and that provided people have equal resources they should live with the consequences of their choices. They argue, for instance, that people who choose to work hard to earn more income should not be required to subsidize those choosing more leisure and hence less income.

Resource-theorists also make a related complaint that the Difference Principle is not sufficiently 'endowment-sensitive.' While part of Rawls' motivation for the Difference principle is that people have unequal endowments, resource-theorists explicitly emphasize this feature of their theory though they differ on which endowments are relevant to questions of distributive justice. They agree that, ideally, social circumstances over which people have no control should not adversely affect life prospects or earning capacities. Some resource-theorists further argue that, for the same sorts of reasons, unequal natural endowments should attract compensation. For instance, people born with handicaps, ill-health, or low levels of natural talents have not brought these circumstances upon themselves and hence, should not be disadvantaged in their life prospects.

The most prominent Resource-based theory, developed by Ronald Dworkin, (Dworkin 1981a, 1981b), proposes that people begin with equal resources but end up with unequal economic benefits as a result of their own choices. What constitutes a just material distribution is to be determined by the result of a thought experiment designed to model fair distribution. Suppose that everyone is given the same purchasing power and each use that purchasing power to bid, in a fair auction, for resources best suited to their life plans. They are then permitted to use those resources as they see fit. Although people may end up with different economic benefits, none of them is given less consideration than another in the sense that if they wanted somebody else's resource bundle they could have bid for it instead.

As mentioned above, many resource-theorists, including Dworkin, add to this system of equal resources and ambition-sensitivity, a sensitivity to inequalities in natural endowments. They note that natural inequalities are not distributed according to people's choices, nor are they justified by reference to some other morally relevant fact about people. Dworkin proposes a hypothetical compensation scheme in which he supposes that, before the hypothetical auction described above, people do not know their own natural endowments. However, they are able to buy insurance against being disadvantaged in the natural distribution of talents and they know that their payments will provide an insurance pool to compensate those people who are unlucky in the 'natural lottery'.

Because the Resource-based theory has a similar motivation to the Difference Principle the moral criticisms of it tend to be variations on those levelled against the Difference Principle. However, unlike the Difference Principle, it is not at all clear what would constitute an implementation of Resource-based theories and their variants in a real economy. It seems impossible to measure differences in people's natural talents — unfortunately, people's talents do not neatly divide into the natural and developed categories. A system of special assistance to the physically and mentally handicapped and to the ill would be a partial implementation of the compensation system, but most natural inequalities would be left untouched by such assistance while the theory requires that such inequalities be compensated for. It is simply not clear how to implement equality of resources in a complex economy and hence despite its theoretical advantages, it is difficult to see it as a practical improvement on the Difference Principle.

Welfare-Based Principles

Welfare-based principles are motivated by the idea that what is of primary moral importance is the level of welfare of people. Advocates of Welfare-based principles view the concerns of other theories-equality, the least advantaged, resources, desert-claims, or liberty as derivative concerns.

Resources, equality, desert-claims, or liberty are only valuable in so far as they increase welfare, so that all distributive questions should be settled according to which distribution maximizes welfare. However, 'maximizes welfare' is imprecise, so welfare theorists propose particular welfare functions to maximize. The welfare functions proposed vary enormously both on what will count as welfare and the weighting system for that welfare. For almost any distribution of material benefits there is a welfare function whose maximization will yield that distribution (at least in a one sector period).

Distribution according to some welfare function is most commonly advocated by economists, who normally state the explicit functional form. Philosophers tend to avoid this. Philosophers also tend to restrict themselves to a small subset of the available welfare functions. Although there are a number of advocates of alternative welfare functions (like 'equality of well-being'), most philosophical activity has concentrated on a variant known as Utilitarianism. This theory can be used to illustrate most of the main characteristics of Welfare-based principles.

Historically, Utilitarians have used the term 'utility' rather than 'welfare' and utility has been defined variously as pleasure, happiness, or preference-satisfaction. So, for instance, the principle for distributing economic benefits for Preference Utilitarians is to distribute them so as to maximize preference-satisfaction. The welfare function for such a principle has a simple theoretical form: it involves choosing that distribution maximizing the arithmetic sum of all satisfied preferences (unsatisfied preferences being negative), weighted for the intensity of those preferences.

The basic theory of Utilitarianism is one of the simplest to state and understand. Much of the work on the theory therefore has been directed towards defending it against moral criticisms, particularly from the point of view of 'commonsense' morality. The criticisms and responses have been widely discussed in the literature on Utilitarianism as a general moral theory. Only two of the criticisms will be mentioned here.

The first is that Utilitarianism fails to take the distinctness of persons seriously. Maximization of preference-satisfaction is often taken as prudent in the case of individuals — people may take on greater burdens, suffering or sacrifice at certain periods of their lives so that their lives are overall better. The complaint against Utilitarianism is that it takes this principle, commonly described as prudent for individuals, and uses it on an entity, society, unlike individuals in important ways. While it may be acceptable for a person to choose to suffer at some period in her life (be it a day, or a number of years) so that her overall life is better, it is often argued against Utilitarianism that it is immoral to make some people suffer so that there is a net gain for other people. In the individual case, there is a single entity experiencing both the sacrifice and the gain. Also, the individuals, who suffer or make the sacrifices, choose to do so in order to gain some benefit they deem worth their sacrifice. In the case of society as a whole, there is no single experiential entity — some people suffer or are sacrificed so that others may gain. Furthermore, under Utilitarianism, there is no requirement for people to consent to the suffering or sacrifice.

A related criticism of Utilitarianism involves the way it treats individual preferences or interests referring to the holdings of others. For instance, some people may have a preference that some minority racial group should have less material benefits. Under Utilitarian theories, in their classical form, this preference or interest counts like any other in determining the best distribution. Hence, if racial preferences are widespread and are not outweighed by the minorities' contrary preferences, Utilitarianism will recommend an inegalitarian distribution based on race.

Utilitarians have responded to these criticisms in a number of ways. Utilitarians may apply their theory to the preferences themselves, arguing that utility is best promoted in the long run when people's preferences are shaped (if this is possible) in ways that are harmonious with one another, suggesting racist preferences should be discouraged. However, the utilitarian then must supply an account of why racist or sexist preferences should be discouraged when the same level of total long term utility could be achieved by encouraging the less powerful to be contented with a lower position. It is difficult for utilitarians to explain why the position of the oppressed is aptly described as one of oppression. Utilitarians have also argued that the empirical conditions are such that utility maximizing will rarely require women or racial minorities to sacrifice or suffer for the benefit of others, or to satisfy the prejudices of others. But if their theory on rare occasions does require people sacrifice or suffer in these ways, Utilitarians have defended this unintuitive consequence on the grounds that our judgments about what is wrong provide us with 'rules of thumb' which are useful at the level of commonsense morality but ultimately mistaken at the level of 'critical theory'.

Utilitarian distribution principles, like the other principles described here, have problems with specification and implementation. Most formulations of Utilitarianism require interpersonal comparisons of utility. This means, for instance, that we must be able to compare the utility one person gains from eating an apple with that another gains from eating an apple. Furthermore, Utilitarianism requires that differences in utility be measured and summed for widely disparate goods (so, for instance, the amount of utility a particular person gains from playing football is measured and compared with the amount of utility another gains from eating a gourmet meal). Critics have argued that such interpersonal utility comparisons are impossible, even in theory, due to one or both of the following: (1) It is not possible to combine all the diverse goods into a single index of 'utility' which can measured for an individual; (2) Even if you could do the necessary weighing and combining of the goods to construct such an index for an individual, there is no conceptually adequate way of calibrating such a measure between individuals.

Utilitarians face a greater problem than this theoretical one in determining what material distribution is prescribed by their theory. Those who share similar Utilitarian theoretical principles frequently recommend very different material distributions to implement the principle. This problem occurs for other theories, but appears worse for Utilitarian and Welfare-based distribution principles. Recommendations for distributions or economic structures to implement other distributive principles commonly vary among advocates with similar theoretical principles, but the advocates tend to cluster around particular recommendations. This is not the case for Utilitarianism, with adherents dispersed in their recommendations across the full range of possible distributions and economic structures. For instance, many Preference Utilitarians believe their principle prescribes strongly egalitarian structures with lots of state invention while many other Preference Utilitarians believe it prescribes a *laissez faire* style of capitalism.

There is an explanation for why Utilitarians are faced with greater difficulties in implementation. Other distributive principles can rule out, relatively quickly, some practical policies on the grounds that they clearly violate the guiding principle, but Utilitarians must examine, in great detail, all the policies on offer. For each policy, they must determine the distribution of goods and services yielded by the policy and at least three other factors: the identity of each person in the distribution (if individuals' utility functions differ); the utility of each person from the goods and services distributed to them; the utility of each person from the policy itself. The size of the information requirements make this task impossible. Hence, broad assumptions must be made and each different set of assumptions will yield a different answer, and so the answers range across the full set of policies on offer. Moreover, there is no obvious way to arbitrate between the different sets of assumptions. For instance, suppose three Utilitarians agree on the same Utilitarian distributive principle. Utilitarian 1 however, asserts that the population's utility function conforms to function A (e.g. people's marginal utility is linear in the goods and services they consume) and is maximized by Policy 1; while Utilitarian 2 asserts that half the population's utility function conforms to function A and half to function B (e.g. people's marginal utility is diminishing) and is maximized by Policy 2; Utilitarian 3 asserts Utilitarian 2 is correct about the utility functions of the population but claims that Policy 3 will maximize utility. What seems impossible for advocates of Utilitarian-distribution principles to answer is how we would arbitrate these claims. If Utilitarian principles are to play a role in debates about distributive justice then this is the most important question to answer.

Desert-Based Principles

Another complaint against welfarism is that it ignores, and in fact cannot even make sense of, claims that people *deserve* certain economic benefits in light of their actions. The complaint is often motivated by the concern that various forms of welfarism treat people as mere containers for well-being, rather than purposeful beings, responsible for their actions and creative in their environments.

The different desert-based principles of distribution differ primarily according to what they identify as the basis for deserving. Most contemporary proposals for desert-bases fit into one of three broad categories:

1. Contribution: People should be rewarded for their work activity according to the value of their contribution to the social product. (Miller 1976, Miller 1989, Riley 1989)
2. Effort: People should be rewarded according to the effort they expend in their work activity. (Sadurski 1985a,b, Milne 1986)
3. Compensation: People should be rewarded according to the costs they incur in their work activity. (Dick 1975, Lamont 1997)

Aristotle argued that virtue should be a basis for distributing rewards, but most contemporary principles owe a larger debt to

John Locke. Locke argued people deserve to have those items produced by their toil and industry, the products (or the value thereof) being a fitting reward for their effort. His underlying idea was to guarantee to individuals the fruits of their own labor and abstinence. According to the contemporary desert theorist, people freely apply their abilities and talents, in varying degrees, to socially productive work. People come to deserve varying levels of income by providing goods and services desired by others. (Feinberg) Distributive systems are just insofar as they distribute incomes according to the different levels earned or deserved by the individuals in the society for their productive labors, efforts, or contributions.

Contemporary desert-principles all share the value of raising the standard of living — collectively, 'the social product'. Under each principle, only activity directed at raising the social product will serve as a basis for deserving income. The concept of desert itself does not yield this value of raising the social product; it is a value societies hold independently. Hence, desert principles identifying desert-bases tied to socially productive activity (productivity, compensation, and effort all being examples of such bases) do not do so because the concept of desert requires this. They do so because societies value higher standards of living, and therefore choose the raising of living standards as the primary value relevant to desert-based distribution. This means that the full development of desert-based principles requires specification (and defence) of those activities which will or will not count as socially productive, and hence as deserving of remuneration. (Lamont 1994)

It is important to distinguish desert-payments from entitlements. For desert theorists a well-designed institutional structure will make it so that many of the entitlements people have are deserved. But, of course, entitlements and just deserts can come apart — a person can be entitled to a payment without it being deserved, just as a person can be entitled to assume the presidential office without deserving it. (Feinberg 1970, 86) Similarly, a person may deserve a payment but not being entitled to it (such instances are potential areas for institutional reform for a desert theorist). Payments designed to give people incentives are a form of entitlement particularly worth distinguishing from desert-payments as they are commonly confused. Incentive-payments are 'forward-looking' (Barry 1965, 111-112) in that they are set up to create a situation in the future, while desert-payments are 'backwards-looking' that they are justified with reference to work in the present or past. Even though it is possible for the same payment to be both deserved and an incentive, incentives and desert provide distinct rationales for income and should not be conflicted. (Lamont 1997)

While some have sought to justify current capitalist distributions via desert-based distributive principles, John Stuart Mill and many since have forcefully argued the contrary claim — that the implementation of a productivity principle would involve dramatic changes in modern market economies and would greatly reduce the inequalities characteristic of them. It is important to note, though, that contemporary Desert-based principles are rarely complete distributive principles. They usually are only designed to cover distribution among working adults, leaving basic welfare needs to be met by other principles.

The specification and implementation problems for desert-based distribution principles revolve mainly around the desert-bases: it is difficult to identify what is to count as a contribution, an effort or a cost, and it is even more difficult to measure these in a complex modern economy.

The main moral objection to desert-based principles is that they make economic benefits depend on factors over which people have little control. John Rawls has made one of the most widely discussed arguments to this effect (Rawls 1971), and while the strong form of this argument has been clearly refuted (Zaitchik, Sher), it remains a problem for desert-based principles. The problem is most pronounced in the case of productivity-based principles — a person's productivity seems clearly to be influenced by many factors over which the person has little control.

It is interesting to note that under most welfare-based principles, it is also the case that people's level of economic benefits depend on factors beyond their control. But welfarists view this as a virtue of their theory, since they think the only morally relevant characteristic of any distribution is the welfare resulting from it. Whether the distribution ties economic benefits to matters beyond our control is morally irrelevant from the welfarist point of view. (As it happens, welfarists often hold the empirical claim that people have little control over their contributions to society anyway.) However, for people's benefits to depend on factors beyond their control is a more awkward result for desert theorists who emphasize the responsibility of people in choosing to engage in more or less productive activities.

Libertarian Principles

Most contemporary versions of the principles discussed so far allow some role for the market as a means of achieving the desired distributive pattern — the Difference Principle uses it as a means of helping the least advantaged; utilitarian principles commonly use it as a means of achieving the distributive pattern maximizing utility; desert-based principles rely on it to distribute goods according to desert, etc. In contrast, advocates of Libertarian distributive principles rarely see the market as a means to some desired pattern, since the principle(s) they advocate do not ostensibly propose a 'pattern' at all, but instead describe the sorts of acquisitions or exchanges which are themselves just. The market will be just, not as a means to some pattern, but insofar as the exchanges permitted in the market satisfy the conditions of just exchange described by the principles. For Libertarians, just outcomes are those arrived at by the separate just actions of individuals; a particular distributive pattern is not required for justice. Robert Nozick has advanced this version of Libertarianism (Nozick 1974), and is its most well-known contemporary advocate.

Nozick proposes a 3-part "Entitlement Theory".

If the world were wholly just, the following inductive definition would exhaustively cover the subject of justice in holdings:

a. A person who acquires a holding in accordance with the principle of justice in acquisition is entitled to that holding.
b. A person who acquires a holding in accordance with the principle of justice in transfer, from someone else entitled to the holding, is entitled to the holding.
c. No one is entitled to a holding except by (repeated) applications of (a) and (b).

The complete principle of distributive justice would say simply that a distribution is just if everyone is entitled to the holdings they possess under the distribution (Nozick, p.151).

The statement of the Entitlement Theory includes reference to the principles of justice in acquisition and transfer. The principle of justice in transfer is the least controversial and is designed to specify fair contracts while ruling out stealing, fraud, etc. The principle of justice in acquisition is more complicated and more controversial. The principle is meant to govern the gaining of exclusive property rights over the material world. For the justification of these rights, Nozick takes his inspiration from John Locke's idea that everyone 'owns' themselves and, by mixing one's labors with the world, self-ownership can generate ownership of some part of the material world. However, of Locke's mixing metaphor, Nozick legitimately asks: '...why isn't mixing what I own with what I don't own a way of losing what I own rather than a way of gaining what I don't? If I own a can of tomato juice and spill it in the sea so its molecules... mingle evenly throughout the sea, do I thereby come to own the sea, or have I foolishly dissipated my tomato juice?' Nozick concludes that what is significant about mixing our labor with the material world is that in doing so, we tend to increase the value of it, so that self-ownership can lead to ownership of the external world in such cases.

The obvious objection to this claim is that it is not clear why the first people to acquire some part of the material world should be able to exclude others from it (and, for instance, be the land owners while the later ones become the wage labourers). In response to this objection, Nozick puts a qualification on just acquisition, called the *Lockean Proviso*, whereby an exclusive acquisition of the external world is just, if, after the acquisition, there is 'enough and as good left in common for others'. One of the main challenges for Libertarians has been to formulate a morally plausible interpretation of this proviso. According to Nozick's interpretation, an acquisition is just if and only if the position of others after the acquisition is no worse than their position was when the acquisition was unowned or 'held in common'. For Nozick's critics, his proviso is unacceptably weak. This is because it fails to consider the position others may have achieved under alternative distributions and thereby instantiates the morally dubious criterion of whoever is first gets the exclusive spoils. For example, one can satisfy Nozick's proviso by 'acquiring' a beach and charging $1 admission to those who previously were able to use the beach for free, so long as one compensates them with a benefit they deem equally valuable, such as a clean up or life-guarding service on the beach. However, the beach-goers would have been even better off had the more efficient organizer among them acquired the beach, charging only 50 cents for the same service, but this alternative is never considered under Nozick's proviso. (Cohen, 1995)

Will Kymlicka has given a summary of the steps in Nozick's self-ownership argument:

1. People own themselves.
2. The world is initially unowned.
3. You can acquire absolute rights over a disproportionate share of the world; if you do not worsen the condition of others.
4. It is relatively easy to acquire absolute rights over a disproportionate share of the world. Therefore:
5. Once private property has been appropriated, a free market in capital and labor is morally required.

The assessment of this argument is quite complex, but the difficulties mentioned above with the proviso call into question the step from (3) to (4).

The challenge for Libertarians then is to find a plausible reading of (3) which will yield (4). Moreover, at one point, Nozick claims the proviso must apply to both acquisitions and transfers, compounding the problem.

Of course, many existing holdings are the result of acquisitions or transfers which at some point did not satisfy principles (a) and (b) above. Hence, Nozick must supplement those principles with a principle of rectification for past injustice. Although he does not specify this principle he does describe its purpose:

This principle uses historical information about previous situations and injustices done in them... and information about the actual course of events that flowed from these injustices, until the present, and it yields a description (or descriptions) of holdings in the society. The principle of rectification presumably will make use of its best estimate of subjunctive information about what would have occurred... if the injustice had not taken place. If the actual description of holdings turns out not to be one of the descriptions yielded by the principle, then one of the descriptions yielded must be realized.

Nozick does not make an attempt to provide a principle of rectification. The absence of such a principle is much worse for a historical theory than for a patterned theory. Past injustices systematically undermine the justice of every subsequent distribution in historical theories. Nozick is clear that his historical theory is of no use in evaluating the justice of actual societies until such a theory of rectification is given:

> In the absence of [a full treatment of the principle of rectification] applied to a particular society, one *cannot* use the analysis and theory presented here to condemn any particular scheme of transfer payments, unless it is clear that no considerations of rectification of injustice could apply to justify it.

Unfortunately for the theory, no such treatment will ever be forthcoming because the task is, for all practical purposes, impossible. The numbers of injustices perpetrated throughout history, both within nations and between them, are enormous and the necessary details of the vast majority of injustices are unavailable. Even if the details of the injustices were available, the counterfactual causal chains could not be reliably determined and, as Derek Parfit has pointed out, in a different context, even the people who would have been born would have been different. (Parfit 1986) As a consequence, Nozick's entitlement theory will never provide any guidance as to what the current distribution of material holdings should be nor what distributions or redistributions are legitimate or illegitimate. (Indeed Nozick suggests, for instance, the Difference Principle may be the best implementation of the principle of rectification.) Although Nozick is fairly candid about this consequence, many of his supporters and critics have ignored it and have carried on a vigorous debate as though his theory is an attempt to tell us something about the justice of current economic distributions.

Libertarians inspired by Nozick usually advocate a system in which there are exclusive property rights, with the role of the government restricted to the protection of these property rights. The property rights commonly rule out taxation for purposes other than raising the funds necessary to protect property rights. The strongest critique of any attempt to institute such a system of legally protected property rights comes, as we have seen, from Nozick's theory itself — there seems no obvious reason to give strong legal protection to property rights which have arisen through violations of the just principles of acquisition and transfer. But putting this critique to one side for a moment, what other arguments are made in favour of exclusionary property rights?

As already noted, Nozick argues that because people own themselves and hence their talents, they own whatever they can produce with these talents. Moreover, it is possible in a free market to sell the products of exercising one's talents. Any taxation of the income from such selling, according to Nozick, 'institute[s] (partial) ownership by others of people and their actions and labor'. People, according to this argument, have these exclusive rights of ownership. Taxation then, simply involves violating these rights and allowing some people to own (partially) other people. Moreover, it is argued, any system not legally recognizing these rights violates Kant's maxim to treat people always as ends in themselves and never merely as a means. The two main difficulties with this argument have been: (1) to show that self-ownership is only compatible with having such strong exclusive property rights; and (2) that a system of exclusive property rights is the best system for treating people with respect, as ends in themselves.

Nozick candidly accepts that he does not himself give a systematic moral justification of the exclusionary property rights he advocates: 'This book does not present a precise theory of the moral basis of individual rights.' But others have tried to provide more systematic justifications of similar rights (Lomasky, Steiner) or to develop, more fully, justifications to which Nozick alludes.

In addition to the arguments from self-ownership, and the requirement to treat people as ends in themselves, the most common other route for trying to justify exclusive property rights has been to argue that they are required for the maximization of freedom and/or liberty or the minimization of violations of these. (Hayek) As an empirical claim though, this appears to be false. If we compare countries with less exclusionary property rights (e.g. more taxation) with countries with more exclusionary property regimes, we see no systematic advantage in freedoms/liberties enjoyed by people in the latter countries. Now if Libertarians restrict what counts as a valuable freedom/liberty (and discount other freedoms/liberties people value), it will follow that exclusionary property rights are required to maximize freedom/liberty or to minimize violations of these. But the challenge for these Libertarians is to show why only their favoured liberties and freedoms are valuable, and not those which are weakened by a system of exclusive property rights.

Feminist Principles

There is no one feminist conception of distributive justice; theorists who name themselves feminists defend positions across the political spectrum. Hence, feminists offer distinctive versions of all the theories considered so far as well as others. One way of thinking about what unifies many feminist theorists is an interest in what difference, if any, the practical experience of gender makes to the subject matter or study of justice; how different feminists answer this question distinguishes them from each other and from those alternative distributive principles which most inspire their thinking.

The distributive principles so far outlined, with the exception of strict egalitarianism, could be classified as liberal theories — they both inform, and are the product of, the liberal democracies which have emerged over the last two centuries. Lumping them together this way, though clumsy, makes the task of understanding the emergence of feminist critiques (and the subsequent positive theories) much easier.

John Stuart Mill in *The Subjection of Women* (1869) gives one of the clearest early feminist critiques of the political and distributive structures of the emerging liberal democracies. His writings provide the starting point for many contemporary liberal feminists. Mill argued that the principles associated with the developing liberalism of his time required equal political status for women. The principles Mill explicitly mentions include a rejection of the aristocracy of birth, equal opportunity in education and in the marketplace, equal rights to hold property, a rejection of the man as the legal head of the household, and equal rights to political participation. Feminists who follow Mill believe that a proper recognition of the position of women in society requires that women be given equal and the same rights as men have, and that these primarily protect their liberty and their status as equal persons under the law. Thus, government regulation should not prevent women from competing on equal terms with men in educational, professional, marketplace and political institutions. From the point of view of other feminisms, the liberal feminist position is a conservative one, in the sense that it requires the proper inclusion for women of the rights, protections, and opportunities previously secured for men, rather than a fundamental change to the traditional liberal position. The problem for women, on this view, is not liberalism but the failure of society and the State to properly instantiate liberal principles.

One phrase or motto around which a whole range of feminists have rallied, however, marks a significant break with Mill's liberalism: 'the personal is political.' Feminists have offered a variety of interpretations of this motto, many of which take the form of a critique of liberal theories. Mill was crucial in developing the liberal doctrine of limiting the state's intervention in the private lives of citizens. Many contemporary feminists have argued that the resulting liberal theories of justice have fundamentally been unable to accommodate the injustices that have their origins in this 'protected' private sphere. This particular feminist critique has also been a primary source of inspiration for the broader multicultural critique of liberalism. The liberal commitments to government neutrality and to a protected personal sphere of liberty, where the government must not interfere, have been primary critical targets.

While issues about neutrality and personal liberty go beyond debates about distributive justice they also have application within these debates. The feminist critics recognize that liberalism correctly identifies the government as one potential source of oppression against individuals, and therefore recommends powerful political protections of individual liberty. They argue, however, that liberal theories of distributive justice are unable to address the oppression which surfaces in the so-called private sphere of government non-interference. Susan Moller Okin, for example, documents the effects of the institution of the nuclear family, arguing that the consequence of this institution is a position of systematic material and political inequality for women. Standard liberal theories, committed to neutrality in the private sphere, seem powerless to address (or sometimes even recognize) striking and lasting inequalities for women, minorities, or historically oppressed racial groups, when these are merely the cumulative effect of individuals' free behaviour. Okin and others demonstrate, for example, that women have substantial disadvantages in competing in the market because of childrearing responsibilities which are not equally shared with men. As a consequence, any theory relying on market mechanisms, including most liberal theories, will yield systems which result in women systematically having less income and wealth than men. Thus, feminists have challenged contemporary political theorists to rethink the boundaries of political authority in the name of securing a just outcome for women and other historically oppressed groups.

While the political effects of personal freedom pose a serious challenge to contemporary liberal theories of distributive justice, the feminist critiques are somewhat puzzling because, as Jean Hampton puts it, many feminists appear to complain in the name of liberal values. In other words, their claims about the fundamental flaws of liberalism at the same time leave in tact the various ideals of liberty and equality which inspire the liberal theories of justice. Moreover, the task of defining feasible pathways for modifying the structure of liberal democracies without undermining their virtues and protections has proved more difficult than the setting out the criticisms of liberalism. Indeed, despite a legitimate feminist worry about the effects of so-called government neutrality on women's material status, the relative neutrality of liberal democracies compared to non-liberal societies has been one of the significant contributing factors both to the flourishing of feminist theory and to the many significant practical gains women in liberal democracies have made relative to women in other parts of the world. The challenge, being taken up by many, is to navigate both a coherent theoretical and practical path in response to the best feminist critiques available.

Methodology and Empirical Beliefs about Distributive Justice

How are we to go about choosing between the different distributive principles on offer, and respond to criticisms of the principles? Unfortunately, few philosophers explicitly discuss the methodology they are using. The most notable exception is John Rawls (1971, 1974) who explicitly brought the method of wide reflective equilibrium to political philosophy. This method has been brilliantly discussed by Norman Daniels over the years and the reader is strongly encouraged to refer to his entry to understand how to evaluate, revise and choose between normative principles. While there is no point in reiterating the method here there are some supplementary issues worth noting.

Empirical data on the beliefs of the population about distributive justice was not available when Rawls published *A Theory of Justice* (Rawls 1971) but much empirical work has since been completed. Swift (1995, 1999) and Miller (1999, chaps. 3-4) have provided surveys of this literature and arguments for why those committed to the method of reflective equilibrium in distributive justice literature should take the beliefs of the population seriously, though not uncritically. Indeed, some go even further, arguing that the distributive decisions arising through the legitimate application of particular democratic processes might even, at least in part, constitute distributive justice.(Walzer 1984) Data on people's beliefs about distributive justice is also useful for addressing the necessary intersection between philosophical and political processes. Such beliefs put constraints on what institutional and policy reforms are practically achievable in any generation — especially when the society is committed to democratic processes.

Two final methodological issues need to be noted. The first concerns the distinctive role counterexamples play in debates about distributive justice. As noted above, the overarching methodological concern of the distributive justice literature must be, in the first instance, the pressing choice of how the benefits and burdens of economic activity should be distributed, rather than the mere uncovering of abstract truth. Principles are to be implemented in real societies with the problems and constraints inherent in such application. Given this, pointing out that the application of any particular principle will have some, perhaps many, immoral results will not by itself constitute a fatal counterexample to any distributive theory.

Such counter-evidence to a theory would only be fatal if there were an alternative, or improved, version of the theory, which, if fully implemented, would yield a morally preferable society overall. So, it is at least possible that the best distributive theory, when implemented, might yield a system which still has many injustices and/or negative consequences. This practical aspect partly distinguishes the role of counterexamples in distributive justice theory from many other philosophical areas. Given that distributive justice is about what to do now, not just what to think, alternate distributive theories must, in part, compete as comprehensive systems which take into account the practical constraints we face.

The second and related methodological point is that the evaluation of alternate distributive principles requires us (and their advocates) to consider the application of the distributive principle in the world. If it is uncertain or indeterminate how a particular distributive principle might in practice apply to the ordering of real societies, then this principle is not yet a serious candidate for our consideration. This is also true of principles whose implementation is practically impossible given the institutional/psychological/informational/technical constraints of a society. Distributive justice is not an area where we can say an idea is good in theory but not in practice. If it is not good in practice, then it is not good in theory either.

Distributive Justice

Distributive justice concerns what some consider to be socially just with respect to the allocation of goods in a society. Thus, a community in which incidental inequalities in outcome do not arise would be considered a society guided by the principles of distributive justice. Allocation of goods takes into thought the total amount of goods to be handed out, the process on how they in the civilization are going to dispense, and the pattern of division. Civilizations have a narrow amount of resources and capital; the problem arises on how the goods should be divided. The common answer to this question is that every individual receives a fair share. Often contrasted with just process, which is concerned with just processes such as in the administration of law, distributive justice concentrates on just outcomes and consequences. A prominent contemporary theorist of distributive justice is the philosopher John Rawls, although this subject matter has now received wide treatment across philosophy and the social sciences.

Distributive Justice and Wealth

Distributive justice considers the distribution of goods among members of society at a specific time, and on that basis, determines whether the state of affairs is subjectively acceptable. For example, someone who evaluates a situation by looking at the standard of living, absolute wealth, wealth disparity, or any other such utilitarian standard, is thinking in terms of distributive justice. Generally, those people who hold egalitarianism to be important, even implicitly, rely on notions of distributive justice. Distributive justice could be considered a means that addresses the burdens and benefits to some norm of equality to members. The definition of distributive justice has stayed constant, compared to other concepts in macro marketing and social economics.

However, not all advocates of consequentialist theories are concerned with an equitable society. What unites them is the mutual interest in achieving the best possible results, or in terms of the example above, the best possible distribution of wealth

Distributive Justice in Real Life Policies

Proponents of distributive justice link it to the concepts of human rights, human dignity, and the common good. The concept of distributive justice entails what civilization is said to owe its individual members in a proportion:

- Resources that are available to the society. This includes financial and market considerations.
- Everyone in society will receive equitable access to basic health care needs.

Distributive justice theory argues that societies have a duty to individuals in need and that all individuals have duties to help others in need. Many governments are known for dealing with issues of Distributive justice, especially countries with ethnic tensions and geographically distinctive minorities. Post-apartheid South Africa is an example of a country that deals with issues of re-allocating resources with respect to the distributive justice framework.

The Common Good

Commenting on the many economic and social problems that American society now confronts, Newsweek columnist Robert J. Samuelson recently wrote: "We face a choice between a society where people accept modest sacrifices for a common good or a more contentious society where group selfishly protect their own benefits." Newsweek is not the only voice calling for a recognition of and commitment to the "common good." Daniel Callahan, an expert on bioethics, argues that solving the current crisis in our health care system—rapidly rising costs and dwindling access—requires replacing the current "ethic of individual rights" with an "ethic of the common good".

Appeals to the common good have also surfaced in discussions of business' social responsibilities, discussions of environmental pollution, discussions of our lack of investment in education, and discussions of the problems of crime and poverty. Everywhere, it seems, social commentators are claiming that our most fundamental social problems grow out of a widespread pursuit of individual interests.

What exactly is "the common good", and why has it come to have such a critical place in current discussions of problems in our society? The common good is a notion that originated over two thousand years ago in the writings of Plato, Aristotle, and Cicero. More recently, the contemporary ethicist, John Rawls, defined the common good as "certain general conditions that are...equally to everyone's advantage". The Catholic religious tradition, which has a long history of struggling to define and promote the common good, defines it as "the sum of those conditions of social life which allow social groups and their individual members relatively thorough and ready access to their own fulfillment." The common good, then, consists primarily of having the social systems, institutions, and environments on which we all depend work in a manner that benefits all people. Examples of particular common goods or parts of the common good include an accessible and affordable public health care system, and effective system of public safety and security, peace among the nations of the world, a just legal and political system, and unpolluted natural environment, and a flourishing economic system. Because such systems, institutions, and environments have such a powerful impact on the well-being of members of a society, it is no surprise that virtually every social problem in one way or another is linked to how well these systems and institutions are functioning.

As these examples suggest, the common good does not just happen. Establishing and maintaining the common good require the cooperative efforts of some, often of many, people. Just as keeping a park free of litter depends on each user picking up after himself, so also maintaining the social conditions from which we all benefit requires the cooperative efforts of citizens. But these efforts pay off, for the common good is a good to which all members of society have access, and from whose enjoyment no one can be easily excluded. All persons, for example, enjoy the benefits of clean air or an unpolluted environment, or any of our society's other common goods. In fact, something counts as a common good only to the extent that it is a good to which all have access.

It might seem that since all citizens benefit from the common good, we would all willingly respond to urgings that we each cooperate to establish and maintain the common good. But numerous observers have identified a number of obstacles that hinder us, as a society, from successfully doing so.

First, according to some philosophers, the very idea of a common good is inconsistent with a pluralistic society like ours. Different people have different ideas about what is worthwhile or what constitutes "the good life for human beings", differences that have increased during the last few decades as the voices of more and more previously silenced groups, such as women and minorities, have been heard. Given these differences, some people urge, it will be impossible for us to agree on what particular kind of social systems, institutions, and environments we will all pitch in to support.

And even if we agreed upon what we all valued, we would certainly disagree about the relative values things have for us. While all may agree, for example, that an affordable health system, a healthy educational system, and a clean environment are all parts of the common good, some will say that more should be invested in health than in education, while others will favour directing resources to the environment over both health and education. Such disagreements are bound to undercut our ability to evoke a sustained and widespread commitment to the common good. In the face of such pluralism, efforts to bring about the common good can only lead to adopting or promoting the views of some, while excluding others, violating the principle of treating people equally. Moreover, such efforts would force everyone to support some specific notion of the common good, violating the freedom of those who do not share in that goal, and inevitably leading to paternalism (imposing one group's preference on others), tyranny, and oppression.

A second problem encountered by proponents of the common good is what is sometimes called the "free-rider problem". The benefits that a common good provides are, as we noted, available to everyone, including those who choose not to do their part to maintain the common good. Individuals can become "free riders" by taking the benefits the common good provides while refusing to do their part to support the common good. An adequate water supply, for example, is a common good from which all people benefit. But to maintain an adequate supply of water during a drought, people must conserve water, which entails sacrifices. Some individuals may be reluctant to do their share, however, since they know that so long as enough other people conserve, they can enjoy the benefits without reducing their own consumption. If enough people become free riders in this way, the common good which depends on their support will be destroyed. Many observers believe that this is exactly what has happened to many of our common goods, such as the environment or education, where the reluctance of all person to support efforts to maintain the health of these systems has led to their virtual collapse. The third problem encountered by attempts to promote the common good is that of individualism. our historical traditions place a high value on individual freedom, on personal rights, and on allowing each person to "do her own thing". Our culture views society as comprised of separate independent individuals who are free to pursue their own individual goals and interests without interference from others. In this individualistic culture it is difficult, perhaps impossible, to convince people that they should sacrifice some of their freedom, some of their personal goals, and some of their self-interest, for the sake of the "common good". Our cultural traditions, in fact, reinforce the individual who thinks that she should not have to contribute to the community's common good, but should be left free to pursue her own personal ends.

Finally, appeals to the common good are confronted by the problem of an unequal sharing of burdens. Maintaining a common good often requires that particular individuals or particular groups bear costs that are much greater than those borne by others. Maintaining an unpolluted environment, for example, may require that particular firms that pollute install costly pollution control devices, undercutting profits. Making employment opportunities more equal may require that some groups, such as white males, sacrifice their own employment chances. Making the health system affordable and accessible to all may require that insurers accept lower premiums, that physicians accept lower salaries, or that those with particularly costly diseases or conditions forego the medical treatment on which their live depend. Forcing particular groups or individuals to carry such unequal burdens "for the sake of the common good", is, at least arguably, unjust. Moreover, the prospect of having to carry such heavy and unequal burdens leads such groups and individuals to resist any attempts to secure common goods.

All of these problems pose considerable obstacles to those who call for an ethic of the common good. Still, appeals to the common good ought not to be dismissed. For they urge us to reflect on broad questions concerning the kind of society we want to become and how we are to achieve that society. They also challenge us to view ourselves as members of the same community and, while respecting and valuing the freedom of individuals to pursue their own goals, to recognize and further those goals we share in common.

Subaltern (Postcolonialism)

Subaltern is a term that commonly refers to persons who are socially, politically, and geographically outside of the hegemonic power structure.

History

In the 1970s, the term began to be used as a reference to colonized people in the South Asian subcontinent. It provided a new perspective on the history of a colonized place from the perspective of the colonized rather than from the perspective of the hegemonic power. Marxist historians had already begun to view colonial history from the perspective of the proletariat, but this was unsatisfying as it was still a Eurocentric way of viewing the globe. "Subaltern Studies" began in the early 1980s as an "intervention in South Asian historiography." While it began as a model for the Subcontinent, it quickly developed into a "vigorous postcolonial critique." Subaltern is now regularly used as a term in history, anthropology, sociology, human geography, and literature.

Meanings

The term subaltern is used in postcolonial theory. The exact meaning of the term in current philosophical and critical usage is disputed. Some thinkers use it in a general sense to refer to marginalized groups and the lower classes-a person rendered without agency by his or her social status. Others, such as Gayatri Chakravorty Spivak use it in a more specific sense. She argues that subaltern is not just a classy word for oppressed, for Other, for somebody who's not getting a piece of the pie....In postcolonial terms, everything that has limited or no access to the cultural imperialism is subaltern-a space of difference. Now who would say that's just the oppressed?

The working class is oppressed. It's not subaltern....Many people want to claim subalternity. They are the least interesting and the most dangerous. I mean, just by being a discriminated-against minority on the university campus, they don't need the word 'subaltern'...They should see what the mechanics of the discrimination are. They're within the hegemonic discourse wanting a piece of the pie and not being allowed, so let them speak, use the hegemonic discourse. They should not call themselves subaltern."

Subaltern was first used in a non-military sense by Marxist Antonio Gramsci. Some believe that he used the term as a synonym for proletariat, possibly as a code word in order to get his writings past prison censors, while others believe his usage to be more announced and less clearcut.

In several essays, Homi Bhabha, a key thinker within postcolonial thought, emphasizes the importance of social power relations in his working definition of 'subaltern' groups as oppressed, minority groups whose presence was crucial to the self-definition of the majority group: subaltern social groups were also in a position to subvert the authority of those who had hegemonic power.

Boaventura de Sousa Santos uses the term 'subaltern cosmopolitanism' extensively in his 2002 book *Toward a New Legal Common Sense*. He refers to this in the context of counter-hegemonic practices, movements, resistances and struggles against neoliberal globalization, particularly the struggle against social exclusion. He uses the term interchangeably with cosmopolitan legality as the diverse normative framework for an 'equality of differences'. Here, the term subaltern is used to denote marginalised and oppressed people(s) specifically struggling against hegemonic globalization.

Theory

Postcolonial theory tries to understand the power and continued dominance of Western ways of knowing. Joanne Sharp, following Spivak, argues that other forms of knowing are marginalised by Western thinkers reforming them as myth or folklore. In order to be heard the subaltern must adopt Western thought, reasoning and language. Because of this, Sharp and Spivak argues that the subaltern can never express their own reasoning, forms of knowledge or logic, they must instead form their knowledge to Western ways of knowing.

The academic engagement with the "other." To truly engage with the subaltern they argue that an academic would need to decentre themselves as the expert. Traditionally the academic wants to know about the subaltern's experiences but not their own explanations of those experiences. Hooks argues that in Western knowledge a true explanation can only come from the expertise of the academic. The subordinated subject, gives up their knowledge for the use of the Western academic. Hooks describes the relationship between the academic and the subaltern subject:

No need to hear your voice when I can talk about you better than you can speak about yourself. No need to hear your voice. Only tell me about your pain. I want to know your story. And then I will tell it back to you in a new way. Tell it back to you in such a way that it has become mine, my own. Re-writing you I write myself anew. I am still author, authority. I am still colonizer the speaking subject and you are now at the centre of my talk.

Edward Said's work on Orientalism is related to the idea of the subaltern in that it explains the way in which Orientalism produced the foundation and the justification for the domination of the "other" through colonialism. Europeans, Said argues, created an imagined geography of the Orient before European exploration through predefined images of savage and monstrous places that lay outside of the known world. During initial exploration of the Orient these mythologies were reinforced as travellers brought back reports of monsters and strange lands. The idea of difference and strangeness of the Orient continued to be perpetuated through media and discourse creating an "us" and "them" binary through which Europeans defined themselves by defining the differences of the Orient. This laid the foundation for colonialism by presenting the Orient as backward and irrational and therefore in need of help to become modern in the European sense. The discourse of Orientalism is Eurocentric and does not seek to include the voices of the Orientals themselves.

Stuart Hall argues for the power of discourse to create and reinforce Western dominance. The discourses on how Europe described differences between itself and others used European cultural categories, languages and ideas to represent the other. The knowledge produced by a discourse gets put into practice and then becomes reality. By producing a discourse of difference Europe was able to maintain its dominance over the "other" thereby creating a subaltern by excluding the "other" from the production of the discourse.

Development Discourse

Mainstream development discourse built on colonial and Orientalism knowledges. It focuses on modernization theory which follows the idea that in order to modernize underdeveloped countries should follow the path of developed Western countries. It is characterized by free trade, open markets and capitalist systems as the way to development. Mainstream development discourse focuses on applying universal policies at a national level.

Victoria Lawson critiques mainstream development discourse as recreating the subaltern. The discourse does this by: being disengaged from other scales such as the local or community level; not considering regional, class, ethnic, gender etc. differences between places; continuing to treat the subjects of development as subordinate and lacking knowledge; and by not including the subjects voices and opinions in development policies and practices.

While the subaltern by definition are groups who have had their voice's silenced, they can speak through their actions as a way to protest against mainstream development and create their own visions for development. Subaltern groups are creating social movements which contest and disassemble Western claims to power. These groups use local knowledge and struggles to create new spaces of opposition and alternative futures.

Feminist Perspectives on the Self

The topic of the self has long been salient in feminist philosophy, for it is pivotal to questions about personhood, identity, the body, and agency that feminism must address. In some respects, Simone de Beauvoir's trenchant observation, "He is the Subject, he is the Absolute—she is the Other," sums up why the self is such an important issue for feminism. To be the Other is to be the non-subject, the non-person, the non-agent—in short, the mere body. In law, in customary practice, and in cultural stereotypes, women's selfhood has been systematically subordinated, diminished, and belittled, when it has not been outright denied. Since women have been cast as lesser forms of the masculine individual, the paradigm of the self that has gained ascendancy in U.S. popular culture and in Western philosophy is derived from the experience of the predominantly white and heterosexual, mostly economically advantaged men who have wielded social, economic, and political power and who have dominated the arts, literature, the media, and scholarship. Responding to this state of affairs, feminist philosophical work on the self has taken three main tacks: (1) critique of established views of the self, (2) reclamation of women's selfhood, and (3) reconceptualization of the self to incorporate women's experience. This entry will survey feminist perspectives on the self from all three of these angles.

Critique

Two views of the self have been prominent in contemporary Anglo-American moral and political philosophy—a Kantian ethical subject and homo economicus. Both of these conceptions see the individual as a free and rational chooser and actor—an autonomous agent. Nevertheless, they differ in their emphasis. The Kantian ethical subject uses reason to transcend cultural norms and to discover absolute moral truth, whereas homo economicus uses reason to rank desires in a coherent order and to figure out how to maximize desire satisfaction. Whether the self is identified with pure abstract reason or with the instrumental rationality of the marketplace, though, these conceptions of the self isolate the individual from personal relationships and larger social forces. For the Kantian ethical subject, emotional bonds and social conventions imperil objectivity and undermine commitment to duty. For homo economicus, it makes no difference what social forces shape one's desires provided they do not result from coercion or fraud, and one's ties to other people are to be factored into one's calculations and planning along with the rest of one's desires. Some feminist philosophers modify and defend these conceptions of the self. But their decontextualized individualism and their privileging of reason over other capacities trouble many feminist philosophers.

Twentieth century philosophy's regnant conceptions of the self minimize the personal and moral import of unchosen circumstances and interpersonal relationships. They eclipse family, friendship, passionate love, and community, and they downplay the difficulty of resolving conflicts that arise between these commitments and personal values and aspirations. Since dependency is dismissed as a defective form of selfhood, caregiving responsibilities vanish along with children, the disabled, and the frail elderly. Prevailing conceptions of the self ignore the multiple, sometimes fractious sources of social identity constituted by one's gender, sexual orientation, race, class, age, ethnicity, and so forth. Structural domination and subordination do not penetrate the "inner citadel" of selfhood. Likewise, these conceptions deny the complexity of the intrapsychic world of unconscious fantasies, fears, and desires, and they overlook the ways in which such materials intrude upon conscious life. The homogenized—you might say sterilized—rational subject is not prey to ambivalence, anxiety, obsession, prejudice, hatred, or violence. A disembodied mind, the body is peripheral—a source of desires for homo economicus to weigh and a distracting temptation for the Kantian ethical subject. Age, looks, sexuality, and physical competencies are extraneous to the self. As valuable as the capacities for rational analysis and free choice undoubtedly are, it is hard to believe that there is nothing more to the self.

Feminist philosophers have charged that these views are, at best, incomplete and, at worst, fundamentally misleading. Many feminist critiques take the question of who provides the paradigm for these conceptions as their point of departure. Who models this free, rational self? Although represented as genderless, sexless, raceless, ageless, and classless, feminists argue that the Kantian ethical subject and homo economicus mask a white, healthy, youthfully middle-aged, middle-class, heterosexual man. He is pictured in two principle roles—as an impartial judge or legislator reflecting on principles and deliberating about policies and as a self-interested bargainer and contractor wheeling and dealing in the marketplace. It is no accident that politics and commerce are both domains from which women have historically been excluded. It is no accident either that the philosophers who originated these views of the self typically endorsed this exclusion. Deeming women emotional and unprincipled, these thinkers advocated confining women to the domestic sphere where their vices could be neutralized, even transformed into virtues, in the role of submissive wife and nurturant mother.

Feminist critics point out, furthermore, that this misogynist heritage cannot be remedied simply by condemning these traditional constraints and advocating equal rights for women, for these conceptions of the self are themselves gendered. In western culture, the mind and reason are coded masculine, whereas the body and emotion are coded feminine (Lloyd 1992). To identify the self with the rational mind is, then, to masculinize the self. If selfhood is not impossible for women, it is only because they resemble men in certain essential respects—they are not altogether devoid of rational will. Yet, feminine selves are necessarily deficient, for they only mimic and approximate the masculine ideal.

Problematic, as well, is the way in which these gendered conceptions of the self contribute to the valorization of the masculine and the stigmatization of the feminine. The masculine realm of rational selfhood is a realm of moral decency—principled respect for others and conscientious fidelity to duty—and of prudent good sense—adherence to shrewd, fulfilling, long-range life plans. However, femininity is associated with emotionally rooted concern for family and friends that spawns favoritism and compromises principles. Likewise, femininity is associated with immersion in unpredictable domestic exigencies that forever jeopardize the best-laid plans and often necessitate resorting to hasty retreats or charting new directions. By comparison, the masculinized self appears to be a sturdy fortress of integrity. How flattering! The self is essentially masculine, and the masculine self is essentially good and wise.

Feminists object that this philosophical consolidation of the pre-eminence of the masculine over the feminine rests on untenable assumptions about the transparency of the self, the immunity of the self to noxious social influences, and the reliability of reason as a corrective to distorted moral judgment. Today people grow up in social environments in which culturally normative prejudice persists, even in communities where overt forms of bigotry are strictly proscribed (Meyers 1994). Although official cultural norms uphold the values of equality and tolerance, cultures continue to transmit camouflaged messages of the inferiority of historically subordinated social groups through stereotypes and other imagery. These deeply ingrained schemas commonly structure attitudes, perception, and judgment despite the individual's conscious good will (Valian 1998). As a result, people often consider themselves objective and fair, and yet they systematically discriminate against "different" others while favouring members of their own social group (Piper 1990; Young 1990). Fortified by culture and ensconced in the unconscious, such prejudice cannot be dispelled through rational reflection alone (Meyers 1994). In effect, then, the Kantian moral subject countenances "innocent" wrongdoing and occluded reinforcement of the social stratification that privileges the minority of men whom this conception takes as paradigmatic.

These oversights necessitate reconceptualizing the self in two respects. To account for the residual potency of this form of prejudice, feminists urge, the self must be understood as socially situated and murkily heterogeneous. To account for the self's ability to discern and resist culturally normative prejudice, the moral subject must not be reduced to the capacity for reason.

Complementing this line of argument, a number of feminists argue that conceptualizing the self as a seamless whole has invidious social consequences. To realize this ideal, it is necessary to repress inner diversity and conflict and to police the boundaries of the purified self. Alien desires and impulses are consigned to the unconscious, but this unconscious material inevitably intrudes upon conscious life and influences people's attitudes and desires. In particular, the feared and despised Other within is projected onto "other" social groups, and hatred and contempt are redirected at these imagined enemies (Scheman 1993; Kristeva 1991). Misogyny and other forms of bigotry are thus borne of the demand that the self be unitary together with the impossibility of meeting this demand. Worse still, these irrational hatreds cannot be cured unless this demand is repudiated, but to repudiate this demand is to be resigned to a degraded, feminized self. Far from functioning as the guarantor of moral probity, the Kantian moral subject is the condition of the possibility of intractable animosity and injustice.

Another strand of feminist critique targets homo economicus's preoccupation with independence and planning. In an eery suspension of biological reality, selves are conceived as sufficient unto themselves. No one seems to be born and raised, for birth mothers and caregivers are driven offstage. The self appears to materialize on its own, endowed with a starter set of basic desires, ready to select additional desires and construct overarching goals, and skilled in performing instrumental rationality tasks. No one's powers ever seem to deteriorate either, for time is suspended along with biology. Since dependency is denied, no morally significant preconsensual or nonconsensual entanglements at the beginning or the end of life need be acknowledged. All affiliations are to be freely chosen, and all transactions are to be freely negotiated. The repudiation of feminine caregiving underwrites the illusion of independence, and the illusion of independence underwrites homo economicus's voluntarism.

To achieve maximal fulfillment, homo economicus must organize his chosen pursuits into a rational life plan. He must decide which desires are most urgent; he must ensure that his desires are co-satisfiable; and he must ascertain the most efficient way to satisfy this set of desires. Madcap spontaneity and seat-of-the-pants improvisation are registered as defeats for "The Man with the Plan." Not only is this vision of a life governed by a self-chosen plan distinctly middleclass, it is gendered. The mother coping with the vagaries of early childhood and the wife accommodating her man's plan are the antitheses of this conception of the self.

Uncertain of where they are ultimately headed and seldom sure how to achieve the goals they embrace as they go along, these women violate norms of selfhood. Ironically, middleclass men who grow old also have difficulty measuring up to homo economicus's standards of control. Unable to count on continued health and vigor, unable to anticipate the onset of serious disease or disabling conditions, unable finally to outwit the grim reaper, affluent elderly men violate norms of selfhood along with women and the poor. The price of denying the relationality of the self and idolizing rational self-regulation is that full selfhood eludes all but a lucky, albeit transitory, male elite.

A further problem with this view from a feminist standpoint is that it fails to furnish an adequate account of internalized oppression and the process of overcoming it. It is common for women to comport themselves in a feminine fashion, to scale down their aspirations, and to embrace gender-compliant goals. Feminists account for this phenomenon by explaining that women internalize patriarchal values and norms—that is, these pernicious values and norms become integrated in the cognitive, emotional, and conative structure of the self. Once embedded in a woman's psychic economy, internalized oppression conditions her desires. To maximize satisfaction of her desires, then, would be to collaborate in her own oppression. Paradoxically, the more completely she fulfills these desires, the worse off she becomes. Advantaged as he is, homo economicus can safely accept his desires as given and proceed without ado to orchestrate a plan to satisfy them. But women and members of other subordinated groups can ill-afford such complacency, and homo economicus's instrumental reason is too superficial a form of mastery to serve their interests (Babbitt 1993). They need a conception of the self that renders emancipatory transformation of one's values and projects intelligible.

Feminist critique exposes the partiality of the ostensibly universal Kantian ethical subject and homo economicus. These conceptions of the self are: 1) androcentric because they replicate masculine stereotypes and ideals; 2) sexist because they demean anything that smacks of the feminine; and 3) masculinist because they help to perpetuate male dominance. I leave the heterosexist, racist, ethnocentric, ableist, and classist dimensions of these conceptions to other encyclopedia articles.

Reclamation

Feminist critiques, we have seen, accuse regnant philosophical accounts of masculinizing the self. One corollary of this masculinized view of selfhood is that women are consigned to selflessness—that is, to invisibility, subservient passivity, and self-sacrificial altruism.

This nullification of women's selfhood was once explicitly codified in law. The legal doctrine of coverture held that a woman's personhood was absorbed into that of her husband when she married (McDonagh 1996). The wife's assuming her husband's surname symbolizes this revocation of her separate identity. In addition, coverture deprived the wife of her right to bodily integrity, for rape within marriage was not recognized as a crime, nor was it illegal for a husband to beat his wife. She lost her right to property, as well, for her husband was entitled to control her earnings, and she was barred from making contracts in her own name. Lacking the right to vote or to serve on juries, she was a second-class citizen whose enfranchised husband purportedly represented her politically.

Although coverture has been rescinded, vestiges of this denial of women's selfhood can be discerned in recent legal rulings, and the doctrine remains influential in culture. For example, pregnant women remain vulnerable to legally sanctioned violations of their right to bodily integrity. Courts have forced pregnant women to submit to invasive medical procedures for the sake of the fetuses they were carrying, although no court would compel any other woman or man to undergo comparable procedures for the sake of a living individual, including a family member (Bordo 1993). Selflessness remains the pregnant woman's legal status. Moreover, the stereotype of feminine selflessness still thrives in the popular imagination. Any self-confident, self-assertive woman is out of step with prevalent gender norms, and a mother who is not unstintingly devoted to her children is likely to be perceived as selfish and face severe social censure. Despite the fact that it is no longer legally mandatory for wives to give up their maiden names, many women adhere to this custom and perpetuate this traditional gesture of self-renunciation.

A tension within feminism complicates the project of reclaiming women's selfhood, however. The claim that women are systematically subordinated and that this subordination has a grievous impact on women's lives is central to feminism. Yet, this key insight seems to belie the claim that women's selfhood and agency have been overlooked. To be unjustly subordinated, it would seem, is to be diminished in one's selfhood and to have one's agency curtailed. Otherwise, what's the harm? Some feminists have endorsed this very position. Arguing that moral virtues have no gender, Mary Wollstonecraft regards "feminine" virtues as perversions of true human virtues and laments women's conscription into a bogus ideal (Wollstonecraft 1792). Similarly but more vividly, Simone de Beauvoir labels women "mutilated" and "immanent" (Beauvoir 1952). Socialized to objectify themselves, women become narcissistic, small-minded, and dependent on others' approval. Excluded from careers, waiting to be chosen by their future husbands, taken over by natural forces during pregnancy, busy with tedious, repetitive housework, women never become transcendent agents. Indeed, they are content not to assume the burden of responsibility for their own freedom. Cast in the role of man's power and at the mercy of feminine vices, women succumb to bad faith and surrender their agency.

This portrayal of women as abject victims has been challenged and modulated in contemporary feminist philosophy. I shall review four major reclamation strategies: 1) rethinking the activities of mothering, 2) developing an ethic of care, 3) exploring separatist practices, and 4) reconceiving autonomy.

The conventional view of pregnancy and birth classifies them as merely biological processes, and the conventional view of mothering classifies it as a merely instinctual activity. Feminists demonstrate that these assessments are sorely mistaken. Both pregnancy and birthgiving engage women's agentic powers. Not only does pregnancy raise the question of whether to have an abortion, but also a woman's decision to proceed with a pregnancy entails learning to care for herself in previously unnecessary ways (Held 1989). In the last few decades, medical technologies, such as sonography and fetal surgery, have raised new issues for pregnant women and sometimes confront them with wrenching choices that test their agentic resilience. Arguably, routine pregnancy and birthgiving mobilize specific agentic capacities, such as "active waiting" and coping with "chosen and predictable pain" (Ruddick 1994).

A related feminist innovation focuses on analyzing the discipline of mothering to grasp its aims, its forms of thought, its ideal form, and its characteristic values and disvalues (Ruddick

1989). Caring for a child imposes a set of demands—for preservation (survival), for growth (development into a healthy adult), and for acceptability (enculturation that ensures fitting into a community). Meeting these demands involves a range of activities that are governed by a distinctive set of values: protecting a fragile existence, acknowledging the limits of one's power and the unpredictability of events, cheerful determination to persist despite setbacks, responsive adaptability, sensitivity to the child's subjective viewpoint, and tolerance for inconclusive processes of disclosure. Although the practice of mothering places no premium on independence, self-interest, free choice, power, advance planning, or control, it clearly calls upon a wide range of interpersonal and reflective skills and enlists caregivers' agentic capacities. Dumb instinct hardly suffices for good childcare.

Like feminists who have reclaimed women's agency as mothers, feminists who have developed different versions of care ethics insist on taking women's experience seriously and use this experience as a basis for new approaches to morality and social policy. The aim of the psychological studies that first made the voice of care audible was to recognize and understand the capacities for moral judgment of women whose competency had been underrated. Previous research comparing boys' and girls' moral development had concluded that girls' development was stunted, but Carol Gilligan argues that this assessment misconstrued the data (Gilligan 1982). According to Gilligan, there are two paths of moral development. Many girls and women but almost no men follow the care trajectory (Gilligan 1987). Since earlier investigations first studied U.S. boys and men and used these interviews to generalize about people's moral development, researchers noticed only one path, namely, the justice trajectory. By repudiating the assumption that the masculine is the human norm and by studying girls and women, Gilligan discovered an alternative mode of moral cognition—the Care Perspective. Constituted by a distinctive set of framing concepts and a distinctive set of reflective skills, the morality of care is not translatable into the morality of justice that Gilligan's predecessors had taken to be the gauge of moral development. The Care Perspective, in Gilligan's view, is a different and equally good way to interpret moral situations and to decide how to act. Moreover, by noticing this alternative, we are able to recognize women's moral agency and defend women against the age-old charge that they are morally inferior to men.

Although some feminist philosophers criticize Gilligan's investigations on empirical or philosophical grounds (Moody-Adams 1991; Friedman 1993; Card 1996; Fraser and Nicholson 1990), her research prompted a number of feminist philosophers to develop moral theories marked by quite different emphases from those of traditional moral theories. The theme of human interconnectedness and the value of intersubjectivity are prominent in contemporary feminist moral philosophy. A climate of trust forms an indispensable background for all sorts of undertakings, but no voluntaristic ethic can account for trust (Baier 1986). The ability to empathize with other individuals and imaginatively reconstruct their unique subjective viewpoints is vital to moral insight and wise moral choice, but ethics that base moral judgment on a universal conception of the person marginalize this skill (Meyers 1994). By developing narratives of one's moral identity, one's relationships, and one's values and sharing those narratives with one's associates, one endows one's life with moral meaning and integrity, but rationalistic ethics overlook this process of self-disclosure and interpersonal mediation (Walker 1998). Taking responsibility for who one is and how one shall respond is a salient feature of informal personal relationships, yet justice oriented ethics focus exclusively on being held responsible for what one has done and the credit or blame one's actions may deserve (Card 1996). Appreciating the inevitability of dependency and the need for care demonstrates the poverty of conceiving justice exclusively in terms of rights not to be interfered with and the urgency of developing a theory of justice that includes provisions for care (Kittay 1999). In each instance, feminist moral theorists revalue that which is traditionally deemed feminine—feeling, intimacy, nurturance, and so forth. By highlighting these contexts and values, they reclaim the venues traditionally associated with women as morally significant sites, and they reclaim the moral agency of the individuals whose lives are centred in these sites.

A third approach to reclaiming women's agency spotlights several types of separatist practice—including friendship among women, lesbianism, support groups for rape victims and battered women, and women's consciousness raising and activist groups. Establishing and maintaining such affiliations presupposes self-willed defiance of norms of heterosexual fidelity and familial commitment. Thus, the very existence of these relationships testifies to women's awareness of their own needs and their capacity to act on them despite a repressive social context. Moreover, noting that unchosen relationships and communities of origin often prove oppressive to women and inimical to their agency, some feminists stress that it is important not to underestimate the role of chosen relationships and communities as sites of women's agency (Friedman 1993; Brison 1997; Hoagland 1988; Ferguson 1987; Frye 1983; MacKinnon 1982; Hartsock 1983). By cordoning off a social sphere of mutually attuned, mutually concerned women, separatism in all its forms turns down the racket of patriarchy. Separatist associations provide forums in which women can exchange personal confidences, secure in the knowledge that other participants will empathize with their dissatisfactions and frustrations as well as their joys and triumphs and that others will be receptive to their worries and complaints. Isolation often confounds women's subjectivity and agency, for in isolation their problems appear to be personal failings if not pathologies. Separatism overcomes isolation. It affords women the opportunity to develop language that makes sense of their anomalous experience and that restores their self-esteem together with the opportunity to reflect on the social meanings of their experience. Within separatist contexts, women find support for their resistance to social norms and their struggles to overcome personal privations or pressures.

Separatist practices relieve women of the burden of Otherness. Each woman is an equal among equals. Each woman's subjectivity and agency are affirmed. Thus, feminist philosophers seek not only to chronicle the ways in which women have created pockets of separatism within patriarchal systems but also to theorize the forms of subjectivity and agency that flourish in these sites.

Autonomy is a key issue for this theoretical project. Although some feminists dismiss autonomy as an androcentric relic of modernism (Jaggar 1983; Addelson 1994; Hekman 1995; Card

1996), others assert women's need for self-determination (de Lauretis 1986; King 1988; Lugones and Spelman 1983; Govier 1993). In light of the history of figuring women as driven by their reproductive biology and in need of rational male guidance and the history of women's enforced economic dependence on men or relegation to poorly paid, often despised forms of labor, feminists can hardly ignore the topic of self-determination. Thus, a number of feminist philosophers take up this challenge and present accounts of autonomy that do not devalue the interpersonal capacities and social contributions that are conventionally coded feminine (Nedelsky 1989; Meyers 1989 and 2000; Benhabib 1995 and 1999; Weir 1995). In feminist accounts, autonomy is not conflicted with self-sufficiency and free will, but rather it is seen to be facilitated by supportive relationships and also to be a matter of degree.

Whereas standard philosophical accounts of autonomy confine their social critique to the observation that pluralistic societies that respect basic rights are more conducive to autonomy, feminist accounts point up how subordination constrains autonomy and how egalitarian communities augment it (Meyers 1989; Babbitt 1993; Benhabib 1995).

Whereas standard philosophical accounts intellectualize autonomy and stress rational decision making, feminist accounts accent the role of feelings in autonomous lives. Whereas standard philosophical accounts spotlight the autonomous individual's independence and immunity to others' influence, feminist accounts stress the autonomous individual's need for constructive feedback, advice, and encouragement. Whereas standard philosophical accounts trace autonomy to endorsing and prioritizing a coherent set of desires and goals and to scheduling fulfillment of these objectives, feminist accounts view autonomy as an ongoing and improvisational process of exercising self-discovery, self-definition, and self-direction skills (Meyers 1989 and 2000). Whereas standard philosophical accounts see autonomy as an all-or-nothing achievement, feminist accounts note how autonomy skills piggyback on seemingly unrelated ancillary skills, how autonomy skills may be exercised in certain contexts yet deactivated in others, and how different degrees of skillfulness yield varying degrees of autonomy.

Feminist accounts of autonomy strike a balance between recognizing the injury that subordination does to women's sense of self and agency and respecting the measure of autonomy women gain despite this subjugation. Subordination endangers women's autonomy in a number of ways. Not only does internalized oppression mold women's desires and alienate them from themselves, but also those in subordinate positions are offered all sorts of incentives to minimize friction and ease their lot by placating those with power (Card 1996). Likewise, well-meaning friends are all too likely to counsel the course of least resistance, namely, compliance with convention regardless of one's personal values and aspirations. Another effect of systematic subordination is that women's autonomy skills may be poorly developed or poorly coordinated, and exercising these skills is rarely rewarded and generally discouraged (Meyers 1989). Deficient autonomy skills compound the threat internalized oppression poses.

Still, feminist accounts of autonomy enable us to understand why women do not completely lack autonomy and how women's autonomy can be augmented. The self-discovery, self-definition, and self-direction skills that secure autonomy are commonplace (Meyers 1989). Indeed, some of them,such as introspective attunement to feelings and receptiveness to others' feedback, are gender-compatible for and often promoted in women. Although others, such as rational planning and self-assertion, are coded masculine, many women in fact have considerable proficiency in these areas. All too often, however, they exercise these skills only in narrowly restricted, gender-appropriate contexts. For example, a homemaker may demonstrate remarkable instrumental reason skills in running her household, or a mother may exhibit effective self-assertion skills in dealing with a teacher who has mistreated her child. Yet, these women may come off as inept, helpless, and meek in other situations. Thus, augmenting women's autonomy is often a matter of emboldening women to extend the range of application of their existing autonomy skills and fostering the development of weak skills. It is evident, then, why separatist practices of various kinds are conducive to women's autonomy. By inviting women to marshall their autonomy skills and reinforcing women's determination to carry out their decisions, they function as autonomy workshops.

Still, from a feminist perspective, separatist practices are merely transitional and ameliorative. In addition, the patriarchal social structures that relentlessly undermine women's autonomy must be changed, and women's selfhood and agency must be legally and culturally affirmed. Thus, feminist philosophers defend a variety of social policy initiatives that expand the scope of women's choices and that respect women as self-directing individuals. Feminist philosophers have been in the forefront in arguing for egalitarian families, in legitimating economic opportunity for women, in opposing harassment of women in workplaces, in defending women's reproductive rights, and in condemning violence against women in all its forms. In each instance, greater justice for women strikes a blow against the masculinized self of traditional philosophy by securing greater social recognition for the female agentic self.

Reconceptualizations

The Nature of the Self

The primary task of a philosophy of the self is to clarify what makes something a self. Feminist philosophers are acutely aware that this is not a value-free task. To get an analysis of the nature of the self off the ground, one must decide which entities count as selves (or, at least, which entities are noncontroversially counted as selves within one's linguistic community). Since we regard selves as valuable—as members of our moral community and as worthy of respect—these judgments are in part judgments about which entities are valuable. Moreover, values enter into these judgments because we consider selves to be the sorts of things that can achieve (or fail to achieve) ideals of selfhood. Thus, philosophical accounts of the self have implications for conceptions of what it is to lead a good life. As we have seen, many feminist philosophers argue that it is a mistake to hold that rationality alone is essential to the self and that the ideal self is transparent, unified, coherent, and independent, for they discern misogynist subtexts in the atomistic individualism of the Kantian ethical subject and homo economicus. It is incumbent on feminist philosophers, then, to develop more satisfactory accounts of the self—accounts that are compatible with respect for women. Thus, a number of feminist philosophers propose reconstructions of alternative theories of the nature of the self.

Three traditions have been especially influential in recent feminist thought—classic psychoanalysis, object relations theory, and poststructuralism. Feminist philosophers gravitate toward these approaches to understanding selfhood because they do not share the drawbacks that prompt feminist critique of the Kantian ethical subject and homo economicus. None of these approaches regards the self as homogeneous or transparent; none supposes that a self should be coherent and speak in a single voice; none removes the self from its cultural or interpersonal setting; n one sidelines the body. In appropriating these views, feminists bring out their implications in regard to gender, incorporate feminist insights into these theories, and modify the theories to address feminist concerns.

Julia Kristeva transposes the classic Freudian conception of the self and the distinction between consciousness and the unconscious into an explicitly gendered discursive framework (Kristeva 1980). For Kristeva, the self is a subject of enunciation—a speaker who can use the pronoun 'I'. But speakers are not unitary, nor are they fully in control of what they say because discourse is bifurcated. The symbolic dimension of language, which is characterized by referential signs and linear logic, corresponds to consciousness and control. The clear, dry prose of scientific research reports epitomizes symbolic discourse. The semiotic dimension of language, which is characterized by figurative language, cadences, and intonations, corresponds to the unruly, passion-fueled unconscious. The ambiguities and nonstandard usages of poetry epitomize semiotic discourse. These paradigms notwithstanding, Kristeva maintains that all discourse combines elements of both registers. Every intelligible utterance relies on semantic conventions, and every utterance has a tone, even if it is a dull monotone. This contention connects Kristeva's account to feminist concerns about gender and the self. Since the rational orderliness of the symbolic is culturally coded masculine while the affect-laden allure of the semiotic is culturally coded feminine, it follows that no discourse is purely masculine or purely feminine. The masculine symbolic and the feminine semiotic are equally indispensable to the speaking subject, whatever this individual's socially assigned gender may be. It is not possible, then, to be an unsulliedly masculine self or an unsulliedly feminine self. Every subject of enunciation—every self—amalgamates masculine and feminine discursive modalities.

Like the unconscious in classic psychoanalytic theory, the semiotic decenters the self. One may try to express one's thoughts in definite, straightforward language, yet because of the semiotic aspects of one's utterances, what one says carries no single meaning and is amenable to being interpreted in more than one way. In Kristeva's view, this is all to the good, for accessing the semiotic—that which is conveyed, often inadvertently, by the style of an utterance—kindles social critique. The semiotic gives expression to repressed, unconscious material. According to Kristeva, what society systematically represses provides clues to what is oppressive about society and how society needs to be changed. Thus, she discerns a vital ethical potential in the semiotic (Kristeva 1987). Since this ethical potential is explicitly linked to the feminine, moreover, Kristeva's account of the self displaces "masculine" adherence to principle as the prime mode of ethical agency and recognizes the urgent need for a "feminine" ethical approach. Viewing the self as a "questionable-subject-in-process"—a subject who is responsive to the encroachments of semiotic material into conscious life and who is therefore without a fixed or unitary identity—and valorizing the dissident potential of this decentered subjectivity, Kristeva seeks to neutralize the fear of the inchoate feminine that, in her view, underwrites misogyny. In one respect, Nancy Chodorow's appropriation of object relations theory parallels Kristeva's project of reclaiming and revaluing femininity, for Chodorow's account of the relational self reclaims and revalues feminine mothering capacities. But whereas Kristeva focuses on challenging the homogeneous self and the bright line between reason, on the one hand, and emotion and desire, on the other, Chodorow focuses on challenging the self-subsisting self with its sharp self-other boundaries. Chodorow's claim that the self is inextricable from interpersonal relationships calls into question the decontextualized individualism of the Kantian ethical subject and homo economicus.

Chodorow sees the self as relational in several respects (Chodorow 1981). Every child is cared for by an adult or adults, and every individual is shaped for better or worse by this emotionally charged interaction. As a result of feelings of need and moments of frustration, the infant becomes differentiated from its primary caregiver and develops a sense of separate identity. Concomitantly, a distinctive personality emerges. By selectively internalizing and recombining elements of their experience with other people, children develop characteristic traits and dispositions. Moreover, Chodorow attributes the development of a key interpersonal capacity to nurturance. A caregiver who is experienced as warmly solicitous is internalized as a "good internal mother" (Chodorow 1980). Children gain a sense of their worthiness by internalizing the nurturance they receive and directing it toward themselves, and they learn to respect and respond to other people by internalizing their experience of nurturance and projecting it toward others. Whereas Kristeva understands the self as a dynamic interplay between the feminine semiotic and the masculine symbolic, Chodorow understands the self as fundamentally relational and thus linked to cultural norms of feminine interpersonal responsiveness. For Chodorow, the rigidly differentiated, compulsively rational, stubbornly independent self is a masculine defensive formation—a warped form of the relational self—that develops as a result of fathers' negligible involvement in childcare.

Feminist philosophers have noted strengths and weaknesses in both of these views. For example, Kristeva's questionable-subject-in-process seems to enshrine and endorse the very gender dichotomy that causes women so much grief. Yet, Chodorow's relational self seems to glorify weak individuation and scorn the independence and self-assertiveness that many women desperately need. Still, Kristeva's analyses of the psychic, social, and political potency of gender figurations underscore the need for feminist counter-imagery to offset culturally entrenched, patriarchal images of womanhood. And Chodorow's appreciation of the relational self together with her diagnosis of the damage wrought by hyperindividuation advances feminist demands for equitable parenting practices. These contributions notwithstanding, both of these views have come under attack for heterosexist biases as well as for inattention to other forms of difference among women.

Critical race theorists and poststructuralists have been particularly vocal about this failure to come to grips with the diversity of gender, and they have offered accounts of the self designed to accommodate difference. Poststructuralist Judith Butler maintains that personal identity—the sense that there are answers to the questions 'who am I?' and 'what am I like?'—is an illusion (Butler 1990). The self is merely an unstable discursive node—a shifting confluence of multiple discursive currents—and sexed/gendered identity is merely a "corporeal style"—the imitation and repeated enactment of ubiquitous norms. For Butler, psychodynamic accounts of the self, including Kristeva's and Chodorow's, camouflage the performative nature of the self and collaborate in the cultural conspiracy that maintains the illusion that one has an emotionally anchored, interior identity that is derived from one's biological nature, which is manifest in one's genitalia. Such accounts are pernicious. In concealing the ways in which normalizing regimes deploy power to enforce the performative routines that construct "natural" sexed/gendered bodies together with debased, "unnatural" bodies, they obscure the arbitrariness of the constraints that are being imposed and deflect resistance to these constraints. The solution, in Butler's view, is to question the categories of biological sex, polarized gender, and determinate sexuality that serve as markers of personal identity, to treat the construction of identity as a site of political contestation, and to embrace the subversive potential of unorthodox performances and parodic identities.

African American feminists are less sanguine than poststructuralists about the felicitous social impact of playful deviations from norms and the laughter they may prompt (Williams 1991; Crenshaw 1993). Nevertheless, some of them have adapted poststructuralist theory to the purposes of critical race theory. Noting that gender, race, and class stratification do not operate in isolation from one another but rather interact to produce compound effects, these theorists conceive of the individual as an intersectional subject—a site where structures of domination and subordination converge. Intersectional theory does not purport to offer a comprehensive theory of the self. Its aim is to capture those aspects of selfhood that are conditioned by membership in subordinated or privileged social groups. Accenting the liabilities of belonging to more than one subordinated group, Kimberle Crenshaw likens the position of such individuals to that of a pedestrian hit by several speeding vehicles simultaneously, and Maria Lugones likens their position to that of a stateless border-dweller who is not at home anywhere. Nevertheless, some theorists of mixed ancestry embrace border-dwelling as a model of positive identity. Moreover, proponents of the intersectional self credit multiply oppressed people with a certain epistemic advantage. In virtue of their suffering and alienation, these individuals are well situated not only to discern which values and practices in their heritage deserve allegiance but also to identify shortcomings in the traditions of the groups to which they belong. Thus, African American women are acutely aware of racism within feminism and sexism within the struggle for racial justice. Their intersectional positioning and subjectivity makes such insight virtually unavoidable.

By and large, recent feminist philosophy of the self reflects skepticism about modernist, unitary accounts of the self. In seeking to remedy the androcentric biases of the latter views, feminist philosophers emphasize features of selfhood that other philosophical schools neglect, including intersubjectivity, heterogeneity, and social construction. Still, some contemporary feminist philosophers express concern that the sorts of conceptions I have sketched are detrimental to feminist aims. Influenced by Jurgen Habermas's communicative ethics, Seyla Benhabib refuses to join poststructuralists in declaring the death of the autonomous, self-reflective individual who is capable of taking responsibility and acting on principle (Benhabib 1995). Although Benhabib is committed to viewing people as socially situated, interpersonally bonded, and embodied, she is also committed to the feasibility of rational philosophical justification of universal moral norms. Moreover, she argues that a narrative conception of the self renders the idea of a core self and coherent identity intelligible without suppressing difference and without insulating the self from social relations (Benhabib 1999). Autobiographical stories can include the many voices within us and the many relationships we have experienced, and these stories are constantly under revision, for they are always being contested by our associates' disparate self-narratives with their divergent versions of events. Nevertheless, these narratives do not collapse into incoherence, and they presuppose a core capacity to describe and reflect on one's experience. For Benhabib, this view of selfhood and reason is indispensable to feminist emancipatory objectives.

Gender and Identity

Postmodern challenges to the idea of a stable self and to the coherence of the category woman' have sparked a lively debate about the relation between gender and the self. If there is no such thing as a self with persistent attributes, it seems that gender cannot be a feature of every woman's identity. But if there is nothing that all women have in common, it seems that there are no interests that all women share, and there is nothing for feminism to be about. Several feminist philosophers have proposed accounts of the relation between gender and the self that aim to rescue feminism from this reductio. Linda Alcoff rejects both the universalized conceptions of gender that cultural feminists advocate and the deconstructions of the category 'woman' that poststructuralist feminists tender. Her alternative is to construe femininity as "positionality." Positionality has two dimensions (Alcoff 1994). First, it is the social context that locates the individual and that deprives her of power and mobility. Second, it is a political point of departure—the affirmation of women's collective right to take charge of their gendered identity. To be a woman is, then, to be deprived of equality, and to be a feminist is to take responsibility for redressing this wrong and for redefining the meaning of being a woman. Alcoff salvages the category 'woman' by defending an interpretation of the social meaning of being assigned to that category.

Iris Young introduces an additional layer of analysis. To explain gender, Young invokes Jean-Paul Sartre's idea of seriality (Young 1994). A social series is "a social collective whose members are unified passively by the objects around which their actions are oriented or by the objectified results of the material effects of the actions of others." In other words, a series is constituted by a behaviour-directing, meaning-defining environment. The lives of series members are affected by being assigned to particular social series, for serial existence is experienced as a "felt necessity." People feel impelled to act in ways that are consonant with their series memberships. Yet, series membership "does not define the person's identity in the sense of forming his/her individual purposes, projects, and sense of self in relation to others." Indeed, a woman "can choose to make none of her serial memberships important for her sense of identity." For Young, then, a gendered self is optional although membership in the series 'woman' is not.

Sally Haslanger underscores three conceptions of 'gender', and her distinctions clear up much of what seems puzzling in Alcoff's and Young's views (Haslanger 2000). Haslanger argues in favour of a "critical analytical" approach to gender—that is, focusing on the "work the concepts of gender and race might do for us in a critical—specifically feminist and antiracist—social theory" and suggesting "concepts that can accomplish at least some important elements of that work." To pursue this politicized approach to gender, it is necessary to decide which conception of gender best serves the aims of emancipatory political theory and politics. As Haslanger points out, feminist theorists have interpreted gender as the experience of sexed embodiment, a broad psychological orientation to the world, a set of internalized norms, a system of sexual symbolism, a set of traditional roles, and a social position or class. In her view, the principal task for feminist theory is to provide an analysis of gender as a "pattern of social relations that constitute the social classes of men as dominant and women as subordinate." The other forms of gender, including gendered identity, should be explained in terms of this fundamental structure.

Like Alcoff and Young, Haslanger is acutely aware of the political damage essentialist theories of gender have done—especially, the alienation of women of color and lesbians from feminism—and also the factual shortcomings of essentialist theories of gender—that is, many women do not fit the proposed accounts of what it is to be a woman. Although none of these feminist philosophers repudiates the conception of gender as a gendered self, each treats this conception as secondary or derivative. Alcoff politicizes gendered identity and ties it to a self-ascribed commitment to progressive social change. Young stresses the indeterminacy of gendered identity and allows that women's gender-based political commitments can be antifeminist as well as feminist. Although Haslanger insists that the connections between gender as social class and gendered identities are highly variable, she claims that gender "implicates each of us at the heart of our self-understandings," and she advocates conscientious reflection on "who we think we are."

Alcoff remarks that every woman's subjectivity is engendered; Young observes that every woman's identity is marked by gender; and Haslanger notes that every woman is invested in her gender. From the standpoint of a feminist philosophy of the self, it is crucial to account for this engendering, marking, and investment. In my view, the alternative to a common homogeneous feminine identity is gendered and individualized identities (Meyers forthcoming 2000). Individualization does not, however, entail optionality, for gender insinuates itself into identity in ways that we may not be conscious of and in ways that we may not be able to change no matter how much we try. Gender is constitutive of who we are—our personalities, our capabilities and liabilities, our aspirations, and how we feel about all of these attributes. Yet, there is no feature of identity that all women share. How is this possible? Nancy Chodorow uses psychoanalytic theory to make sense of individualized, gendered identities (Chodorow 1995). Psychoanalysis explains how individuals' affective dispositions, unconscious fantasies, and interpersonal relationships filter the culturally entrenched conception of gender they encounter. Through various psychic processes—projection and introjection together with the defence mechanisms—gender acquires a "personal meaning" that is inspired by, but that does not wholly replicate culturally transmitted strictures and iconography.

It is a mistake to picture gender as a toxic capsule full of norms and interpretive schemas that individuals swallow whole and that lodges intact in their psychic structure. The diversity of individuals' experience of gender belies this view. But it is also a mistake to picture attributes like gender as systems of social and economic opportunities, constraints, rewards, and penalties that need not impinge upon individual identity. The seeming naturalness of enacting gendered characteristics, the passion with which people cling to their sense of their gender, and the intractability of many gendered attributes when people seek to change them testify to the embeddedness of gender in identity. Still, it is important to recognize, as Alcoff, Young, Haslanger, and Chodorow do, that the potency of the impact of gender on the self does not altogether deprive women of control over their gendered attributes. Neither personal resistance to one's own gendered dispositions and evaluative standards nor political resistance to the social structures that gender women's identities is ruled out on this view. As this article attests, there is tremendous foment and variety within the field of feminist work on the self. Yet, in reviewing this literature, I have been struck by a recurrent theme—the inextricability of metaphysical issues about the self from moral and political theory. Feminist critiques of regnant philosophical theories of the self expose the normative underpinnings of these theories. Feminist analyses of women's agentic capacities both acknowledge traditional feminine social contributions and provide accounts of how women can overcome oppressive norms and practices. Feminist reconstructions of the nature of the self are interwoven with arguments that draw out the emancipatory benefits of conceiving the self one way rather than another. There is nothing surprising, to be sure, about the salience of normative concerns in feminist philosophizing. Still, I mention it because I believe that feminists' attention to political concerns leads to fresh questions and also that asking novel questions enriches philosophical understanding of the self. Moreover, I would urge that this forthrightness about the political viewpoint that informs philosophy is a virtue, for overlooking the political suppositions and implications of esoteric philosophical views has led to considerable mischief.

The Right to Private Property

The right to private property is the social-political principle that adult human beings may not be prohibited or prevented by anyone from acquiring, holding and trading (with willing parties) valued items not already owned by others. Such a right is, thus, unalienable and, if in fact justified, is supposed to enjoy respect and legal protection in a just human community.

Why Private Property?

The right to private property is the social-political principle that adult human beings may not be prohibited or prevented by anyone from acquiring, holding and trading (with willing parties) valued items not already owned by others. Such a right is, thus, unalienable and, if in fact justified, is supposed to enjoy respect and legal protection in a just human community.

In the development of classical liberalism there emerged in Western political thought a shift of focus as to the prime value in social-political matters, from the group–a tribe, class, state or nation–to the human individual. It started with the effort to gradually transfer power from a few or even one person as the source of collective authority and power to more segments of society involved in exercising such authority and power, leading, eventually, to the sovereignty of the human individual. The way in which power is diffused when individuals are sovereigns rather than groups is through the fact that individuals have only a little and highly diversified power to wield. In consequences, they aren't likely to impose themselves on others by, say, starting a war, even when they disagree very seriously. That, in essence, was the initial motivation for moving toward individualism, which, when implemented via law and public policy, is much more conducive to peace and, as a result, to prosperity than is any form of collectivism. Thus classical liberalism has had some considerable support on practical grounds–its usefulness to attaining various widely sought after objectives.

A major reason, however, that individualism makes better sense than its competitors is that the view that *human beings are primarily parts of a social whole* is wrong. This last is a false notion. When invoked, arguably it tends to serve as a disguise for certain special or vested privileges of some members of society. Generalizing such special or vested interests, the values or goals pursued in their name, has been a major source of political acrimony throughout human history. It even continues to drive much of contemporary democratic politics.

There is, however, the problem that as far as its ethical presuppositions and implications are concerned, individualism and in consequences also classical liberalism have not fared all that well. These views are constantly being charged with opposition to community life and human fellowship, hedonism, materialism, and so forth. Even though this is wrongheaded, without a solid moral case it is difficult to show that to be true. The reason is that morality is extremely important in human affairs. Most people do not confidently embrace a political stance unless it manages to embrace certain basic moral principles. Pragmatic reasons thus never suffice to establish the soundness of political systems and public policies.

It is part of the point of this essay to show that private property rights accord with certain basic moral principles. These are the indispensability of human agency in any sensible moral framework and the moral virtue of prudence. I will argue that individualism embraces these principles and that the right to private property makes their actual realization possible in human community life.

Individuality and Humanity

Human beings have, as one of their distinctive features, a significant element of individuality. Notice, for example, how this comes through in some thought experiments. If a friend dies, it is nonsense to think, "Oh well, I'll just get another friend." You cannot just replace a person with another if you regard him as he really is, most basically, not just as some member of a class of people, such as dentists or auto mechanics. (Even with pets it's difficult to replace them because they become sort of humanized around us.)

On the other hand, with a cow, fly, rock and most other things in the world, replacing them is no problem in one sense because they aren't important *individually*. They're important in their relationship to other things, whereas in the case of human beings it is everyone's individuality that matters most, especially in those most significant personal or intimate relationships. You fall in love with an individual, not a banker–when you really fall in love, that is. (Some people "fall in love" with a type, true enough, but there's something perverse about that — it is somewhat sad to hear, "Well, I love him because he's in uniform or has a big car.")

Even apart from such common sense observations there is the clear evidence that whenever we consider human beings, we cannot avoid their volitional conduct, actions they choose to bring about on their own. In intellectual discussions this is evident in the fact that we criticize one another about what we think, holding our adversaries directly or indirectly responsible for alleged misjudgments.

It is a reasonable view, then, that human beings are first and foremost individuals who cause much of what they do. Their actions flow from their thinking and their thinking is the sphere in which they are free, self-determined.

Individualism: True and False

Now individualism is associated somewhat uncomfortably with classical liberalism. The reason is that some have overemphasized the element of individuality, making it seem that we are not also members of communities, even of the human race. Such "atomistic" individualism has made it seem that classical liberalism is tied to a misguided social philosophy. An example of it may be found in the oft repeated story, by economists, of Robinson Crusoe. If one models human life on Crusoe's story and his interaction with Friday, it appears that we are born capable of self-sufficient productive conduct and from the start choose whether to associated with others. Yet this idea is patently absurd, considering that all human beings are born helpless and grow up in the company of others on whose support they vitally depend.

Yet it is not true that individualism is necessarily committed to atomism. One can fully admit to the communal aspects of human life while insisting that we are essentially individuals, as well. Such a robust, what I have called "classical" individualism, also stresses the importance of the private realm and insists that all bona fide human communities must adhere to the terms individuals set for themselves.

The crucial individualist ingredient of classical liberal social and political theory stresses not some arid independence or isolation of the individual human being but the fact that everyone can make what in principle can be independent judgments as to the kind of communities suitable to one's membership. Given human nature, the element of choice must be preserved in every suitable human community. This is the source of the classical liberal political principles that demands that the consent of the governed be upheld in public policy as well as personal relations. The criminal nature of murder, assault, kidnapping, rape, robbery, burglary and so forth all make sense in terms of this classical or moderate individualism first found in Aristotle philosophy.

Individuality and Privacy

The gist of individualism is, then, that everyone must consent to being used by another. This is because each is important, valuable in his or her own right. And if an individual is important as such, then there is a sphere that constitutes the individual's realm of sovereignty and others ought to respect it, the realm within which one must make effective judgments about one's life. And indeed in classical liberal, political, and legal theory there's a great deal of emphasis on individual rights rather than rights of families or other groups, bearing on this individualist element of the position. The right to private property is, in turn, the most practically relevant of those individual rights.

The term "privacy," then, underlines this emphasis of the importance of individuals. The right to private property is really just an extension, within the framework of a naturalist world view, of the right to one's own life. It is when one('s life) engages with the rest of the world in the unique way one will do so, and when another will do this in his or her unique way, then privacy becomes important. It will then be possible to actualize and to protect who one is and one's manifestation in the world–one's own art, productivity, creativity, innovation and so forth. None of those, as well, may be used by others without the individual's consent to whom they belong.

Socialism and Humanity

Now consider that one of the interesting things about socialism is that in deep-seeded socialist theory there are no individuals. Marx said it directly: "The human essence is the true collectivity of man." He also noted that human beings constitute specie-beings and comprise "an organic whole" in the collectivity we call humanity. What is important about you and me for a consistent, thoroughgoing socialist is that we belong to the human race, somewhat analogously to the way a bee belongs to its hive or an ant to its colony, only in this case the constituent parts are intelligent persons.

This is especially true of international socialism, but National Socialism and even more restrictive, local forms of socialism, emphasize the group as a whole and *its* plan, telos or destiny. Even communitarians, as vague as their conception of a community comes to (so that one cannot pin them down as socialists because they leave room for some elements of individualism), speak mostly of concerns in behalf of "us" and use the term "we" to designate the primarily valued party when discussing public policy. The individual can then, at times, be sacrificed if some gains are made for the group, collective or community.

Classical Liberalism, Human Nature & Individuality

Yet, if we examine human life carefully, we notice clearly that there is something irreducibly, inescapably, individual about everybody. Just think about yourself. How do you insist on being regarded by friends and others close to you? As a student? An American or Rumanian or Hispanic? Or as a woman or basketball player? Is there not in fact something unique that is the *you* that captures who you are? One's *identity* isn't racial, ethnic, religious or even professional. It is individual. As John Quincy Adams said in the motion picture *Amistad*, ask not *what* someone is but *who* someone is to come to know the person.

It's in classical liberalism that this is acknowledged more than in any other political philosophy. There's always been a little bit of emphasis on individuality, of course, in various rebellious political movements, but it's very difficult to maintain the supremacy of the tribe or, later, the state if one admits that what is truly important in a human society is the individuals who comprise it, as individuals. Because then one can't reasonably say, "Well, we can do away with that individual or with that group of individuals or their projects so as to benefit some others, including some collective such as the state, community, culture or race."

Indeed, with the recognition and acknowledgment of the supreme value of the individual, the very definition of a "good" or "just" society would have to emphasize the freedom and happiness of individuals. In fact, a characteristic of the classical liberal political ethos is that one scrutinizes a society for its quality, its goodness, and its justice on the basis of how loyal it is to the mission of securing the rights of individuals to their liberty and pursuit of happiness. This is actually a very prominent movement in the world today. It's not done consistently and purely, but all those human rights organizations that go from country to country to check whether they adhere to tenants of justice are at least rhetorically committed to the examination of whether the countries treat their citizens as individuals with rights. Are their projects respected or are they neglected and treated with callous disregard for the choices of individuals?

This is one of the reasons that in a largely liberal–or, for the sake of avoiding confusion with American liberalism, a libertarian–society membership in a class looses its moral and political significance. In the United States of American, for example there are matters that may make no difference to most people, but when they matter to even just one, it is appreciated. I, for one, once worked as a busboy in Cleveland, Ohio, and noticed that when paid, I could go back to the same restaurant and eat a meal there. There was no frowning and shaking of the head and saying, "Wait a minute, you don't belong here." In much of Europe, in contrast, if you work in a restaurant you don't get to eat there–it is not illegal now but it's certainly gosh.

Fluctuating Classes

In a more or less libertarian social-political society the divisions that are based on incidental attributes–one's wealth, color, national origin, ethnicity, race, and so forth–tend to be less significant because one's individual worth trumps all these and classes, at any rate, are always in a flux. Even racial and ethnic, not to mention religious or economic categories tend to shift because there is no widespread and well entrenched legally enforced barriers to either entry to or exit from any of them.

Such categories and the behaviour associated with them may still prevail in certain special contexts. For example, a professor will usually attain special respect in the classroom, but when one meets the professor at a restaurant, one will not need to carry over the behaviour associated with that classroom status. No "Her Doctor, Doctor," as, for example, in much of Germany, in or outside the classroom. In most American schools, however, one says, "Hello Professor," but outside the label isn't usually used.

All this can be a bit disturbing because it can sometimes spill over into disrespect for people who in fact deserve respect. Rampant individualism can corrupt into disrespect for all authority. The corruption can but by no means need be generated by the notion that individuals matter primarily as individuals, not so much as members of classes. It is also evident enough that we are social beings, members of the class of human beings, and there are some matters very important about that, too.

The Moral Standing of Private Property Rights

Individualism does, however, underlie the regime of private property rights. But why do we need a separate discussion of the merits of the right to private property? What will such an inquiry yield?

There are at least two answers to that question. One is that when you resist people taking something from you, by taxation, theft or any other means, it is important to know, even if only implicitly, that the resistance is justified. That it is a kind of self-defence, akin to resisting someone assaulting or raping someone else. It is vital to learn that one is in the right and is not doing something merely willful or stubborn or prejudicial, that one is not just being a recalcitrant, antisocial person, when one insists on the integrity of ownership. This is a point widely contested by opponents of classical liberal or libertarian legal orders.

When all things are considered, the most important questions about liberalism and its various tenants is, "Is it true?" "Is classical liberalism or, its purest versions, libertarianism, the way a society ought to be organized?" And, in order to answer that question, one must examine whether its various tenets can withstand challenges, criticisms and so on. Individualism is one of these tenets but the right to private property is the most important practical, public policy element of it.

The second reason we need to examine private property rights is whether system of individual rights, including the right to private property, is a just system? Or is it, as many critics claim, just a figment of some people's imagination?

One of the most prominent and oft-repeated criticisms levelled at classical liberalism, especially by students of various configurations of Marxism–there are about 300 versions now—is that this whole emphasis on individuality is a kind of a historical glitch. It's only a temporary phase in history which had its role but now can be dispensed with.

Individualism and Historicism

The Marxists and many others, some who follow them without knowing it, claim that in the 16th century the individual was *invented*, not merely discovered or his existence politically affirmed, for the sake of sustaining economic productivity. In order to create motivation for wealth-creation, the individual had to be made seem significant. It's a myth, but it's a useful myth. It's like telling someone that she is beautiful when she isn't so that she will do certain things from which certain advantages derive. According to Marxists, there was a period of human history where the belief in the importance of the individual had an objective historical function, not because it's true, but because it contributes to certain crucial elements of capitalism.

There are people who look at history in this way, as if it is the record of the growth of humanity from infancy to full maturity. They then take it that the bourgeois epoch is like the adolescence of an individual. It's a temporary stage and has its usefulness because, typically, adolescents embark upon all sorts of useless ventures–such as getting up at four o'clock to drive some place not because there's something important to do as a sort of exercise to prepare for adulthood. It trains them for the eventual serious challenges of maturity. When one treats humanity this way, so that it has these various historical stages, individualism can be regarded to be one of those stages. It's a somewhat appealing picture–it fits some images we have of humankind. Ecologists encourage this, as do some moral visionaries who see humanity as a big family or some other kind of collectivity.

Marx explicitly said that the Greek era was the childhood of humanity. He, as I have noted already, and many of those who have been influenced by his thinking believe that humanity is some kind of organism, a being of which individuals are the parts. Humanity goes through stages of organic development, the tribalism its first and communism its final stage. And while the individualist stage in a necessary one, it is certainly not the completed stage of humanity.

Individualist Alternative to Organicism

These challenges have to be answered because they are extremely well developed, plausible enough, and with enormous influence in the world intellectual community. It is a little like when one meets a friend and asks them to explain some event such as their recent divorce and they proceed to give you a very well worked out and sincerely held rationalization as to how things happened. Now, in order to cope with one of these rationalizations, one must get to the heart of the actual situation and demonstrate beyond all reasonable doubt that the story is a different one. One must show that one's understanding of what's going on is more rational, coherent, comprehensive, and explains much more than does theirs. Otherwise the deceptive story will be the only viable account making the rounds, despite its conflict with common sense. Unless liberalism is able to identify a better story than what those who champion the organic view advance, it will be defeated, at least theoretically. And while that isn't always decisive, it certainly has an impact on the confidence with which the position can be supported and implemented.

Indeed, one of the advantages of anti-liberal doctrines is that so many intellectuals are enchanted by them. They create elaborate and smart stories around them, stories that are extremely appealing and intellectually challenging. For one, such a story gives the intellectual a privileged position. Only intellectuals are in the position to grasp such a complex story, after all. Common sense does not support it. (For example, Marx thought only communists could really understand the truth of such a story, the rest of us having been blinded by our class outlook.)

The Appeal of Collectivism

The idea, for example, that we are all mere parts of a large human organism, humanity, has very a strong intellectual standing in our time. A great many people make reference to humanity–as when they talk about sacrificing oneself or one's private interests or one's materialistic goals for humanity. And others refer to smaller groups–the community or ethnic group or the race–as the organisms that are of significance.

So it's almost a feature of the mainstream to think of us not as individuals but as parts of some larger whole. "Don't you have something more important to live for than yourself?" "Isn't there something greater than yourself to which your life must be devoted for it to be worthwhile?" Less loosely, some, such as the philosopher Charles Taylor, argue that we all must *belong* to a group, by dint of our very humanity, our nature as human beings. He tells us that "Theories which assert the primacy of rights are those which take as the fundamental, or at least a fundamental, principle of their political theory the ascription of certain rights to individuals which deny the same status to a principle of belonging or obligation, that is a principle which states our obligation as men to belong to or sustain society, or a society of a certain type, or to obey authority or an authority of a certain type." Never mind that Taylor cannot give us any such theories–John Locke, for example, rested basic human rights on ethics or natural law. What is important in what Taylor says is not only that if you just live to make the most of *your* life, you're not really living a *significant enough* life. A significant life must not only fulfil a greater purpose and humanity's purpose is one of the candidates. God's purpose is another candidate. Ecologists have a biological purpose in mind. But a significant life but belong to the effort to pursue this purpose and thus our lives, to be properly significant, may be subordinated, by force, to such purposes.

There's a very prominent tradition of selecting alternative wholes larger than ourselves as the proposed beneficiaries of significant human actions. And this can lead to the whole process of forcing individuals to be used for purposes to which they do not consent. This is the greatest source of coercive thinking in human history. Once it is accepted that human individuals are part of a larger whole they, as members of a partnership or team, have enforceable obligations to the goals of that large whole. They belong to it.

Consider, to appreciate this, how in certain cases we treat such wholes as ourselves. If something happens to one's ear, for example, and yet one prizes one's appearance with an intact ear, then one takes another part of one's body that's not visible and takes part of it so as to replace the ear. The famous Welsh actor, Richard Harris, had his nose destroyed in a fight, so doctors took a part of his hip bone and replaced it, clearly because the nose was more important to an actor than that little part of the hip bone.

Well, if humanity is the larger organism, then maybe a given individual may not be so important a part of it as another. So the less important individual can be sacrificed for the more important one (or the goals of the less important can be sacrificed for those of the more important). One may be an eye and the other just a useless thumb. That picture is widely embraced because of the belief that humanity is some organic whole.

If one recognizes collectivism as a misguided picture of human life, one must carefully and effectively argue in response to these well worked out and often honestly and sincerely meant doctrines. One must demonstrate that it is indeed individuals who count for the most in the human picture. It needs to be proven, some of the widespread opinion to the contrary notwithstanding, that notions such as "individual rights" are universal and not stuck to some limited historical epoch.

The Right to Private Property

One reason that it must be shown that the social regulative principle of a right to private property is sound and that it ought to be respected and protected in human community life is that it is a vital conceptual or logical implication of the individualist story. If individualism is indeed sound, so is the principle of private property rights. When the right to private property is not respected and not sufficiently protected, then there is something wrong with a community.

This means that it is not quite fit for human inhabitation, given the individuality of every person and how respect for this is a precondition for his or her flourishing.

There are many different ways in which private property has been supported in the history of political economy. Most prominent has been the claim that there should be legal protection of the right private property because this facilitates productivity–a point that's in agreement with Marx, only universalized beyond a given epoch. Protecting this right helps society get rich–not only in the 16th century but always. Both Adam Smith and John Stuart Mill tended to argue along these lines: It's a good thing to have these rights because if we act in terms of them we will have greater prosperity. Many economists today argue a similar point. Indeed, that is one reason many governments engage in privatization, so as to encourage economic growth.

All of this is vital but it isn't what is most important. What needs to be shown is that the individual has these rights regardless of what's done when simply exercising them. Even if individuals waste away their lives, they have that right. It is theirs to waste away, not someone else's, because they are the important element of society, not some outsider, not some other being such as society, the community, the tribe or the ethnic group. It is this element of liberty, the right to choose how one lives, that is most central to human community life, even if, indeed because, as a matter of one's personal life it is equally important to make the right choice, to choose to do the right thing.

That is exactly why the right to private property is vital. When effectively protected, it secures for human individuals a sphere of personal jurisdiction, the right to acquire and hold the props, as it where, with which to order one's life.

Moral virtues such as generosity, kindness, courage, moderation, prudence and the rest are all imperatives the practice of which engage one with the natural world. If one is not in charge of some of that world, at least oneself, one cannot conduct oneself virtuously. So the right to one's life, liberty and property are necessary conditions for a morally significant or meaningful life in human communities.

It needs to be noted here, as a significant aside, that even if we are essentially individuals, this doesn't mean we are not also naturally members of societies. But, as moral agents and as candidates for membership in some human communities or societies, we are morally responsible to take into consideration and never neglect the fact that we must judge those societies as to whether they do adequate justice to our individuality, most generally, and whether they best serve our flourishing.

No Carte Blanche to Communities

From this it follows that we must always keep in focus the question of whether we ought to live in a given community. Do we–ought we to–want to support this kind of public policy, this kind of a legal system? What is the standard by which we make that kind of decision when we have the chance? At the most basic level of community concern must lie the issue of what principles should govern human communities. The right to private property is one of those principles.

Very often we don't have a direct practical option to act on the choice we make about basic principles. But at least we can think about them so that when we do get a chance to make a significant decision, then we will know where to stand. We owe it to ourselves, to a life of integrity, not to forget about that issue, ever. That is the highest duty of citizenship!

Property Rights, Individuality and the Moral Life

So what does the right to private property do in connection with the essential human element of individuality?

Well, as already suggested, the right to private property secures for one a sphere of sovereignty. See, if we are individuals, required, morally, to lead our lives by our judgements, it is crucial that we control the elements with which our lives are lived. Indeed, it becomes the most crucial thing.

The question, "How ought I to live?" becomes the foremost question to which you then seek an answer. While we aren't moral theoreticians and ethical philosophers and so on, that question still is always near the forefront of our minds. No matter what you do, even reading these lines, the question will arise: "Should I sleep or should I pay attention? Should I consider this point or should I just glide over it?"

All of those are questions having to do with your ethical agency, with one's governance of one's life, with one's sovereignty. One's feeling that one is doing the right thing becomes crucial if one is indeed the master of one's existence.

No Private Property Rights, No Full Moral Agency

Now, without the right to private property, without having some props, some elements of reality that are under our jurisdiction, our ethical decisions cannot be effectual. Consider for example, if it turns out to be true that a good human being ought to be generous. Well, if we do not have the right to private property how are we going to be generous? Are we going to be like politicians and bureaucrats and expropriate what belongs to others and give this to the poor and needy? That's not generosity. That's theft.

In short, then, in order to have a effective life of moral virtue, for example the virtue of generosity, we must have the right to property, to hold and then to be free to part with values, on your own terms.

Moral Individualism

Although collectivism has some currency, especially among intellectuals and social theorists, so does a particular version of individualism. The author have in mind the sort that pertains to moral responsibility.

Few people ever quite let go of the idea that some things they and others do are good and some bad things and that those doing them are responsible. When others judge our lives, or when we reflect upon ours, we say, "I did or didn't do the right thing." Moreover, we can go on to consider what we did with what belongs to us–use it well or badly.

Without our sphere of sovereignty, that's manifest in the actual world where we live our lives, we would not be able to act on most moral principles, especially those that involve allocating resources. Are we stingy? But one has to be stingy with something. If one is a neat person, one has to be neat within some sphere that one keeps orderly. If a slob, one will need something that belongs to one that one isn't taking good care of. If those items don't belong to you, if you always have to ask permission of society or the clan or the tribe of the nation as to what to do with these things, the you are not the effective agents in the disposition of them. And you are then not an effective moral agent either. You cannot take pride in what you achieve, nor feel guilt for your failings. You are basically just a little bit of a cell in this larger organism.

The Virtue of Prudence

Prudence is one of the virtues identified in classical Greece. We want now to discuss it in a little more detail than thus far.

First, in the modern era prudence has been demeaned because the task of taking care of oneself and one's own has been deemed to be instinctual ever since Thomas Hobbes argued that we are all driven to preserve ourselves. But Hobbes rested his case on extrapolating the principles of classical mechanistic physics to human life, a move that is not at all justified. Human beings must choose their conduct, including whether they will serve others' or their own well-being. Prudence, as the ancients saw it, is the virtue one needs to take decent care of oneself.

Later Immanuel Kant argued that since prudence is a motivation that is aligned to one's own interest or inclinations, it is not a moral virtue. Only motives that are totally indifferent as to one's own interest or inclinations can have moral significance, even though we can not know whether we are ever so purely motivated.

Neither Hobbes nor Kant had it right. Prudence is a moral virtue, though not the only or highest on. In any case, a prudent person acts, among other ways, economically. Such a person realizes that one must reserve for the future, put resources away for a rainy day. Such a person isn't reckless in the disposition of the resources over which he or she has control.

But now if we have no right to acquire or hold things then we can't be prudent. We then don't have the decision-making authority to allocate resources in accordance with standards of prudence. On the other hand, if we do have this authority, then we can choose to act prudently.

Prudence and Justice

If in fact it is a moral virtue to be prudent, but it's politically impossible for one to act on that virtue, then there is a basic conflict between ethics and politics. Then the political sphere is not properly *adjusted* to the ethical sphere. Then our ethical agency has not been done sufficient justice by the legal system in which we act. And, indeed, that is one of the things that is so frustrating in societies where one does not have the right to private property.

Not only that one is going to be thwarted in one's efforts to acquire life's necessities, but that one cannot act responsibly. Here what happens is a version of the tragedy of commons.

The tragedy of commons is a problem usually associated with managing the environment. The reason is that most spheres where there are environmental problems are public. The atmosphere, oceans, rivers, large forests and so on are spheres wherein no one is individually responsible. To put it another way, everyone is responsible for the management of such spheres but no one has a clear idea what to do about this responsibility because the limits imposed by private property rights are missing.

When you have a distinct or definite sphere of jurisdiction, however complicated it may be–with various layers of responsibility and delegation–then when something is done wrong, it can be traced to the agent or agents who did it. And when things are done right, again it can be traced to the agent or agents whose responsibility it was to do them right. Without the right to private property this is impossible.

This is one of the reasons that no society can completely abolish private property. It is impossible to act in any sort of responsible way without some sphere of personal jurisdiction.

Moral Responsibility and Private Property

So the right to private property is the concrete manifestation of the possibility of responsible conduct in a community where there are lots of people who need to know what they ought to do and with what they ought to do it. We are talking about a life lived within the context of the natural world. If our bodies are non-existent and we are just living in an illusionary material world, then these matters are of no significance. There is an assumption underlying the right to private property, and indeed many other elements of classical liberalism or libertarianism, namely, that we have a task to live properly in the midst of a natural environment, a natural world. We are not just living a purely immaterial life. Food needs to be grown and distributed, production has to occur. All sorts of concrete, natural tasks need to be carried out in order to facilitate our human lives. If this natural life turns out to be either illusionary or insignificant, then some of these things loose their importance. Then politics might indeed be subject to different principles, ones that facilitate different goals, different aims from prosperity, flourishing, or other kinds of earthly success. It's not easy to imagine what that would be. Yet, in a philosophical discussion of these issues, one has to contend with the fact that there are alternative basic ideas that are proposed concerning the basic elements of human living. Liberalism has to stand the test of being compared with these alternative pictures.

Naturalism and Politics

The naturalist approach, in the sense we are preparing and forging ways of living within the natural world, is, I am convinced, demonstrably sound. The alternatives tend to be very vaguely and confusedly supported.

There are doctrines in the world that say that all individuality, for example, is a myth. There are Eastern religions that contend that the natural, individual self is an illusion and that in truth, we're all just part of the universal consciousness.

In order to test this, one has to have some criteria by which truth needs to be determined. The naturalist approach rests on the application of criteria that are universally accessible, available to all human beings with their rational faculties intact.

Commerce and Property

Private property rights, of course, makes for the institution of commerce. If you trade goods and services, if you sell them, if you produce them, if you hoard them, if you save them, you have to have some level of jurisdiction over them. If I wanted to trade you my watch for your shirt, then it has to be my watch. Or I have to have delegated to me the authority of someone whose watch it is. And it has to be your shirt; otherwise there would be no ability or justification in engaging in this trade. I can't sell you this; this belongs to this hotel. But if it belongs to nobody, then I can't even ask the permission of the hotel whether I can sell it or even give it away. So commerce, as well as charity and generosity presuppose the institution of private property rights. Without that institution, these activities cannot be undertaken smoothly, without confusion.

Moral Standing of Political-Economic Systems

One of the questions that arises in the discussion of political philosophy and political economy is whether they have moral standing. When the Left criticizes classical liberals morally because the liberal or libertarian polity makes profit-making possible, what is the answer?

It's not enough to just say, "Well, we just like to make profit." A murderer can just say, "We just like to kill people." That is no justification, clearly.

There are those who argue that a social science such as economics requires nothing from morality–indeed, it is entirely amoral, purely positive or descriptive in its central thrust. But this is a mistake. All human affairs, including economic ones, are permeated with moral issues. In economics, for example, there is the moral (or as Rasmussen and Den Uyl have called it, the meta-normative) element of private property rights.

If one does not own anything, no trade can ensue and all the talk of supply and demand must be abandoned in favour of what collectivists tend to support, a sort of share-and-share alike "economy." But to own something means to be in a distinctively normative relationship with others. They are prohibited from taking what belongs to one. They ought not do so and will be penalized, furthermore, if they do.

So the amoral stance on the market economy is doomed to failure. What is needed is a moral or other normative justification of the institution of private property rights.

To do that we must analyse human nature as it is manifest in the natural world. Will such an analysis support the institutions of freedom and free markets and give them a stronger moral standing in human society than alternative ones possess?

Morality and Public Affairs

Now there are some who would dismiss all this because there are cases in human community affairs involving innocent helpless persons, one's who meet with natural disaster and may find themselves without any voluntary help when they need it. And that is certain a possibility, even if not a likelihood in a free society.

James Sterba, for example, has been arguing for decades that because such cases are possible, the people who find themselves in them have a right to welfare that the legal order may protect. These positive rights, whereby others are required to work for such persons – or part with goods they have worked for in order to support them–come about because it would not be reasonable, Sterba argues, to demand that such people respect private property rights. It would be more reasonable to expect of them to strive to obtain the goods they need – ones Sterba calls, in a question-begging fashion, surplus wealth. (As if someone is justified in identifying what constitutes surplus – a term from classical Marxism that makes no sense outside the Marxist framework.)

If one recognizes, however, that an individual's life is his or her own and he or she does not belong to anything or anyone outside of memberships to which he or she consents, then even the most dire needs of others does not support any institutional arrangement that fails to recognize individual rights–to life, liberty, and, yes, property (that one comes by without violating the rights of others even if one does not strictly deserve the property for some kind of service rendered or other achievement–for instance, come by because others want to purchase some talent or other attribute one naturally has). Just as it is unjustified to use others as a shield against natural danger, regardless of how little use one may make of them, one may not use others against their will, including wealth they own. One must find ways around this prohibition, as indeed most do when they engage in trade rather than theft in the effort to acquire their own wealth.

It is reasonable to demand this of everyone, even those in dire straits. If, however, in desperate circumstances such people do not honour this prohibition, there can be some measure of forgiveness, even within the purview of the legal authority (as per some cases that have been subject to unusual judicial discretion). But such exceptions, as hard cases in general, make bad general law.

Law and Common Sense

Let me go back to where we started. When somebody robs another who resists, the latter has a common sense idea of doing the right thing, that the resistance is not merely some immature, capricious and wilful conduct. It is not as if one were simply engaged in feet stomping and crying, "I want it! I want it! I want it!" No, one senses that there is right on one's side, not just an arbitrary wish and desire.

That is one reason it is vital to consider whether the free system can be given justification. What has been said here is by no means a thorough defence of the right to private property, but it does furnish some hints as to how such a defence would have to be presented if the issue ever arises, which is quite often in our world. First, this right, if protected, preserves one's moral agency in this natural world in which community life occurs. Furthermore, it punctuates the fact that striving to prosper is a morally valid goal for human beings. So, the moral virtue of prudence, of taking the requisite actions to care for oneself and one's intimates, supports the right to private property as well.

One thing that respect and protection of private property rights makes possible is the pursuit of wealth. Oddly, however, that is a *criticism* many offer against the system of free market capitalism that is built on the legal infrastructure of private property rights. They say, as we have already seen Marx do so, that private property rights–if they are protected, maintained, developed as law–encourage a hedonistic, narrowly selfish life, one that is concerned exclusively with acquisition of worldly goods. As he said, "the right of man to property is the ? right of selfishness." Freedom is supposed to make too much self-indulgence, including pleasure, possible.

So another question that arises here turns out to be, "Is pleasure justified?" For even if the right to private property could be used for purposes quite different from obtaining pleasure in life, if pleasure is something loathsome and this right somehow encourages its relentless pursuit, perhaps it is an institution that is much more harmful than benign.

We cannot enter this topic at length but this much should suffice for now. If we are indeed natural beings in this world, one of our important values will be pleasure, the good feelings we experience *via* our bodies. This is so even if there are higher goods the attainment of which may require giving up some pleasure. So, now, if wealth brings with it the possibility of pleasure, then wealth itself is a worthy good, provided it is not stolen but created, produced, and that it is not chosen as the highest good if a higher one can also be identified.

Abandon the Divided Self Idea

If one has a completely different view of human nature, whereby only the spiritual side of human life is of significance, then one will embrace a different system of values and probably also champion different institutions. We have a powerful tradition in most civilizations whereby there is an uneasiness about facilitating the flourishing of the human body. And that is often what stands, at a most basic level, against the free society!

One reason underlying that stand is the lack of a clear, unambiguous and benign acceptance of our earthly selves. We often think ourselves to be so unique, so extraordinary that we believe we must be partly divine or other worldly. St. Augustine said it well when he cried out, "How great, my God, is this force of memory, how exceedingly great! It is like a vast and boundless subterranean shrine.... Yet this is a faculty of my mind and belongs to my nature; nor can I myself grasp all that I am. Therefore the mind is not large enough to contain itself. But where can that uncontained part of it be?" And he then answered, as have millions of others, that it must be somewhere apart from nature.

Business, too, has a bad reputation because of this, as well as the free market place, because if our natural selves are somehow inferior, than servicing it with the vigor with which people in business do must be misguided. People who pursue profit or material wealth, would then be pursuing trivia. They would be mere hedonists. As the title of one articles put it, "Praise Mother Teresa and then Hit the Shopping Malls." In other words, we live a schizophrenic life. We embrace the value of prosperity, economic success, wealth on the one hand but then we deny it on the other. Yet, if in our lives we embrace our bodies, minds, emotions, sensations and so on, then we suggest by this that a more integrated view of how to live and how to protect our values is right, not one that tears us into warring pieces.

The private property rights system rests, in part, on such an integrated understanding of human life, not the schizophrenic one. It rejects the idea that each human being is divided, a view that much of our literature embraces. It places us squarely on this earth, even though it is by no means hostile to anyone who chooses to look elsewhere for fulfillment, quite the contrary. (Indeed, the right to private property has made religious pursuits extremely fruitful as well as abundant, especially in the United States of America where churches can purchase their own land and welcome parishioners where they will not be disrupted by their foes.

The divided self idea started with Plato, at least with a certain reading of him, where he takes our minds to be divided from our bodies and where the mind is supposed to hold the rest of ourselves in check, rule it firmly. Major writers, especially theologians, have ever since stressed this drama and it is reflected in our society's institutions. Victor Hugo made note of this point:

On the day when Christianity said to man: You are a duality, you are composed of two beings, one perishable, the other immortal, one carnal, the other ethereal, one enchained by appetites, needs, and passions, the other lofted on wings of enthusiasm and reverie, the former bending forever to earth, its mother, the latter soaring always toward heaven, its fatherland–on that day, the drama was created. Is it anything other, in fact, than this contrast on every day, this battle at every moment, between two opposing principles that are ever-present in life and that contend over man from the cradle to the grave?

As a result of this, sadly, we are often apologetic for pursuing a satisfactory, happy life here on earth. And then we find it difficult if not impossible to defend the political regime that most clearly enhances such a life, having to accept it when others maintain that, well, it is a mundane, materialist life that such a regime supports.

All of this must be seriously re-thought. Without it, the best socioeconomic system human beings have ever identified will fail to flourish.

7

Democracy and Political Participation

Democracy

A system of government in which effective political power is vested in the people. In older usage (for example, in the writings of the classical Greek and Roman philosophers or in the Federalist Papers), the term was reserved exclusively for governmental systems in which the populace exercised this power directly through general assemblies or referenda to decide the most important questions of law or policy. In more contemporary usage, the term has been broadened to include also what the American Founding Fathers called a republic—a governmental system in which the power of the people is normally exercised only indirectly, through freely elected representatives who are supposed to make government decisions according to the popular will, or at least according to the supposed values and interests of the population.

Representative Democracy

Representative democracy is a form of government founded on the principle of elected individuals representing the people, as opposed to either autocracy or direct democracy.

The representatives form an independent ruling body (for an election period) charged with the responsibility of acting in the people's interest, but *not* as their proxy representatives; that is, not necessarily always according to their wishes, but with enough authority to exercise swift and resolute initiative in the face of changing circumstances. It is often contrasted with direct democracy, where representatives are absent or are limited in power as proxy representatives. In many representative democracies (Canada, Australia, UK, etc.), representatives are most commonly chosen in elections by a plurality of those who are both eligible to cast votes and actually do so. A plurality means that a winning candidate has to win more votes than any other candidate in the race, but does not necessarily require a majority of the votes cast.

While existing representative democracies hold such elections to choose representatives, in theory other methods, such as sortition (more closely aligned with direct democracy), could be used instead. Also, representatives sometimes hold the power to select other representatives, presidents, or other officers of government (indirect representation). A representative democracy that emphasizes individual liberties is called a liberal democracy. One that does not is an illiberal democracy. There is no necessity that individual liberties are respected in a representative democracy.

Today, in liberal democracies, representatives are usually elected in multiparty elections that are free and fair. The power of representatives in a liberal democracy is usually curtailed by a constitution (as in a constitutional republic or a constitutional monarchy) or other measures to balance representative power:

- An independent judiciary, which may have the power to declare legislative acts unconstitutional (e.g. constitutional court, supreme court)
- It may also provide for some deliberative democracy (e.g., Royal Commissions) or direct popular measures (e.g., initiative, referendum, recall elections). However, these are not always binding and usually require some legislative action-legal power usually remains firmly with representatives.
- In some cases, a bicameral legislature may have an "upper house" that is not directly elected, such as the Canadian Senate, which was in turn modeled on the British House of Lords.

The term republic may have many different meanings. Today, it often simply means a state with an elected or otherwise non-monarchical head of state, such as the Islamic Republic of Iran or Republic of Korea. It may also have a meaning similar to liberal democracy. For example, "the United States relies on representative democracy, but its system of government is much more complex than that. It is not a simple representative democracy, but a constitutional republic in which majority rule is tempered by minority rights protected by law".

Criticisms

The major problem with representative democracies is that voter apathy is more common than political interest. This often means that governments are in power without a mandate, suggesting that they do not have electoral legitimacy, or the right to rule, while in office. Real world represenative democracies are not always that represenative. Measures such as the Gallagher_Index attempt to quantify the extent to which parliaments are representative. Voting based on local electorates tends to creates a high degree of Stratified sampling which selects parliamentarians with centrist views. As such radical views are somewhat excluded from parliamentary debates much more so that if parliamentarians were a random selection from the population.

United Kingdom

In the 2005 election in the UK, voter turnout was only 61.36% of the electorate, albeit an increase from the from 59.4% turnout in 2001. In Britain of late, there has been considerable discussion as to how the electoral system might be reformed to increase its representativeness. Significant proposals have included:

1. introducing more technologically advanced, elector friendly, and secure voting/political communication methods;
2. holding two-stage elections or run-off ballots in multi-candidate constituencies so that no candidate can get elected on the basis of just a small portion of the total vote. (Modern developments in tele-voting have enormously increased the speed and reduced the cost and effort of holding such ballots);
3. legislating for equal-sized constituencies and adopting measures to ensure more accurate and up-to-date electoral registers;

4. halting and reversing recent experiments in Continental European-type indirect (party proportional, corporatist) representation which reduce political competition and voter choice and influence compared with the traditional Anglo-American system of direct (territorial, local community) representation;
5. scrapping various protectionist-type curbs on the private funding boom and advertising of political parties;
6. further extending the franchise; and
7. increasing the ratio of significant elected to non-elected political posts: creating substantially more elected as opposed to appointed or hereditary positions.

Political Participation

Taking part in politics. The general level of participation in a society is the extent to which the people as a whole are active in politics: the number of active people multiplied by the amount of their action, to put it arithmetically. But the question of what it is to take part in politics is massively complex and ultimately ambiguous. It raises the question of what constitutes politics. We would, for example, assume that activity within a political party or an organization which regarded itself as a pressure group should count as political participation. But what about activity in other sorts of organization, such as sports associations and traditional women's organizations?

Although not overtly political, these organizations set the context of politics, give their active members administrative experience and are capable of overt political action if their interests or principles are threatened.

There is an opposite problem about political losers: if people act, but ineffectively, perhaps because they are part of a permanent minority in a political system, can we say they have participated in the making of decisions? One implication of this doubt is that possessing power is a necessary condition or logical equivalent of true political participation. If one is merely consulted by a powerful person who wants one's views for information, or if one is mobilized or re-educated within the control of another, one has not participated in politics in any significant sense. — *Lincoln Allison*

Participation (Decision Making)

Participation in social science is an umbrella term including different means for the public to directly participate in political, economic, management or other social decisions. Ideally, each actor would have a say in decisions directly proportional to the degree that particular decision affects him or her. Those not affected by a decision would have no say and those exclusively affected by a decision would have full say. Likewise, those most affected would have the most say while those least affected would have the least say. Participatory decision making infers a level of proportionate decision making power and can take place along any realm of human social activity, including economic (ie Participatory economics), political (ie Participatory democracy or parpolity), cultural (ie intercommunalism) or familial (ie Feminism).

The term is used in management theory (as in "participatory management") to denote a style of management that calls for a high level of participation of workers and supervisors in decisions that affect their work. The term is also used in Participatory Economics or "parecon" as it is theorized and elaborated in that model.

For well-informed participation to occur, some version of transparency, e.g. radical transparency, is necessary, but not sufficient. It has been suggested in the participatory economics model that for full and meaningful participation to exist, some form of Balanced job complex is necessary: self-confidence, empowerment and information must be equitably distributed.

Sherry Arnstein discusses types of participation and "nonparticipation" in *A Ladder of Citizen Participation* (1969). She defines citizen participation as the redistribution of power that enables the havenot citizens, presently excluded from the political and economic processes, to be deliberately included in the future. Multiple other *"ladders"* of participation have been presented, most notably Connor's "A new ladder of citizen participation" (1988), Wiedemann and Femers' "Public Participation in waste management decision making: analysis and management of conflicts" (1993) and Dorcey et al. "Public Involvement in government decision making: choosing the right model" (1994) and Rocha's "A Ladder of Empowerment" (1997).

An Analysis of the Theories of Democracy

One of the theories of the limits of democracy is Democratic Elitism. Developed by Max Weber and Joseph Schumpeter, Democratic Elitism is the theory that in a large-scale society, democratic participation is limited to the electing of political leaders. Weber believed that participatory democracy can only succeed when things that need to be done are very simple, and that specialized skills and knowledge are required for more complicated decisions.

According to Weber, the development of mass citizenship makes it very necessary to have bureaucratic officials. A representative multiparty democracy will help keep a balance in the system and help prevent both political leaders from arbitrarily making decisions and power being completely taken by bureaucrats.

Weber argued that in order for democratic systems to be effective there must be more than one political party that each represents different interests so that voters have a variety of choices, and there has to be political leaders who are able to abstain from the rule of bureaucracy. He believes that rule by elites is inevitable and that hopefully those elites will effectively represent our interest in an innovative and insightful fashion.

Joseph Schumpeter's view was pretty much the same as Weber's. He felt that democracy can only offer the possibility of Replacing one political leader or party with another.

The pluralist theory was influenced by Weber and Schumpeter, although they developed their ideas somewhat differently. They believed that interest groups limit the centralization of power in the hands of government officials. Competing interest groups or factions are necessary to democracy because they reduce the sole influence of any one group or class. There needs to be a balance among competing interests in order to be considered in democratic political order. This situation influences elections because parties need to be responsive to many different interest groups. The US is considered to be the most pluralistic of industrialized societies, and, therefore, is the most democratic.

8

The Political Process and Social Change

Social Change

Social change is a general term which refers to:

- A change in social structure: the nature, the social institutions, the social behaviour or the social relations of a society, community of people and so on.
- When behaviour patterns change in large numbers, and this change is visible and sustained: once there is deviance from culturally-inherited values, rebellion against the established system may result, resulting in a change in the social order.
- Any event or action that affects a group of individuals who have shared values or characteristics.
- Acts of advocacy for the cause of changing society in a way subjectively perceived as normatively desirable.

One of the most popular and succinct definitions of social change is supplied by Charles L. Harper in his *Exploring social change* (1993), where it is characterised as the "significant alteration of social structure and cultural patterns through time." He goes on to explain that this social structure is made up of "a persistent network of social relationships" in which interaction between people or groups has become repetitive. The resultant changes can effect everything from population to the economy, which, as it so happens, alongside such others as industrialisation and shifting cultural norms and values, are also established agents of social change. The term is used in the study of history, sociology, economies and politics, and includes such topics as the success or failure of different political systems, globalization, democratisation, development and economic growth. The term can encompass concepts as broad as revolution and paradigm shift, right down to narrow changes such as a particular cause within small-town government. The concept of social change implies measurement of some of the characteristics of a group of individuals. While the term is usually applied to changes that are beneficial to society, it may also result in negative side-effects and consequences that undermine or eliminate existing ways of life that are considered positive. Social change is a topic in sociology and social work, but also involves political science, economics, history, anthropology and many other social sciences. Among the many means of creating social change are direct action, protest, advocacy, community organisation, community practice, revolution, and political activism. According to Anthony Giddens, Sociology was born of the transformations that wrenched the industrializing social order of the West away from the ways of life characteristic of preceding societies. The world that was created by these changes is the primary object of concern of sociological analysis. The pace of social change has continued to accelerate, and it is possible that we stand on the threshold of transitions as significant as those that occurred in the late eighteenth and nineteenth centuries.

Models of People

Generally there are two sources or dimensions of change (Shackman, Liu, Wang, 2002). One source is non-systematic change, such as climate change, some kind of technological innovation from the outside, or changes forced by foreign countries.

The other source is a systems change: Eisenstadt (1973) argued that modernisation required a basic level of free resources and the development of standardised and predictable institutions, such as a stable but flexible market system and political process. An additional requirement was that governing institutions be flexible enough to adapt to the changes that come up. Most of the time, changes to society come about through some combination of both systematic and non-systematic processes.

- Hegelian: The classic Hegelian dialectic model of change is based on the interaction of opposing forces. Starting from a point of momentary stasis, Thesis countered by Antithesis first yields conflict but subsequently results in a new Synthesis.
- Kuhnian: Thomas Kuhn in *The Structure of Scientific Revolutions* argued with respect to the Copernican Revolution that people are unlikey to jettison an unworkable paradigm, despite many indications that the paradigm is not functioning properly, until a better paradigm can be presented.
- Heraclitan: The Greek philosopher Heraclitus used the metaphor of a river to speak of change thus, "On those stepping into rivers staying the same other and other waters flow" (DK22B12). What Heraclitus seems to be suggesting here, later interpretations notwithstanding, is that, in order for the river to remain the river, change must constantly be taking place. Thus one may think of the Heraclitan model as parallel to that of a living organism, which, in order to remain alive, must constantly be changing.
- Daoist: The Chinese philosophical work Dao De Jing, I.8 and II.78 uses the metaphor of water as the ideal agent of change. Water, although soft and yielding, will eventually wear away stone. Change in this model is to be natural, harmonious and steady, albeit imperceptible.

The Functionalist Perspective

Functionalists perceive society to be a system comprising various functions that operate collectively to maintain order and stability. According to Talcott Parsons, one of the leaders of this school, change stems from other social systems (through, for instance, cultural influence, as in the case of English education in the former colonies of the British Empire) and tensions and strains within the system itself, especially those related to economic activities. Functionalism, writes Michael Haralambos, holds that the economy is solely responsible for resolving societal problems, with industrialism playing an especially crucial role. He explains how, through production and various other economic activities, social change is accelerated such that society has to adapt as a whole: a change in one part effects all the others. These activities include improvements in technology, whereby new innovations come to the fore, and trade with other countries. Social change in the functionalist view can also occur at different levels, be it on a micro scale (involving the groups and people within one's immediate environment) or at a macro level (economic, political and educational systems, for instance). Functionalists also believe that cultural norms and values unite society, which is largely resistant to change, and thus ensure that change in social structure is likely to be slow if it conflicts with entrenched cultural, religious or political principles. The time frame of change also plays a significant role, and the distinction between long-term and short-term change is important. According to Harper, short-term changes, as in family developmental stages, may be obvious and easy to comprehend, but they may not actually constitute changes at all in the long run.

Shortcomings

There are two main criticisms of the functionalist perspective to which most sociologists subscribe:

1. The theory places too much emphasis on external sources of social change, being based largely on the premise that society operates in a state of equilibrium, and that the various changes that take place can be accounted for uniformly by the various political, religious and especially the economic activities that are dominant at the time.
2. Society does not meet the needs of all its members. Emphasis is laid in this regard on the fact that ethnic and gender segregation that occurs politically and economically is created by these structures.

A Theory of Social Change and Implications for Practice, Planning, Monitoring and Evaluation

Who Needs Theories of Change?

We need good theories of social change for building the thinking of all involved in processes of development, as individuals, as communities, organisations, social movements and donors. The conventional division in the world today between policy-makers (and their theorising) and practitioners is deeply dysfunctional, leaving the former ungrounded and the latter unthinking.

Good concepts help us to grasp what is really happening beneath the surface. In the confusing detail of enormously complex social processes, we need to turn down the volume of the overwhelming and diverse foreground and background "noise" of social life, to enable us to distinguish the different instruments, to hear the melodies and rhythms, the deeper pulse, to discover that "simplicity on the other side of complexity." We need help to see what really matters.

As social development practitioners we need theory to help us to ask good questions, more systematically and rigorously, to guide us to understanding, to discovering the real work we need to be doing, primarily assisting communities and their organisations to understand and shape their own realities.

A theory of social change is proposed through this paper as one small contribution to a larger body of theorising. It can be seen as an observational map to help practitioners, whether field practitioners or donors, including the people they are attempting to assist, to read and thus navigate processes of social change.

There is a need to observe and understand the change processes that already exist in a living social system. If we can do this before we rush into doing our needs analyses and crafting projects to meet these needs, we may choose how to respond more respectfully to the realities of existing change processes rather than impose external or blind prescriptions based on assumed conditions for change.

Theories in Context

Economic and cultural globalization, climate change, competition for markets and for strategic and scarce resources are forcing new complexities on all sectors of societies the world over. Yet entrenched structures and patterns of power are still playing themselves out in old managerialist and militaristic ways. We are in the thrall of a global economic and political system that is increasingly inappropriate and self-contradictory, unable to come to terms with itself. The most powerful are at odds with themselves, neither able to comprehend the consequences of what they do nor the complexities of social change they become mired in, unable to respond, even in their own interest, threatening to lead everyone to ruin.

While millions have been lifted out of dire poverty in the last decade, particularly through the rapid industrialisation of Asia in the image of the West, these may be only temporary gains, with serious doubts emerging about the ecological and economic sustainability of this path. And global warming threatens to turn our development efforts into "sand-castles at low tide".

Many counter-trends can be found where millions of the most marginalised, on all continents, are becoming more threatened than ever as local sovereignty, diversity and eco-systems disappear under multiple forces of change that are not easily visible to them and seemingly out of their reach to influence. Social movements of all kinds – economic, social, cultural, political and religious – have developed out of these conditions and are burgeoning in opposition, with some promise but mixed success and with many facing cooption or suppression.

There are some, North and South, pursuing intolerant fundamentalist and sectarian agendas which serve to deepen rather than to resolve the crises. So while the world is globalising and homogenising in many ways, it is at the same time polarising in reaction. The most marginalised and voiceless in the South continue to pay the heaviest price for this.

Poverty is now being perceived as a large enough threat to gain the attention of the rich and powerful. Development is becoming a global Project. The Millennium Development Goals (MDGs) and plans to roll these out have been taking centre stage in global and national development initiatives. A particular role for civil society is emerging: *"Civil society organisations (CSOs) are recognised as having access to and knowledge of those aspects of society that are being defined as 'targets for change'. Yet, in the power dynamics of the world CSOs are not seen as drivers of change but as potential delivery agents of solutions, of programmes and practices developed and promoted by those at the centre. There are a number of mechanisms now firmly in place (some subtle and some crude) to direct and control NGOs and CBOs towards fulfilling agendas other than their own."*

The relationship between Governments, donors, NGOs, CBOs, growing legions of freelance international development consultants, private companies and even some social movements is increasingly being shaped by this trend of putting projects to tender, paying people as service providers to achieve centrally determined outcomes. Development funding is fast becoming a marketplace governed by tender processes and business-talk.

The "development sector" of NGOs and CBOs, who struggle to be businesslike, is under renewed pressure to show results and justify its existence, to compete in this new marketplace. There are less and less funds for them from politicians who are looking for more convincing ways to put money into development that can quickly and easily display 'measurable impact'.

Enter the private sector, initially as suppliers of goods and services to development organisations, but now increasingly winning the tenders as prime service providers. The marketplace of development Projects has never been so clearly visible as it is today.

This projectization of development work has a deeper consequence. Short-term Projects are effectively replacing established organisations with temporary organisations that can be turned on and off, like taps. Organisations, that have become vehicles for Projects live under the same threat, the same taps. Projects are the casual labour of the sector, apparently low risk. This contrasts with indigenous organisations driven by their own needs, that can be resilient and can learn, adapt and improve and bring sustainability.

It is the season of accountability. Projects promise this. But over the past few years, almost every organisation or project I have visited is stressed with issues of monitoring and evaluation, anxiously shopping around for methodologies to measure and report on impact to satisfy donors. Adverts for M&E specialists abound as donors seek to further outsource this function to experts, robbing organisations of rich learning processes to which M&E should contribute.

Donors themselves face the same pressure to account to their back-donors, who in turn must report to their political masters (supposedly accountable to their electorate), who are, for good and bad reasons, asking harder questions and setting higher standards each year. In an age where the "speak" is becoming more participatory, bottom-up or horizontal there is, paradoxically, a strengthening of pressure for upward, vertical accountability to the North.

But as practitioners, donors and back-donors, we might want to ask ourselves more honestly whether the real reason we are struggling to measure and report on impact might be that as a sector we are simply not achieving the results we have promised each other when we sign Project contracts. Monitoring and evaluation methodologies that are centred on accountability, rather than on honestly learning from practice, will not bring us the measures or the value we want. In other words the problem is not effective measuring and reporting but effective practice itself, as guided by the logic of Projects.

It is ironic that the very Project approaches that donors insist be used for planning, monitoring and evaluating practice and impact, like Logical Framework Analysis and its cousins, have tacitly introduced an unspoken theory of social change that is often misleading and self-defeating. This theory of change is briefly described and critiqued next.

The Current Conventional Theory of Social Change

The "Development Project" is by far the most dominant vehicle for conscious social change, used widely by donors, NGOs and governments the world over. Projects have become the almost unquestionable contracting and managing frameworks for social development practice.

The most prominent format for Projects is the Logical Framework Analysis (Logframe) which has some cousins in ZOPP, Project Cycle Management (PCM), and other business-like tools for managing practice, in particular for planning, monitoring, evaluation and reporting (PME&R).

At a European Union sponsored logframe training workshop in the mid-1990s I learnt that the Logframe approach traces its lineage to the US Pentagon in 1945, created specifically to help the management of the Berlin Airlift in that year – a huge relief Project by any measure. As a military planning tool it migrated into government and business in the 1950s and was eventually picked up and fashioned into its present form by USAID in the 1970s and then carried to Europe by German donors, as ZOPP, in the 1980s, from where it spread widely across the development sector into international NGOs and down into governments and local NGOs of the South. It was introduced into South Africa by several donors in the 1990s on a wave of training workshops which have continued to the present. Despite heavy criticisms from a wide range of field practitioners, it and its cousins have survived and remain the dominant frameworks in the development sector for PME&R. Created to help control the flow of resources, these frameworks have, by default, come to help control almost every aspect of development practice across the globe, subordinating all social processes to the logistics of resource control, infusing a default paradigm of practice closely aligned with conventional business thinking.

As such, Project approaches to change bring their own inbuilt or implicit theory of social change to the development sector, premised on an orientation of simple cause and effect thinking. It goes something like this: In a situation that needs changing we can gather enough data about a community and its problems, analyse it and discover an underlying set of related problems and their cause, decide which problems are the most important, redefine these as needs, devise a set of solutions and purposes or outcomes, plan a series of logically connected activities for addressing the needs and achieving the desired future results, as defined up front, cost the activities into a convincing budget, raise the funding and then implement the activities, monitor progress as we work to keep them on-track, hopefully achieve the planned results and at the end evaluate the Project for accountability, impact and sometimes even for learning. As an implicit theory of change and consequently as an approach to change, this theory unconsciously assumes that:

- Project interventions themselves introduce the change stimulus and processes that matter and are the vehicles that can actually deliver development. (Existing, indigenous social change processes, usually invisible to conventional analysis, are seldom acknowledged and are effectively reduced to irrelevancy – except where resultant active or passive resistance to change cannot be ignored);

- problems (as needs to be addressed) are discernable or visible to the practitioner upfront out of cause and effect analysis. Solutions to the core problems analysed can be posed as predetermined outcomes. (The use of logical problem trees is common, despite that fact that they are incapable of dealing with feedback loops and other complex systemic problems);
- participatory processes in the planning phase can get all stakeholders onboard, paving the way for ownership and sustainability. (This would be nice but people are seldom so compliant!);
- unpredictable factors, whether coming from outside or from within the Project, or even as the knock-on effects of the Project work itself are, at worst, inconveniences to be dealt with along the way;
- desired outcomes, impacts or results, sometimes envisioned several years up the line, can be coded into detailed action plans and budgets and pursued in a logical and linear way. In other words, if the planning is good enough the Project should succeed.

There are situations where some of these assumptions do hold, and so Projects can in some instances be right on the nail, the hammer that is needed. Conditions which are favourable for Projects are described in more detail in the next section.

But more often than not, particularly in situations where there is a greater need for development assistance, conditions do not allow for these assumptions to hold. The use of Projects where the conditions for them are not favourable can be profoundly counter-developmental and destructive for people and their relationships and lead to a real experience of failure and set-back, characterised not by crisis but rather by defeat. Misapplied Projects can also undermine practice and relationships up and down the aid-chain. Inexperienced practitioners tend to be blamed or blame themselves and their lack of Project capacity for such failures and go for more training in Project Management, while more experienced practitioners pursue their own more appropriate ways of doing things but try to keep their donors happy in the belief that they are working dutifully under the agreed Project Logframe.

Some practitioners have even said that Logframes are a useful tool for lying to donors. But in the end everyone is being fooled and missing vital opportunities to engage honestly and to learn about realities and think more deeply about possibilities. Many practitioners, including donors, do acknowledge the limitations of Logframes and other Project-based approaches but in the apparent absence of viable alternatives dub them "necessary evils".

It may be that many Northern donors have experienced enough success with Project approaches in their own countries where conditions for them are more favourable, allowing them to feel confident that they have universal application. Yet, I have met field practitioners in the North who also experience problems with Project approaches in the more complex and usually deprived areas in which they work.

Many donors insist on Project approaches because they are not aware of alternatives and perhaps several are not aware of the power that Projects bring in forcing a narrow concept of change on situations where they do not apply. A less generous analysis might wonder whether some donors and practitioners find Projects to be ideal vehicles of control to impose their own visions of change on communities of the South.

But there is now enough experience in the development sector, and hopefully sufficient honesty, to take another look – a deeper look – at change processes themselves and what they ask of practice and how we lead and manage our work. There are viable alternatives, though they may still take some thinking through and may not present themselves as tools and frameworks to easily work with. Development and social change are deeply complex processes and we should be wary of looking for an overly simple set of tools to help us face the difficulties. The theory in this chapter proposes three distinctly different kinds of change which underpin most social processes of development, namely *emergent change, transformative change* and *projectable change.*

Understanding deeply and respecting what change processes already exist can help us to respond to and work with a deeper sense of reality, rather than its shallowly perceived set of problems and needs. In facing this challenge to observe what we are working with more deeply, we may then be able to develop more successful and measurable practices and impacts, helped by frameworks that enable us to more deftly manage our practice and relationships, including processes and systems for planning, monitoring, learning from, evaluating, rethinking and reporting on practice.

But where are the debates and discussions about how change really happens, where is the research and thinking? I have asked numerous development practitioners and donors from the North and South what their thinking and theories of social change are and for the vast majority it is the first time that they have ever seriously engaged the question! Field practitioners, whose own experience should yield rich insights for theorising about how change happens, seldom have or take the time to think about what they are doing, and so effectively allow donor thinking and implicit theories of and approaches to change to dominate their practice. Many donors do not even know they have this power and many would not want to wield it if they knew of the destructive effects that their insistence on Project approaches are so often responsible for. Instead of forcing their own default theories and approaches on the South should donors not be funding the thinking and theorising by practitioners themselves, their own authentic learning processes, as much as they fund the work practitioners do?

A Theory of Social Change

In its parts the theory presented here draws from other theories of change.

Like the conventional theory described above, these often assume that change has a particular character, associated with its theory. My attempt acknowledges the value of these various theories, including the conventional one, but seeks to bring them together into something that is more integrated, recognising the diversity of social change.

This theory was also developed out of practice and tested in practice, from working on numerous field accompaniments and learning processes over many years.

The three types of change articulated below are not *prescriptions* of social change but rather *descriptions* of different kinds of social change that already exist and are inherently a part of the developing state of a social being. If used to accurately read the nature of change in a social being then they suggest certain approaches working with change that are more likely to respond successfully to unfolding realities on the ground. But the first task must be to understand what is already there before anything is done in response. *3.1 Emergent change – "We make our path by walking it."*

"We do not grow absolutely, chronologically. We grow sometimes in one dimension, and not in another; unevenly. We grow partially. We are relative. We are mature in one realm, childish in another. The past, present, and future mingle and pull us backward, forward, or fix us in the present. We are made up of layers, cells, constellations."

Anais Nin

Emergent change describes the day-to-day unfolding of life, adaptive and uneven processes of unconscious and conscious learning from experience and the change that results from that. This applies to individuals, families, communities, organisations and societies adjusting to shifting realities, of trying to improve and enhance what they know and do, of building on what is there, step-by-step, uncertainly, but still learning and adapting, however well or badly.

This is likely the most prevalent and enduring form of change existing in any living system. Whole books, under various notions of complex systems, chaos theory and emergence, have been written about this kind of change, describing how small accumulative changes at the margins can affect each other in barely noticeable ways and add up to significant systemic patterns and changes over time; how apparently chaotic systems are governed by deeper, complex social principles that defy easy understanding or manipulation, that confound the best-laid plans, where paths of cause and effect are elusive, caught in eddies of vicious and virtuous circles. Emergent change is paradoxical, where perceptions, feelings and intentions are as powerful as the facts they engage with. Emergent change processes take two forms:

Less Conscious Emergent Change

This kind of emergent change tends to occur where there are unformed and unclear identities, relationships, structures or leadership, under shifting and uncertain environments, internally and externally, with no crises or stucknesses being evident and being unfavourable for conscious development Projects. Being less conscious it may be less predictable, more chaotic and haphazard than more conscious emergent change. More conscious emergent change.

Conditions for more conscious emergent change occur where identity, relationships, structures and leadership are more formed, the environment relatively stable and less contradictory. Conditions for emergent change can also materialise after resolution of a crisis (transformative change) or after a period of projectable change (described below). The conditions or even need for emergent change, rather than more organised projectable change, may stem from a number of factors – perhaps change fatigue after a period of transformative or of projectable change, perhaps to consolidate gains made or a need to grow more steadily, a step-at-a-time.

Less conscious emergent change, characteristically chaotic and still in formation and therefore most difficult to grasp, requires a reading of enormous respect and subtlety. Indeed the very act of entering and observing a less conscious emergent situation can provide a centre of gravity – that the system has not yet developed for itself – that shifts the character of a community.

Researchers or practitioners entering a community to observe or to begin a survey are often surprised and appalled by the expectations that get created by their presence, expectations that should be assigned to community leadership (not yet formed or recognised).

Reading more conscious emergent situations should, by definition, be easier as the social being brings its own more coherent understanding of itself to the relationship with the practitioner.

In either case, emergent situations ask for a working relationship with outside practitioners that can be characterised as *accompanying learning*.

Transformative Change – Through Crisis and Unlearning

At some stage in the development of all social beings it is typical for crisis or stuckness to develop. This may be the product of a natural process of inner development, for example the crisis of the adolescent when that complex interplay of hormones and awakening to the hard realities of growing up breaks out into all manner of physical, emotional and behavioural pimples. Another example is of a pioneering organisation growing beyond the limits of its informal structuring and relationships. Crises may be the product of a social beings entering into tense or contradictory relationships with their world, prompted by shifts in external political, economic, cultural or environmental contexts. For example, farming communities in Caprivi in Northern Namibia were devastated in the late 1990s by the lowering of trade barriers agreed upon at SADEC, losing their traditional markets to a flood of cheap maize from across the Zambian border. Or teachers in thousands of South African schools in the late 1990s who faced crises of discipline when corporal punishment was suddenly banned by law.

Crisis or stuckness sets the stage for transformative change. Unlike emergent change, which is characterised as a learning process, transformative change is more about unlearning, of freeing the social being from those relationships and identities, inner and outer, which underpin the crisis and hold back resolution and further healthy development.

A crisis or stuckness can come in many forms and expressions with deep and complex histories and dynamics. They may be "hot" surfaced experiences of visible conflict or "cold" hidden stucknesses which cannot be seen or talked about.

Left alone, crises do get unconsciously resolved over time, tragically or happily or somewhere in-between. But they can also be more consciously and proactively resolved through well led or facilitated transformative change processes.

For practitioners, understanding existing transformative change processes or change conditions demands a surfacing of relationships and dynamics that are by their nature contested, denied or hidden and resistant to easy reading. This reading can take time, effort and require patience and an openness to sudden shifts of perspective as layers of the situation and its story are peeled away. The real needs for change very rarely reveal themselves upfront. When they are revealed they can provoke real resistance to change and require the people to let go deeply held aspects of their identity, both collective and individual. We can characterise the real work of working with transformative change as facilitating unlearning.

Projectable change – Working with a Plan

Human beings can identify and solve problems and imagine different possibilities, think themselves and their present stories into preferred futures, being able to project possible visions or outcomes and formulate conscious plans to bring about change towards these.

As human beings (in or out of the development sector) we pursue projectable approaches to our own development, individually or collectively planning and undertaking projects, from small to large.

Projectable approaches, through projects, tend to succeed where problems, needs and possibilities are more visible, under relatively stable conditions and relationships, which are not fraught with crisis or stuckness. Where the internal and external environments, especially the relationships, of a system are coherent, stable and predictable enough, and where unpredictable outcomes do not threaten desired results, then the conditions for projectable change arise and well-planned projects become possible.

Two orientations where projectable change dominate:

- One is characterised by a problem-based approach, essentially identifying problems and seeking a fix. A broken tap is identified and a fix found. A problem-based approach works logically with plans from the present into the future.
- Another is characterised by a creative approach of people imagining or visioning desired results, not as a direct solution but as a new situation in which old problems are less or no longer relevant – a leap of imagination into the future. Rather than looking for a direct fix, a new source of water may be created or looked for, rendering the broken tap an irrelevant problem. A creative projectable change begins in the future, plans backwards to the present, devising stepping-stones to the desired results. The stepping stones may veer between being tightly planned

or loosely described as the people discover their way, guided and motivated by the vision they have created.

Of the three types and conditions of change, projectable change is possibly the easiest to read by practitioners and indeed by communities themselves.

We can characterise the real work of working with projectable change as supporting planning and implementation.

Interconnecting the Three Types of Change

No unfolding situation contains an exclusive set of change conditions or one particular kind of inherent change process – there are always complex configurations. But certain conditions do dominate and can be said to support or even precipitate one kind of change or impetus over another, to hold the centre of gravity of development processes.

But one or other kind of change or change conditions can and do co-exist with and form a part of the more dominant processes of change. So, for example, a particular developing situation may be characterised as being in a dominant process of emergent change, yet in its parts there may be smaller sub-processes of transformative or projectable change.

Though a particular kind of change may be dominant this will still be subject to the conditions and character of other change forces. For example, a relatively stable community may feel united and confident enough to undertake a development Project but is uncertain of its relationships with local government.

Under this uncertainty it might make sense for it to take the change Project forward carefully, with some sense of emergence, or to consider a succession of smaller Projects, rather than a grand Project for change, as relationships with local government stabilise. The same community may also find that some unseen crises are surfaced through the Project work and have to pause to deal with them as transformative change.

And of course, one dominant form of change paves the way for another to succeed it, as Heraklietos reminds us "...all is one. And yet everything comes in season."

For the practitioner this means that there is no simple reading of change processes and he or she will need to stay alive to the movement of change – a challenge to keep reading the situ^tion and adjust practice accordingly.

A Theory for Revolutionary Change

Phil Walden Challenges the Prejudices of Post-modernism

To change the world we need to understand it. For that we require a way of analysing reality that brings us closer to the movement of economic, political and social life in the 21st century.

This brings us immediately up against the popular prejudice that "reality is what you make of it" and that to argue for any other approach is to "impose" on people. The beauty of this "post-modern" outlook, of course, is that it leaves the status quo unchallenged.

Although Karl Marx developed his approach in the 19th century, the method he outlined, which others like Frederick Engels developed, remains as crucial for today as it was then.

Commentators in papers like the *Financial Times*, in fact, often refer to Marx's concepts when trying to get to grips with the manic logic of global capitalism. Michael Prowse, for example, in his article headlined "Consumption, consumption, consumption", wrote:

"This new Britain is rich in everything that can be readily priced and sold on the market, and poor in everything that cannot be easily commodified. Market forces have turned the urban landscape into a parody of shop-until-you-drop America (which I know well, having spent six years in Washington DC). The London traffic is now relentless seven days a week. Even Sunday has its rush hour as the shoppers flood into the malls to pay their respects to Mammon. When I ventured out this week, I began to understand what Karl Marx meant when he wrote of 'commodity fetishism'. The metropolis seemed to be utterly in thrall to capitalists and their commodities." (September 16, 2000)

Marx developed the approach of historical materialism, which showed that class struggle (the conflict between the productive forces and the existing relations of production) was the main cause of historical transformation. He showed that the main political force for revolutionary change was the working class. So the possibility of overcoming the exploitation of capitalism was located within modern and changing reality.

Marx demonstrated that only social ownership could establish the possibility for cooperative, democratic and planned productive activity. Furthermore, Marx argued that it was not possible to reconcile the different perspectives of reform and revolution. Principled socialism wasn't about accommodation to the state, but its overthrow.

The 19th century saw rapid advances in both natural and social sciences. Marx and Engels championed the discoveries of people like Charles Darwin and his book On the Origin of the Species. Engels established a distinctive Marxist standpoint about these new advances in knowledge.

He developed a dynamic conception of the objective, material world of matter in motion, which showed that the world consisted of change and becoming, and this was expressed by dialectical laws of contradiction and the negation of the negation.

Lenin defended this materialist outlook against the view that 20th century science was showing that matter had disappeared, or that reality could be reduced to the role of the thinking subject, or observer.

He argued that whilst science may continually modify or change our particular conceptions of reality it is still possible to show that the materialist standpoint concerning an independent material reality remains valid. As Gerry Healy later showed, if materialist theory is repudiated we can end up justifying egotistical and self-created images of the world.

The Ideological Climate

The collapse of the Soviet Union in 1991 created the ideological climate for many people to associate Marxism with Stalinist bureaucratic elitism and repression. Francis Fukuyama's *The End of History* and *The Last Man* (Penguin 1992) announced that capitalism had won the class struggle and was now the definitive historical future.

Furthermore, post-modern philosophy maintained that Marxism was now "antiquated" because it allegedly defended monolithic and absolute universal truths about the necessity of revolutionary change.

But the domination of the world by giant corporations is increasingly rejected by people who want to understand how to change things. Engels and Lenin's emphasis on contradiction helps us to understand that reality is presently based upon social antagonism and class conflict. Despite the optimism of the apologists for capitalism the exploitative and oppressive nature of capitalism remains.

We live in a global world economy that is still based upon the exploitation of wage labour by capital. Hence the perspective of world revolution is still necessary, even if it has to be continually modified in accordance with the constant changes within social reality.

The changes in the nature of global capitalism, and other questions about social reality, do not do away with the necessity for Marxist theory as the basis for principled political practice. Rather it is necessary to continually enrich our theory.

One important argument against the above analysis could be: if Marxism is still an intelligible doctrine why don't more people support it? The answer to this question is contained in the Marxist view that social being is the primary basis for understanding social consciousness.

In other words, the existing forms of human activity under capitalist social relations of production continually generate illusions and artificial images that make it difficult for people to understand capitalism and the need to transcend it. Post-modern philosophy is just one form of the adaptation to these idealist images of reality, that is to say it accepts the accomplished fact of capitalism.

Post-modernism equates immediate sensations with reality. By contrast Marxism has the explanatory power to comprehend the objective reality behind these images and to show the full extent of the continuing exploitative character of capitalism. We could add that Marxism is not just against capitalism but continues to show why an alternative system is required in order to realise the human aspiration of a classless society.

The ecology movement basically support the view that small is beautiful and a small-scale economy will realise economic needs in terms that are compatible with the requirements of nature. This sentiment is ethical and noble but it does not tackle the problem that the world economy is dominated by transnational corporations.

It is true that the technological development that occurs under capitalism does create the potential for the material well-being of the people of the world. Marx showed, however, that social improvement is not an automatic or mechanical process but requires the conscious intervention of human beings.

In this context only a democratic plan of production can achieve the aims of humanity. The only social force that can challenge the bastions of global capital remains the international working class.

Globalization, Class and Socialist Development

Human Nature and Social Change

1. For Marx, socialism is only "inevitable" in the sense that people are fundamentally creative beings, whose potentials evolve through their social experience: and when individuals are frustrated from realizing their emergent potentials by social forces beyond their control when people are "alienated" from their "species being" the resultant frustration and anger heralds conflict as people attempt to fulfil their capabilities by asserting their right to democratically participate in the social organization of their existence.

2. This is Marx's fundamental insight for the understanding of social change.

3. Within the capitalist mode of production people's social experience is conditioned by relations of "commodity exchange": What I proceed from is the simplest social form in which the product of labour... manifests itself, and this is the commodity. (Marx, quoted, Dragsted 1976:44).

4. The defining characteristic of the capitalist mode of production, is that labourçpower itself, people's ability to work,

is a commodity; and like all commodities labour power has a "use value" (for the consumer) and an "exchange value" (for the producer). And all (economic) relations of exchange take place between consumers and producers.

5. The use value of a commodity is the reason why it is purchased by the consumer ç in the case of labour power, the consumer is the capitalist who purchases labour power to produce more commodities. The use value is the *product* of labour power. The exchange value of a commodity is the reason why it is sold by the producer, and in this case the producer is the labourer who sells labour power to earn an income to reproduce him/herself. The exchange value is the commodities that produce labour power (the *consumption* of labourers).

6. The difference between the product and the consumption of labourers, is "surplus value": a surplus of commodities over and above the reproduction of society. A surplus which is distributed through market exchange as "profit", "rent" and "interest": all incomes derived from property ownership, not the production of commodities. Surplus value, then, is produced by the commodity labour power, in the production of commodities for exchange in competitive markets.

7. Surplus value is distributed as profit through the process of the competitive market exchange of commodities. And it is precisely the competitive dynamic of commodity exchange, which requires producers to become ever more efficient (that is to reduce the labour time necessary to produce commodities), which leads to a "tendency for the rate of

8. With the squeeze on profitability there is pressure on capitalist producers to open up new markets in which to sell commodities: The need of a constantly expanding market for its products chases the bourgeoisie cver the whole surface of the globe.' Markets are the domain in which surplus value is *realized* as profits, but it is within the production process itself where surplus value is *produced*, and there will be attempts to increase the "rate of exploitation" within this process: to widen the gap between the product of labour power and the consumption of labourers.

9. Labourers are able to be exploited because they have been

"proletarianized": they do not own or control the means of production (factories, tools, technology, raw materials, etc...) and have to work for someone that does ça capitalist. But not only are labourers proletarianized, they are also individualized. They compete with each other to get work, and hence wages can be driven down to the minimum and exploitation increased to the maximum.

Liberalization of Capital Accounts

10. Up until the end of the 1970s, before the introduction of liberalized financial markets, the process of exploitation was essentially nationally defined: the parameters of free exchange were defined within particular currency regimes that could be managed by governments. And because of managed exchange rates it was possible, within pluralist social democracies, for the proletariat to limit the excesses of exploitation. Governments could be pressured for increases in the social wage (health, education and welfare expenditure, full employment policies, etc...), as governments had to manage the economy to win elections.

11. In 1979, the British Conservative government of Margaret Thatcher abolished "foreign exchange controls", what economists call the "liberalization of capital accounts", and so began a...structural transition at the global level... [which was] largely complete by the early 1990s...' (Herold 2002:5/6).

12. Governments henceforth were unable to manage national economies: capital was free to move between nation states/ economies, and to attract investment funds governments had to offer an attractive investment environment (low wages, low taxes. "flexible" labour markets with little or no trade union protection, etc...), an environment in which exploitation (the gap between the product and consumption of labourers) is maximized.

13. International capital markets effectively discipline policymakers çthe threat of economic crisis forces governments to follow "free market" competitive policies. And with the ending of exchange controls competition between labourers for work became international (and governments can only legislate nationally).

14. This is what defines globalization.

The Nature of the State and Class Power

15. This has been interpreted as a "weakening of the state". However, the state is an instrument of class rule and has evolved, becoming internationalized, as the class relations of exploitation have taken on an international guise: The bourgeoisie cannot exist without constantly revolutionizing the instruments of production, and thereby the relations of production, and with them *the whole relations of society*.'

16. Central to capitalist relations of exploitation, and the denial of people's rights to democratically realize their creative potentials, is commodity exchange in general, and labour power as a commodity in particular. And the central aim of (proletarian) class struggle is to decommodify labour. With labour power as a commodity, the fulfilment of people's creative potentials depends upon the vicissitudes of anarchic market forces. But human potentials are "social" potentials, which cannot be realized according to "individual", consumers' market choices.

17. For instance, we now have the most efficient forces of production in human history, but rather than people being better able to realize their creative potentials, more and more people are impoverished and unemployed, and fewer and fewer people work longer and longer hours, to the benefit of a tiny minority who are staggeringly wealthy and are becoming richer and richer.

Socialist Development

19. The struggle for socialism, the process of the social evolution towards communism, is not merely about...the struggle against a certain group of capitalists... it is about overturning capital çthe system of wageç labour [proletarianization] and its basic dynamic, competitive accumulation.' (McNally 1993:181).

20. It is fundamentally a struggle for democracy: the right for people to participate in the social control of their existence. Internationally, this can only be based on proletarian internationalism.

...what on earth are workers of world to unite about unless it is some sense of their fundamental rights as human beings? Connecting the sentiments of the [Communist] Manifesto *with those expressed in the*

Declaration of Human Rights *provides one way to... redefine... the terms and spaces of political struggle...' Harvey 2000:18*

21. Liberation, the right for people to realize their creative potentials, the right to live in dignity, lies beyond the economy and production:...freedom really begins... only where labour determined by expediency and external necessity ends; it lies by its very nature *beyond the sphere of material production proper.'* (Marx 1972:958/9). Only when "necessary" (and expedient) labour has been completed (subsistence, housing, clothing, the necessary requirements for social existence, etc...) can people be free to realize their (emergent) creative potentials.

22. "Necessary" labour should be minimized (and equalized) and wealth shared to allow all people (not just the privileged minority) to fulfil their creative, human potentials.

23. Individuals' potentials are social potentials, which evolve and emerge with social experience. Inevitably, at times, people will be frustrated by social constraints from realizing their capabilities: people will feel frustrated and angry, and possibly there will be conflict in society. In a socialist society such conflicts are resolved democratically.

24. In a capitalist society, where there are contradictory class interests, such conflict tends to become class conflict. The rights of the privileged minority are protected by a legal system which prioritizes "property" over "human rights", and the disadvantaged majority have to try and protect these rights by struggle through social or trade union movements.

Welfare State

There are two main interpretations of the idea of a welfare state:

- A model in which the state assumes primary responsibility for the welfare of its citizens. This responsibility in theory ought to be comprehensive, because all aspects of welfare are considered and universally applied to citizens as a "right".
- Welfare state can also mean the creation of a "social safety net" of minimum standards of varying forms of welfare.

There is some confusion between a "welfare state" and a "welfare society," and debate about how each term should be defined. In many countries, especially in the United States, some degree of welfare is not actually provided by the state, but directly to welfare recipients from a combination of independent volunteers, corporations (both non-profit charitable corporations as well as for-profit corporations), and government services. This phenomenon has been termed a "welfare society," and the term "welfare system" has been used to describe the range of welfare state and welfare society mixes that are found. The welfare state involves a direct transfer of funds from the public sector to welfare recipients, but indirectly, the private sector is often contributing those funds via redistributionist taxation; the welfare state has been referred to as a type of "mixed economy."

Etymology

The English term "welfare state" is believed by Asa Briggs to have been coined by Archbishop William Temple during the Second World War, contrasting wartime Britain with the "warfare state" of Nazi Germany. Friedrich Hayek contends that the term derived from the older German word *Wohlfahrtsstaat*, which itself was used by nineteenth century historians to describe a variant of the ideal of *Polizeistaat* ("police state"). It was fully developed by the German academic *Sozialpolitiker*—"socialists of the chair"—from 1870 and first implemented through Bismarck's "state socialism". Bismarck's policies have also been seen as the creation of a welfare state.

In German, a roughly equivalent term (*Sozialstaat*, "social state") had been in use since 1870. There had been earlier attempts to use the same phrase in English, for example in Munroe Smith's text "Four German Jurists", but the term did not enter common use until William Temple popularized it. The Italian term "Social state" (*Stato sociale*) has the same origin.

The Swedish welfare state is called Folkhemmet and goes back to the 1936 compromise between the Union and big Corporate companies. It is a Mixed economy, built on strong unions and a strong system of Social security and universal health care.

In French, the synonymous term "providence state" *(État-*

providence) was originally coined as a sarcastic pejorative remark used by opponents of welfare state policies during the Second Empire (1854-1870).

In Spanish and many other languages, an analogous term is used: *estado del bienestar*; translated literally: "state of well-being".

In Portuguese, a similar phrase exists: *Estado de Bem-Estar Social;* which means "Social well-being state".

Early Welfare States

The "concept of what one might call a welfare state" appeared during the Abbasid Caliphate in the 8th century. The concepts of welfare and pension were introduced in early Islamic law as forms of *Zakat* (charity), one of the five Pillars of Islam, since the time of Caliph al-Mansur. The taxes (including *Zakat* and *Jizya*) collected in the treasury of an Islamic government were used to provide income for the needy, including the poor, elderly, orphans, widows, and the disabled. According to the Islamic jurist Al-Ghazali (Algazel, 1058-1111), the government was also expected to store up food supplies in every region in case a disaster or famine occurred.

Modern Welfare States

Modern welfare states developed through a gradual process beginning in the late 19th century and continuing through the 20th. They differed from previous schemes of poverty relief due to their relatively universal coverage. The development of social insurance in Germany under Bismarck was particularly influential. Some schemes, like those in Scandinavia, were based largely in the development of autonomous, mutualist provision of benefits. Others were founded on state provision. The term was not, however, applied to all states offering social protection. The sociologist T.H. Marshall identified the welfare state as a distinctive combination of democracy, welfare and capitalism. Examples of early welfare states in the modern world are Germany, all of the Nordic Countries, the Netherlands, Uruguay and New Zealand and the United Kingdom in the 1930s; although even in current times the question is the U.K. a welfare state or not is as hotly debated in the United Kingdom as it is in the United States today.

Changed attitudes in reaction to the Great Depression were instrumental in the move to the welfare state in many countries, a harbinger of new times where "cradle-to-grave" services became a reality after the poverty of the Depression. During the Great Depression, it was seen as an alternative "middle way" between communism and capitalism. In the period following the Second World War, many countries in Europe moved from partial or selective provision of social services to relatively comprehensive coverage of the population.

The activities of present-day welfare states extend to the provision of both cash welfare benefits (such as old-age pensions or unemployment benefits) and in-kind welfare services (such as health or childcare services). Through these provisions, welfare states can affect the distribution of wellbeing and personal autonomy among their citizens, as well as influencing how their citizens consume and how they spend their time.

After the discovery and inflow of the oil revenue, Saudi Arabia, Brunei, Kuwait, Qatar, Bahrain, Oman, and the United Arab Emirates all became welfare states.

In the United Kingdom, the beginning of the modern welfare state was in 1911 when David Lloyd George suggested everyone in work should pay national insurance contribution for unemployment and health benefits from work.

In 1942, the Social Insurance and Allied Services was created by Sir William Beveridge in order to aid those who were in need of help, or in poverty. Beveridge worked as a volunteer for the poor, and set up national insurance. He stated that 'All people of working age should pay a weekly national insurance contribution. In return, benefits would be paid to people who were sick, unemployed, retired or widowed.' The basic assumptions of the report were the National Health Service, which provided free health care to the UK. The Universal Child Benefit was a scheme to give benefits to parents, encouraging people to have children by enabling them to feed and support a family. This was particularly beneficial after the second world war when the population of the United Kingdom declined. Universal Child Benefit may have helped drive the Baby boom. The impact of the report was huge and 600,000 copies were made.

Beveridge recommended to the government that they should find ways of tackling the five giants, being Want, Disease, Ignorance, Squalor and Idleness. He argued to cure these problems, the government should provide adequate income to people, adequate health care, adequate education, adequate housing and adequate employment. Before 1939, health care had to be paid for, this was done through a vast network of friendly societies, trade unions and other insurance companies which counted the vast majority of the UK working population as members. These friendly societies provided insurance for sickness, unemployment and invalidity, therefore providing people with an income when they were unable to work. But because of the 1942 Beveridge Report, in 5 July 1948, the National Insurance Act, National Assistance Act and National Health Service Act came into force, thus this is the day that the modern UK welfare state was founded.

Welfare systems were developing intensively since the end of the World War II. At the end of century due to their restructuration part of their responsibilities started to be channeled through non-governmental organizations which became important providers of social services.

Two Forms of the Welfare State

There are two ways of organizing a welfare state:

According to the first model the state is primarily concerned with directing the resources to "the people most in need". This requires a tight bureaucratic control over the people concerned, with a maximum of interference in their lives to establish who are "in need" and minimize cheating. The unintended result is that there is a sharp divide between the receivers and the producers of social welfare, between "us" and "them", the producers tending to dismiss the whole idea of social welfare because they will not receive anything of it. This model is dominant in the US.

According to the second model the state distributes welfare with as little bureaucratic interference as possible, to all people who fulfil easily established criteria (e.g. having children, receiving medical treatment, etc.). This requires high taxing, of which almost everything is channeled back to the taxpayers with minimum expenses for bureaucratic personnel. The intended – and also largely achieved – result is that there will be a broad support for the system since most people will receive at least something. This model was constructed by the Scandinavian ministers Karl Kristian Steincke and Gustav Möller in the 30s and is dominant in Scandinavia.

Criticisms

Some criticism of welfare states concern the idea that a welfare state makes citizens dependent and less inclined to work. Certain studies indicate there is no association between economic performance and welfare expenditure in developed countries and that there is no evidence for the contention that welfare states impede progressive social development. R. E. Goodin et al., in *The Real Worlds of Welfare Capitalism* (Cambridge University Press, 1999), compares the United States, which spends relatively little on social welfare (less than 17 per cent of GDP), with other countries which spend considerably more. This study claims that on some economic and social indicators the United States performs worse than the Netherlands, which has a high commitment to welfare provision.

However, the United States, until the banking collapse and credit crunch of 2008 which brought a significant fall in GDP, led most welfare states on certain economic indicators, such as GDP per capita (although in 2006 it had a lower GDP per capita than Norway and Denmark). Until the recession of 2008 brought about a significant rise in unemployment in the USA, the United States also had a low unemployment rate (although not as low as Denmark, Norway) and a high GDP growth rate, at least in comparison to other developed countries (its growth rate, however, is lower than Finland's and Sweden's, two nations with relatively small populations but comparatively high commitments to welfare provision; the United States' growth rate is also lower than the world's overall). The United States also had led most welfare states in the ownership of consumer goods. For example, it has more TVs per capita, more personal computers per capita, and more radios per capita than welfare states.

Bibliography

Andre Beteille: *Equality and Universality : Essays in Social and Political Theory*, Oxford University Press, Delhi, 2003.

Ashutosh Kumar and Ravi Ranjan: *Political Theory and Thought*, K.K. Pub, Delhi, 2009.

B N Ray: *Political Theory: Interrogations and Interventions*, Authorspress, Delhi, 2006.

K T Varkey: *Political Theory : An Administrative and Constitutional Perspective*, Indian Pub, Delhi, 2004.

Kundan Kumar: *Ideology and Political Theory : A Study with Special Reference to the Disintegration of the Soviet Union*, Discovery, Delhi, 2003.

N. Jayapalan: *Comprehensive Political Theory*, Atlantic, New Delhi, 2002.

P B Rathod: *Dimensions of Political Theory*, ABD, Delhi, 2008.

P.B. Rathod: *Modern Political Theory*, ABD, Delhi, 2006.

Rethinking Gandhi : *Politics, Symbols and Political Theory*, Rawat, Delhi, 2001.

S L Verma: *Advanced Modern Political Theory : Analysis and Technologies*, Rawat, Delhi, 2008.

S N Singh: *Modern Political Theory*, Shri Sai Printographers, Delhi, 2006.

Santosh Bakaya: *The Political Theory of Robert Nozick*, Kalpaz, Delhi, 2006.

Index

O

P

R

S

T

V

W

□□□